WITHDRAWN
UTSA LIBRARIES

Power:
Its Nature, Its Use, and Its Limits

Edited by
Donald W. Harward

Power:
Its Nature, Its Use, and
Its Limits

G.K. Hall & Co.   Boston, Massachusetts

Schenkman Publishing Co.   Cambridge, Massachusetts

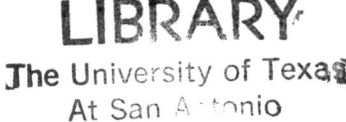

LIBRARY
The University of Texas
At San Antonio

Copyright © 1979 by Schenkman Publishing Company

Library of Congress Cataloging in Publication Data
Main entry under title:

Power, its nature, its use, and its limits.

   Includes lectures presented at the University of
Delaware Honors Program lecture series, held in Newark,
Sept.-Dec., 1977.
   1. Power (Social sciences)—Addresses, essays, lectures. I. Harward, Donald W.
HM131.P674   301.15'5   79-11170
ISBN 0-8161-9011-9

This publication is printed on permanent/durable acid-free paper
MANUFACTURED IN THE UNITED STATES OF AMERICA

Contents

PREFACE … vii

Theme 1: Conceptual Structure of Power

SIDNEY HOOK … 3
The Conceptual Structure of Power—An Overview

Theme 2: Uses of Power

W.W. ROSTOW … 23
The Economic Power of the United States

BRIAN M. JENKINS … 37
Terrorism—A New Dimension of Power

Theme 3: Power and Politics

JAMES MacGREGOR BURNS … 55
Power and Politics—An Overview

HOWARD BAKER … 68
Political Power

BELLA ABZUG … 75
Women and Political Power

NOAM CHOMSKY … 87
Intellectuals and the State

Theme 4: The Powerful and the Powerless

BAYARD RUSTIN   119
Power and Minority Groups

CAROLINE BIRD   130
Women, Power, and Powerlessness

ROLLO MAY   141
Psychoanalysis and Power

THOMAS S. SZASZ   153
Power and Psychiatry

Theme 5: The Limits of Power

CHARLES REICH   161
Power and the Law

WILLIAM REHNQUIST   177
The Nature and Exercise of Power

JOHN R. SILBER   189
The Conceptual Structure of Power—A Review

Preface

"Power: Its Nature, Its Use, and Its Limits" was the topic of the University of Delaware Honors Program Lecture Series, held in Newark, Delaware, September through December 1977. The University Honors Program sponsored the series with the assistance of the Delaware Humanities Forum and the National Endowment for the Humanities.

As an institution of higher learning, the University of Delaware has brought, through the contributions in this series, historical, scientific, social, and philosophical perspectives to the analysis of power and its uses.

Power is sought and avoided, paraded and hidden, accumulated and lost. It can be desirable or offensive, enduring or ephemeral. It is said of power "that those who have it want more of it and those that don't have it want it more."

Power is an enigma; the nature of power remains an unexamined but fundamental concept crucial to understanding the nature of most human institutions and almost all human interactions. Not since Bertrand Russell's 1938 essay have we seen an effort to make a straighforward analysis of power; what it means, how it's used, and the character of its limits. Russell's analysis and others failed because each effort to locate or designate a simple set of properties or characteristics essential to its nature betrayed the fact that the concept of power is complex and any analysis of it must reflect this complexity.

What follows is done in a straightforward and nontechnical way. Power is examined on a conceptual level by Sidney Hook. Its uses are explored in detail by W.W. Rostow in an examination of economic power and by Brian Jenkins's examination of power and terrorism. The theoretical discussion of power and politics is made by James MacGregor Burns and is followed by Howard Baker's and Bella Abzug's attempt to portray power in the practical context of political and social action. Noam Chomsky discusses the critical power of politics and the role of intellectuals in its exercise. Thoughtful essays by Bayard Rustin, Caroline

Bird, Rollo May, and Thomas Szasz focus on the powerless, and the dimensions of power in human interaction. The last essays provided by Charles Reich, William Rehnquist, and John R. Silber attempt to appreciate the limits of power, both personal and legal, and to reconsider the issues presented in the analysis of the very conceptual structure of power itself.

Acknowledgments

Because the pieces that form this volume were originally delivered as lectures, I have edited them but retained their style as lectures—not formal essays. I am grateful to the separate authors for their assistance with this editing.

Many faculty members were generous in their time and suggestions for the publication of this series and I am indebted to them. One person, however, gave direction to the book, supported the series, and aided my thoughts and energy immeasurably: Paul Dolan, professor of political science at the University of Delaware.

Professor Dolan has taught with distinction for over thirty years at the University and his insights into the nature of power, its use, and its limits are so keen that I wish to dedicate the publication of this volume to him and to his spirited pursuit of learning and teaching.

DONALD W. HARWARD
November 1, 1978

Theme 1
Conceptual Structure of Power

Sidney Hook

The Conceptual Structure of Power—an Overview

Sidney Hook is currently a senior research fellow at the Hoover Institution on War, Revolution and Peace, Stanford, California. He is emeritus professor of philosophy and formerly head of the All-University Department at New York University.

He attended the College of the City of New York, where he studied under Morris A. Cohen. In 1926, Professor Hook received his master's degree and in 1927 his doctorate in philosophy from Columbia University, after intensive study with John Dewey and F.J.E. Woodbridge.

Professor Hook twice received Guggenheim Fellowships for research in philosophy in Germany and Russia (1928-29). Upon the publication of his Hero in History, *he won the Nicholas Murray Butler Silber Medal for distinction in the field of philosophy and education. In 1953 he received a third Guggenheim Fellowship for research in European philosophy. A Ford Foundation Travelings Fellowship for the study of Asian philosophy and culture was awarded to him in 1958.*

Professor Hook joined the New York University faculty as instructor in 1927 and became a full professor in 1939. In addition, he has taught at Columbia University, the University of California, and for many years at the New School for Social Research.

Among his numerous publications are: The Metaphysics of Pragmatism, From Hegel to Marx, Reason, Social Myths and Democracy, Political Power and Personal Freedom, *and* Academic Freedom and Academic Anarchy. *His most recent books are* Education and the Taming of Power, Pragmatism and the Tragic Sense of Life, *and* Revolutions, Reform and Social Justice.

> *It is better to be a live jackal than a dead lion—for jackals, not men. Men who have the moral courage to fight intelligently for freedom have the best prospects of avoiding the fate both of live jackals and dead lions. Survival is not the be-all and end-all of a life worthy of man. Sometimes the worst thing we can*

know about a man is that he has survived. Those who say life is worth living at any cost have already written for themselves an epitaph of infamy, for there is no cause and no person they will not betray to stay alive. Man's vocation should be the use of the arts of intelligence in behalf of human freedom.
   (From *Who's Who in America,* Bicentennial Edition, 1976-77, Sidney Hook.)

I want to begin with a disclaimer: I shall not restrict myself to the topic, the conceptual structure of power, but shall discuss to some extent some of the other themes enumerated in the prospectus. The reasons for this are many. One of them is the fact that the usages of the term "power" are so varied that analysis of their conceptual structure would result in a complex formal semantic exercise for which this is not the proper occasion and it may have little bearing on the realities and problems of power relationships that are of primary practical interest, and which I suspect are closer to your concerns.

Second, in exploring a theme central to the various disciplines it is difficult to observe intellectual nontresspass signs. There is no danger I shall exhaust any of these other themes, for at best I can only introduce them and give you perhaps a measure or yardstick to apply to some of the analyses which will follow mine and which I am confident will disagree with mine in some respects.

When I speak of power in the present context, I do not speak of natural energy or of the awesomeness of the powers of nature. I shall speak only of human power, of human beings as subjects and objects of power, and of nature and natural resources only insofar as they are used by man to control the behavior of other men and women. That is what August Blanqui, the French revolutionist, meant when he said, "who has iron has bread." Today he would have said, "who has oil has bread." Potentially, oil was always a source of natural energy, but only recently has it become a source of economic and political power.

In its most generic sense, power is the ability to influence the behavior of others in order to further our desires and purposes. This reference to the production of intended effects means that we cannot literally speak of natural power, if you accept that definition, without anthropormorphising nature. Power in my sense must be either human or divine. In any case, whether it is human or divine, power cannot be omnipotent. Only an existentialist can believe that God can make $2 + 2 = 5$ or unmake the past. Even so, the concept of power as influence on the behavior of others is too vast a theme, and we shall have to delimit it. We shall not, therefore, discuss the purely personal uses of power, whether in friendship, or love, commerce, or sport. No one except a hermit can forgo exercising some power to influence the conduct of others or avoid being influenced in turn by their conduct. But our concern will be with the power exercised in a social context by individual or groups either directly or through events they bring to pass.

There are few more qualifications we must make in the interest of clarification. Power is often used interchangeably with influence and authority. Although they are related, it is a source of confusion to overlook the differences. Not all influence is a form of power in the sense that gives us concern. If I influence someone by rational argument to behave in a manner of which I approve, even if I am a salesman, am I exercising power *over* him? Hardly. If someone is voluntarily taken as a model of deportment or dress or of social behavior, etiquette, or manners, does he or she thereby become a source or wielder of power? Not in an objectionable sense. When we speak of the authority of power the term "power" has a somewhat different meaning from what it has in the phrase "the power of authority." The Pope has an authority among Catholics that is independent of his secular power, although his authority may depend upon the communicants' belief in his spiritual power. When Stalin asked Churchill (who had proposed that the Pope be consulted about the postwar world), "How many battalions has the Pope?", he recognized the difference between authority and power and at the same time revealed his naïveté about the limits of power. Neither God, in whom Stalin did not believe, nor history in which he did, is always on the side of the strongest battalions.

One undesirable consequence of equating power with influence or with authority and persuasion is that, almost by semantic fiat, it converts everyone into a seeker of power. So for example, Professor Hans Morganthau speaks of "the ubiquitous lust for power" as if it were an essential trait of man. By bringing in the unconscious, one can hold on to this view that man is by nature a power-questing creature. This makes the assertion as unempirical a notion as the adolescent view that all human actions are egoistic and that no one acts out of disinterested or unselfish motives. But there are a series of phenomena that would make it difficult to hold to the view that everyone is power hungry, if that were asserted as an empirical proposition. For example, the widespread attitude, when posts of power have to be filled, "Let someone else, let George do it"; or the widespread abstention from the political process altogether is sufficient to refute this oversimple view.

What differentiates "power," as I shall use the term, from mere influence, authority, and persuasion is the element of constraint or the threat of constraint that is integral to its meaning. That is why as necessary as power is in human relationships, we are somewhat fearful of it and seek to curb or tame or limit it. This insight is recognized by Max Weber in his *Theory of Economic and Social Organization*, where the presence of power is defined as (I am quoting from Weber) "The probability that one actor within a social relationship will be in a position to carry out his will despite resistance, regardless of the basis upon which the probability rests." Without implicit reference to the overcoming of actual or potential resistance the power of the command would hardly differ from the gentle solicitation of a wish.

If we return now to a modified formulation of the conception of power, as the ability to impose one's will upon others, even in the face of resistance, it is clear that this may be done in various ways and by varied means. The most obvious way, and to some extent always in the background when conflicts arise, is by the exercise of physical force, or by the threat of its exercise. But this is by far not the only way power shows itself. Otherwise the physically stronger would always be the most powerful in history and social life. Whatever may be the case among the lower animals or the animal kingdom, it is not so in human affairs. Unless we define the physically stronger merely in terms of the victorious outcome of any struggle, it is not true that the physically stronger is always the most powerful. David was certainly not stronger than Goliath. A hypnotist can make his physically stronger subject do things that he would be unable to get him to do outside the hypnotic trance. By playing on the fears, natural or supernatural, of multitudes, secular or religious leaders may impose restraints or taboos on their cohorts without any physical sanctions whatsoever. The sacred is sometimes stronger than even the drive to self-preservation. Men have died in the sight of food that has been forbidden to them by taboo.

History is replete with illustrations that military strength by itself is not always decisive for victory. When the Russian general Kornilov marched against Kerensky in August 1917 at the head of well-armed troops (this was after the February 1917 revolution in Russia), Kerensky could hardly muster a military defense with the only forces available, the war-weary semimutinous garrison of St. Petersburg. But it wasn't necessary. In one of the most remarkable examples of the power of propaganda, the coalition that rallied around him mobilized a horde of agitators against Kornilov's troops whose ranks, subjected to the techniques of fraternization, dissolved like snow under a hot sun. Another illustration: the defeat of the United States military forces in Vietnam was not due to their military weakness vis-à-vis their opponents, but to the absence of resoluteness of American political leadership and the erosion of popular support induced by a variety of factors that had nothing to do with military strength. Two of the most far-reaching turning points in the history of Western civilization, the defeat of the Persian forces at Marathon and 500 years later the triumph of Christianity over the Roman Empire and its mighty legions, may be taken as paradigm cases of the insufficiency of physical force by itself to prevail.

There are many other kinds of power in the world that can be employed to determine if not completely to control the behavior of others. There is the power of money and other forms of wealth, particularly property; the power of social position; the power of offices, public or private; the power of expert skill, especially when it is in short supply; and the power of ideas—which may or may not be rationalizations of individual or class interests—religious ideas, nationalistic ideas, racial and ethical ideals.

Libraries of literature have been written about these varieties of power, a great deal of it in the vain attempt to reduce them to one fundamental form, either material or ideal. Usually those who seek to reduce all types of power to forms of one mean no more than that the effects of different power relations in society are the same, namely, control by a few persons over the destinies of many others. But this seems to me to be another great oversimplification. The *way* power is exercised and the *means* employed in its exercise make a difference both to those who use power and to those against whom it is used. Power won by the speaking of truths (leaving blackmail aside) will be different, at least in some respects, from power won by propaganda or outright coercion. Lord Acton's dictum that all power corrupts, is no more true than that all powerlessness corrupts. But to the extent that it is true, the corruption will vary with the mode of its exercise.

The very fact that all exercise of power is limited by other power shows that power is a matter of degree. We need not worry that it cannot be precisely measured. It is what we call an intensive magnitude. It is sufficient in most contexts without quantifying power to assign it greater or lesser weight and to determine when it is growing stronger or weaker. For example, we can say the power of religious organizations is greater in some periods than in others; no Pope can compel a king or a head of state to crawl to Canossa today. Although power is a matter of degree, so that there is always something that limits it, we cannot lay down any exact limits to its operation. Force or physical power can, by the inflinction of death or suffering, or the threat of such, enforce compliant behavior. However, regardless of how harshly physical force is exercised or threatened, there are some things it cannot do. You cannot successfully compel or even command someone to love or to respect you, although you can make them *say* that they do. At the same time, naked power gets clothed with a kind of authority by sheer endurance, if it is not too intense or is not embroiled in revolutionary struggle. Time guilds naked power with a patina of legitimacy and gives it added weight. The sons of the conqueror become inheritors and their sons legitimate rulers. If a tyranny lasts long enough, the popular mood develops from hostility to indifference to acquiescence, and sometimes, unfortunately, even to acclaim.

Nonetheless, recognizing as we must the limitations of naked power, let us not underestimate how effective a ruthless terror can be. Napoleon is supposed to have said that one can do anything with bayonets except sit on them. That overlooks the ways in which bayonets can insure peaceful and comfortable slumber for tyrants by making others sit on them. In passing, it may be noted that fear of death, or the belief that mere survival is the be-all and end-all of existence, can be the unwitting ally of terror. Power, no matter how arbitrary or absolute, has little hold on those who have no fear of death or unpopularity or public disgrace.

The enumeration of different forms of power should not prevent us from recognizing that they usually reinforce each other in most historical circumstances. At any given time, throne and altar, state and church, economic and cultural—especially educational—institutions, usually tend to support a common structure of values. But rifts and differences always develop in time. Those who have power, or their elites or leadership, may have a common interest, but their conceptions of that common interest often conflict, and may make a difference between war and peace as an expression of national policy. Conflicts among different groups among the ruling classes, the ins and the outs, produce changes in power positions that neither anticipate, like growth in the power of other classes. The struggles between nobles and kings strengthen the middle classes, and the struggle between the agricultural and manufacturing interests in England contributed to the rise of the Labour party. When the need for allies in the struggle requires coalitions, a concessionary price may have to be paid for an increased temporary strength whose consequences may be weakness in the long run. In such situations a small group may exercise a disproportionate power. That is one of the acknowledged drawbacks of proportional representation.

Many writers on the nature of power seek to find its roots, or first cause, in some one psychological or social trait, but this seems to me to be an exercise in futility. There are varying conditions on which different forms of power depend. The successful manifestation of power depends not only on the qualities, physical or mental, of those over whom power is wielded. One cannot plausibly explain the operations of power merely in terms of the amount of physical force available to the power holders. No police force could enforce the law if a sufficiently large number of people chose to disobey. Kingly, presidential, or judicial power is often more effective in virtue of the power of authority than in terms of threatened sanctions. This leads to references to the power of habit, the power of tradition, or the power of imitation in human behavior. The existence of such psychological factors cannot be disputed, but my contention is that they cannot account for variations in power relations that are historical in nature. They do not explain who has power, over whom, when, where, and how. That is why I refer to them as conditions for the exercise of power. The relationship is somewhat like that of literacy to what is called the power of the press. Unless a people is literate and able to purchase newspapers, we cannot properly speak of the power of the press. But the existence of literacy does not generate the power of the press; it makes it possible. Only when the press exhibits in the selection and emphasis of its news, as well as in its editorial policy, a sustained bias can we use the expression "the power of the press" intelligibly.

Because of the tendency to use the term "power" for what are the conditions and causes of power, I believe it is a mistake to assume that by some semantic legislation or fiat we can establish consistency in usage. We must look beyond the words to locate the phenomenon and the problem. For example, we sometimes talk about "the power of the weak" or "the power of the powerless" to get their way in virtue of their weakness to curb the behavior of those who are stronger than they are. But such power is only enjoyed because of the sufferance or tolerance of those who possess the greater power. It can be extinguished in a moment. Like "the power of a woman's tears" to get her way, which novelists used to write about, despite her legal, financial, and social inequality, its success rests on the patronizing indulgence of those who have greater power because of the institutional structure of society. Please do not misunderstand. I am not calling into question the psychological reality of the phenomenon called "the power of the weak," but only the misleading connotations of the expression. The weak have little power in the absence of the sympathy, compassion, or pity of the powerful. It is only where they are in a position to inflict unacceptable harm on those capable of destroying them that they can win concessions from those immune to these emotions.

Granting that there is a plurality of interacting powers that determine human behavior and that they are irreducible to each other, it still may be true that one kind of power may be more decisive than others. It may be taken as the independent variable whose changes have an overriding effect on all other forms of power. It would hardly be an exaggeration to say that today the most pervasive doctrine about the nature of power is the view that economic power is the predominant factor in politics and history. And because of the ambiguities of the term "economic" we must specify that by "economic," here, we mean the mode of economic production. Whether held in sophisticated or vulgarized form, it is undeniable that there has been an amazing recrudescence of the theory of historical materialism not only in the market place but also in academic quarters.

That economic relationships have a profound influence on human behavior can hardly be gainsaid. But that these relationships are necessarily expressed as power *over persons*, in virtue of power over things, and that historical materialism is the foundation that explains not only the distribution of wealth, but everything of cultural importance, is extremely difficult to establish in the light of the historical record. For one thing, it cannot do justice to the economic transformations that have resulted from the exercise of political power. Nonetheless it is widely believed, even among many who have no allegiance to Marxist doctrine, indeed among some who are outspokenly anti-Marxist. Anyone who asserts that the fundamental issue of our age is between capitalism and socialism as economic systems rather than between democracy and totalitarianism as political systems subscribes to some variant of historical materialism. For what he is asserting is that the clue or key to the complex maze of power relationships that prevail in our society, or any society, can be derived from the existing mode of economic production and the legal relations of ownership under which it functions. The Marxists maintain that true democracy can be furthered only by socialization of the means of production. The critics of this school, who are really unconscious crypto-Marxists, contend that socialization will destroy democracy and freedom. But they both agree that the economy is all-determining. Their contrary positions cannot be both true, but both may be false. The most fundamental question of our age, I maintain, is not socialism or capitalism, however they are defined, but the freedom to choose between them. And our free choice may be, and from my part *should be*, not socialism *or* capitalism but *more or less* of one or the other.

There are a number of considerations that make the monistic economic view of history, politics, and culture questionable. Some are rather obvious and were passed over too lightly by Marx himself. In replying to those who stressed the power of ideas of consciousness of history, Marx writes: "it is not consciousness that determines existence, but social existence that determines consciousness." By "social existence" he meant one's class position, the web of economic relations that define the area in which all historical agents act. But it is clear that Marx's own social existence does not explain his ideas or consciousness or that of his lieutenants and leading disciples. The retort that Marx is not speaking of the social existence or the consciousness of individuals but only of classes is beside the point. For after all, classes are made up of individuals and class consciousness would be a mystical and mystifying notion unless it is related at least statistically to the thought and behavior of individuals. In any event, if ideas merely reflected antecedent social existence, the historical influence of Marx's revolutionary ideas would be inexplicable.

Further, if this simplistic view of economic power were valid, nationalism in its varied expressions would be the result of the thrust of economic interests, and religion no more than a mask for such interests. I defy anyone to explain modern nationalist movements in the light of this dogma. Economic interests played a minor role in the movement for Indian independence. And if one essayed to interpret Zionism or Irish nationalism or the budding nationalist movements for independence in terms of economic interest, where independence usually results in a decline in the standard of economic life, he would be cutting the cloth of historical reality to fit an ideological dogma.

Nonetheless, leaving these difficulties aside, I want to restate the view that economic power is the predominant power in its strongest and most plausible form before criticizing it. After all, a theory should be considered in its strongest form.

In this form it locates the source of power in the nature of social property itself, and contends that property over things entails property over persons. The question is "How does property do this?" The analysis runs briefly as follows: Property is not a thing but a legal relation or title, a legal right. A legal right is a claim to goods or services that society, through its authorized agencies, stands ready to enforce. One may have a *moral* right regardless of whether it is enforced. But if over an extended period of time a legal right is not enforced, then for all practical purposes it is nonexistent.

What is the nature of property as a legal right? How do you know you have it? Some say that property is the right to use or abuse whatever you have title to. This is simply not so. The law will not enforce your legal right to harvest your crop or run your factory if you are physically or mentally incapable of doing so. Even if you are in the full possession of all your powers, the law will not enforce your right to harvest your crop of marijuana or construct on your property a slaughterhouse or a horse farm or any other establishment forbidden by the zoning laws. Even the freedom of testamentary disposition is restricted. You can't do anything you want with your property or money.

What then does the legal right of property amount to? To this: the power through law *to exclude* others from the possession or use of what you own. And this brings us to the crux of the argument. If you have property in the social means of production—factories, mines, mills, large tracts of land—then you have the power to exclude others from their use. If their use is necessary for the employment of others, if it is their only or chief means of livelihood, then you have a very real power over the lives of those who must live by their use. The power to deny access to the means of earning a living is power to deny life. Power over economic things gives power over persons.

The paradigm cause of such power is illustrated in the case of a town in which almost all employment centers on one large factory and the service industries that cater to it and its employees. If the owner decides to shut down for any reason, the dislocation in the lives of those who must subsist by their labor radiates to all areas of human experience.

It can be and has been argued that this economic power is the basic form of power, that, therefore, such power must be made responsible, and that the best way of doing this is by sharing economic power by changing the legal ownership of social property from private to a collective basis.

What shall we make of this argument? It is a very powerful argument. We must recognize the truth of the basic insight that the central fact about property is not so much legal title as *control*. But if that be so, then the nature of the control is central, and it's an open question whether the mere fact of title determines control. In our own economy it has been widely recognized, since the publication of *The Modern Corporation and Private Property* by Berle and Means, that in the giant corporations there has been a progressive disassociation between titular ownership and managerial control.

Second, if this analysis is sound, then the owner of property over persons depends upon law and the character of the state. Whoever controls the law and the state ultimately controls the economy in diverse ways by direct and indirect taxation, tariffs, subsidies, and currency reform. The struggle for control of the law and state then becomes a political tug of war in which all sorts of political pressure groups contend. In democratic communities, now one group, now another, or a coalition of power groups acquires preponderant influence. It becomes an empirical question which class or group can impose its will. The economic vector is always present, but the economic vector is not always decisive in some of the great events of our time and our country. For example, the prohibition amendment in the United States, with its fateful cultural consequences and effects, expropriated without compensation a billion dollar industry in 1917 (when a billion dollars represented a lot of money). The result was not due to economic interests but to the pressures of the Women's Christian Temperance Union. This is a classic illustration of an historical situation in which another factor, the religious factor, rather than the economic factor had a decisive cultural impact.

Third, particularly important is the existence of free trade unions as a countervailing force, both to the economic power of corporate management and to the power of the state itself. So long as any entrepreneur decides to stay in business the trade unions can exact concessions to limit his power over the lives of those who work for him. And that is why the right to strike is central to free trade unionism. Without it we have a system tantamount to forced labor. The very existence and survival of trade unions, as history shows, depends on protective legislation. In other words the economic power of both capital and labor stem substantially from political and legal power.

Finally, the same conclusion can be derived from an analysis of the economic system in which the title to ownership of the social means of production is vested in the collectivity. Let us look more closely at the collectivist system. It so happens that today in every country of the world in which a collectivist economy is found, the power to exclude workers from access to the means of production and life is a monopoly of a minority political party, which in the name *of* the proletariat exercises a ruthless absolute dictatorship *over* the proletariat. So that if we define property functionally, as I have done, we can say that, in effect, the leadership of these totalitarian organizations controls the economic plant of its country with much greater power than either the owners or managers control the corporations of so-called capitalist societies. It does not have to contend with free-trade unions, with strikes, interventions by an independent judiciary and the myriads of regulations that limit its activities. Oddly enough, the central point I am making, to wit, that control over access to work and living conditions is of greater significance than titles of ownership, was acknowledged by none other than Leon Trotsky many years ago in his devasting indictment of the Soviet economy. He failed, however, to recognize that his analysis shattered the basic assumptions of his own historical materialist faith. Trotsky writes:

> If a ship is declared collective property, but the passengers continue to be divided into first, second, and third class it is clear to the third class passengers, the overwhelming majority,

that differences in the conditions of life will have infinitely more importance than juridical changes in proprietorship. The first class passengers, on the other hand, the leaders, will propound together with their coffee and cigars the thought that collective ownership is everything and a comfortable cabin for everybody, nothing at all. (*The Revolution Betrayed*)

I draw two important conclusions from this analysis. First, that although they are interrelated in many ways, to the extent that we can distinguish between economics and politics, *the mode of political decision*, that is whether democracy or totalitarianism prevails, has a greater weight in determining the actual power relations in society than the mode of economic production. And, second, with respect to democracy, the existence of political democracy by itself is incomplete in that it does not guarantee, although it makes possible, economic, ethnic, and cultural democracy. But, and this is the nub of the argument, without political democracy, economic, ethnic, cultural, or any other meaningful kind of democracy, is impossible.

Once we acknowledge the centrality of the mode of political decision, we must recognize the variations in the locus and strength of the power determinants in different political systems. To do this we must overcome what seems to me to be a profound error of Mosca, Pareto, Michels, and their many disciples. They argue that, because in every society the actual laws and the exercise of power are derived not from thoughts, passions, and will of the many, but from the decisions of an elite few in legislative, judicial, and executive roles, therefore democracy is a myth, majority rule an empty shibboleth, and all political change consists in a succession of power elites.

This view is mistaken because it overlooks the great dissimilarities that may spell the difference between life and death, between, on the one hand, political systems that enable freely expressed public opinion to alter public policy and peacefully get rid of existing elites, and on the other hand, systems in which public opinion has no institutional voice or effect and ruling elites can be replaced only by force and violence. The position I am criticizing is comparable to arguing that, because no one possesses infallibility or absolute truth, therefore there are no degrees of truth, no principle difference exists between inexactness and error and a barefaced lie.

To be sure, literally no majority can rule. No democracy is possible, not even the direct democracy of ancient Athens or the New England town meeting, without some delegation of power. And delegated power may be usurped or abused. Consequently we must concentrate our attention on the ways in which political power is exercised in democratic societies, the ways in which it must be made more responsible, and also the ways in which, under certain conditions, it must be curbed or tamed without making it vulnerable to anarchy within and totalitarian aggression from without.

It is an important truth—but far from the whole truth—to say that political power in a democracy rests on public opinion that is a compound of majority beliefs, sentiments, and ideals regardless of whether they are true or false. At the end of his life, John Maynard Keynes, the great economist, maintained that the strongest factor in public affairs was the dominant ideas inherited from the past, usually those discredited by contemporary scientific inquiry. In nondemocratic societies, these are the ideas of the dominant elites. In democracies there are plural sources of opinion, greater interplay and interactions, more input for more sources, and at the very least a legally recognized opposition to the positions expressed by the official holders of power.

Nonetheless, unless one subscribes to some form of magical idealism, the power of concepts or ideas to effect human conduct can't be understood without taking note of the channels and media through which they are communicated. Not all ideas get a hearing, and some not much of a hearing. *Whose* ideas predominate and how? Here we must note the growing power of those who control the sources of information, the selective criteria of what constitutes news, and the way in which reporting the news makes the news, not to mention the distortions and bias of what has been called advocacy journalism. There are many problems here that should be explored in depth.

It has been widely alleged that those who control the public media, television, radio, and the press are the true lords of public opinion and that they exercise the greatest single influence on public opinion, and not only an influence, but a one-sided influence. Many illustrations have been cited of this pervasive influence. One of the most recent and impressive is a two-volume study entitled *Big Story*, by Peter Braestrop, sponsored by Freedom House. It is a study of the treatment of the famous 1968 Tet Offensive by the Vietcong by the American press, television, and radio. The actual facts show that this was a disastrous military defeat for the Vietcong. However, it was systemically played up by the public media as a smashing and humiliating defeat of the South Vietnam and American forces. This distortion of the true situation, it is alleged, produced the turning point in the public support of the American involvement in Vietnam and enabled the Vietcong to snatch a political victory out of the jaws of a military defeat, and ultimately contributed to President Johnson's decision not to run again.

Even if true, and the evidence seems convincing to me, it would require more than this and other cases to validate the thesis that public opinion in the United States is at the mercy of those who control the public media. But it points up the problem. Regardless of what a sober empirical analysis of the facts discloses, we take it for granted that the spirit, if not the letter, of democratic self-government is undermined if public opinion, which ultimately should control the direction of public policy, is manipulated. Of course we do not want the government to control the public media. But neither do we want the public media to control the government, or unduly influence it by systematic campaigns against selected targets or by threats of leaks with bureaucratic contrivance for acts of commission or omission that were ignored or played down when commited by friends in previous administrations.

In a democracy, the power of government ultimately rests, so we say, upon the freely given consent of the governed. Where there is no possiblity of effective dissent, there is no democracy, no matter what it calls itself—"new," "higher," "directed," "organic," or "people's" democracy. Power in a democracy, by the very nature of the way in which a freely given consent is established, must be limited. For it must be possible for a minority peacefully to become a majority. No person or group can be permitted to become so powerful as to foreclose that possiblity. That is why majority rule in a genuine democracy must respect the basic human rights of minorities.

From this it follows that the best hope of avoiding the abuse of power in our world is to share it. Sharing power is rendered difficult by the size of our democracy, which generates a feeling of individual helplessness, a sense of not being in control of the domestic events affecting one's life, of not counting, of being subject to the power of others, whether government, bureaucrats, pressure groups, multinational corporations, trade unions, or other vaguely identified groups referred to as "they" or "them" in opposition to "us." I am not referring to the impatience with legislative delays, the price we pay for brakes on ill-considered decisions by the people's representative in a federal system of divided powers. In time the errors of political action yield to better political judgment—it is to be hoped. I am referring to actions outside the legislative process that are sensed by a majority of citizens as arbitrary, unwise, or unfair. They range from trivial matters like denying freedom of choice to individuals about what to eat, drink, or wear, when information is available about the likely or unlikely consequences of their consumption, to very important matters affecting their life careers.

An example of the latter is the use of the quota system, preferential hiring, and reverse discrimination in employment. Time and time again every segment of the population, regardless of race, ethnicity, and sex, has expressed its opposition to such practices. In May 1977, the Gallop poll reported that eighty-five percent of Americans polled opposed preferential treatment by race or sex for jobs or college places. Sixty-four percent of the nonwhite, that is, members of groups whom today's preferential treatment is supposed to benefit, also opposed such preference. Women, who are also favored by many quota practices, opposed them by eighty-three percent. As the pollsters pointed out, there has seldom been such an overwhelming agreement among Americans on a controversial issue. Yet the bureaucrats of the HEW and other government agencies are imposing this practice without any legislative warrant, and in defiance of the Civil Rights Act of 1964, which explicitly forbids preferential hiring or quotas of any kind. I am not discussing the validity of this practice, which violates the merit system or the Civil Service principle, but citing it as the kind of action that produces malaise within our democratic system and the belief that things are out of control and that we are not determining our own destiny.

Strictly speaking, we cannot literally share most forms of power that affect us. What is meant by the phrase "sharing power" is that we want power to be responsible, that it not act arbitrarily in determining our lives, that it not prevent the personal or group initiatives and growth that are not harmful to others. There are various ways of sharing or diffusing power. The first is by decentralizing organizations. Whatever a local association or group can do at no greater cost than a larger association or group should be transferred to its jurisdiction. Decentralization, however, is not a panacea. There are some things that must be centralized, like the monetary system, immigration policy, national defense. The development of our own federal system shows that the protection of the civil rights of all citizens often requires the intervantion of federal laws and power against local tyrants. Nonetheless the current outcry against the growth of big government, reflected in the tremendous increase of public bureaucracy, which expanded three times faster than private employment in the last twenty years, and the regulatory mania that goes beyond honest labeling, are symptomatic of an increase of arbitrary power that needlessly interferes with the styles of personal life.

Second, in addition to reawakening the sense of the strategic importance of local government, stress must be placed upon the varieties of citizen participation that it makes possible. The idea is as old as Thomas Jefferson and its philosophy was elaborated most fully by John Dewey in his theories of shared experience. But it is not enough to cry up "participation." Its forms must be institutionalized. The forms of participation should reflect equality of concern in a common project, informed awareness, and delegation of power, although not necessarily equality of power. As with decentralization, so with participation—it is not a panacea. There are some problems like that of nuclear control that cannot be settled by mass participation. Such participation is more likely to result in confrontation with delegated authority than a resolution of problems. There is participation and participation. In a democracy it cannot take the form, or should not take the form, of mob action. It is one thing for citizens to cooperate with law enforcement agencies, it is quite another to organize vigilante groups to enforce the law. It is one thing to hold mass meetings, draw up petitions, and addresses to legislatures with respect, say, to the construction of nuclear energy plants. It is quite another form of participation to attempt to take possession of nuclear sites and plants in defiance of law. Usually it is a nonrepresentative minority that engages in actions of this sort in the course of which they violate the rights of the majority, which is willing to accept the arbitrament of the democratic process.

It is not only in politics that we must seek to increase participatory activities. It must also be done in the most difficult and yet the most significant area of human experience, one's vocation and career. For the ordinary person who does not live on an inherited income, the points at which he or she feels the impact of power is at his or her place of work. Whether or not one finds fulfillment in one's work is next to satisfactory personal relationships in love and family, the chief determinants of personal happiness. The trade union or professional association may stand between the worker and the arbitrary actions and petty tyrannies of management. Government, through various forms of insurance, may remove the nightmare fear of unemployment. But the problem of finding satisfaction and significance at work so that, as John Dewey put it, "earning one's living is also a form of living one's life," so that work is not a burden in one's life but a meaningful and fulfilling experience, cannot be solved merely by fatter trade union settlements or by hope of early retirement. No one knows how to meet the challenges to vocational self-fulfillment in an industrial society geared to assembly lines. The most fruitful prospect lies in the proposals and practices that would provide incentives for retraining and promotion, and that seek to draw workers into participation with management in considering problems relating not only to health and plant safety but to the industrial operation itself. West Germany has blazed an original path with its policy of codetermination in which representatives of the workers sit on governing or managing boards. But this does not meet the needs of the rank and file. It may be that as work becomes more mechanized, hours can be reduced to make for more leisure. But unless there is a creative use of leisure, killing time, as the telltale expression suggests, can be just as boring as monotonous work. Whether at work or leisure, both education and industry must provide an opportunity for individuals to develop a center around which to organize a pattern of experience that expresses their free reflective choice. The more citizens there are who have succeeded in fulfilling themselves in their callings, the greater the likelihood that the excesses of power will be restrained.

In considering the realities of power today, we must never forget that the democracies of the world represent the smallest segment of the world's population, and that they have existed through an even smaller segment of recorded history than the nondemocratic forms of society and government. In his second inaugural address, Abraham Lincoln observed that democracy with its principles of majority rule and respect for minority rights was the only alternative to despotism, on the one hand, and anarchism, on the other. And as we should know from history, anarchism itself is the rule of a thousand despots.

The perpetual task of democracy is to see to it that in sharing power through the democratic process it does not weaken its power to defend the democratic process against external and internal foes. At the same time we must not treat our opponents within the democratic process as if they were the enemies of that process. We live in a dangerous world, more hazardous than the world of Hobbes, who justified the power of government in order to avoid a life that was nasty, brutish, ugly, and short. Hobbes's greatest fear was of sudden death, not from natural causes, but at the hands of his fellow man. We live in an age much more dangerous than that of Hobbes because, among other reasons, it is one in which as a consequence of scientific and nuclear technology the sudden death of cultures is possible. This means that the use of power cannot intelligently be foresworn by those who love freedom and that its exercise must always be justified in the light of the preservation of the free society.

Copyright © 1979 by Sidney Hook.

Theme 2
Uses of Power

W. W. Rostow

The Economic Power of the United States

W. W. Rowstow received a B.A. degree from Yale University in 1936; a Ph.D. from Yale in 1940; attended Balliol College, Oxford, England, 1936-38, as a Rhodes Scholar.

His career as an educator began in 1940 when he became an instructor of economics at Columbia University. During the Second World War (1942-45) he served as a major in the OSS. After the war, Rostow joined the State Department as assistant chief of the German-Austrian Economic Division. He later returned to teaching, as the Harmsworth Professor of American History, Oxford University, England, 1946-47.

In 1947 he became the assistant to the executive secretary of the Economic Commission for Europe. He returned to England in 1949 to spend a year at Cambridge University as the Pitt Professor of American History.

From 1940-1961, Rostow was professor of economic history at Massachusetts Institute of Technology and from 1951-1961 he was also a staff member of the Center for International Studies, M.I.T.

In January 1961, President Kennedy appointed Professor Rostow as deputy special assistant to the president for national security affairs. He served in the capacity until December 1961, when he was appointed counselor of the Department of State and chairman of the Policy Planning Council, Department of State; in May 1964, the president appointed him to the additional duty of United States member of the Inter-American Committee on the Alliance for Progress (CIAP) with the rank of ambassador. He served in these latter two capacities until early 1966, when President Johnson called him back to the White House as his special assistant for national security affairs, where he remained until January 20, 1969. In February 1969, Professor Rostow returned to teaching at the University of Texas at Austin, as professor of economics and history.

Professor Rostow received the Order of the British Empire (honorary military division, 1945), the Legion of Merit (1945), and the Presidential Medal of Freedom (with distinction, 1969).

His recent publications include The United States in the World Arena, The Stages of Economic Growth, Politics and the Stages of Growth, The Diffusion of Power, How It All Began, The World Economy: History and Prospect, *and* Getting from Here to There.

It is not often that the reality of power is cooly and rationally examined. Moreover, power is not an easy subject to deal with in a university. Intellectual life is taken up, at its highest level of aspiration, with the pursuit of ideas. The use of power is not, of course, wholly unknown in university life. Universities must deal, after all, with their trustees or state legislatures. And power has even been known to raise its ugly head in faculty meetings. But there is an inherent clash between our instinctive feeling as intellectuals that the best ideas (that is, those we agree with) should reign and the active world where the raw capacity to shape events often determines the outcome, in ways that seem impervious to ideas.

But, in the end, the wise intellectual acknowledges the inevitablility and, even, the legitimacy of the role of power. There can be no organized government, no reasonably civilized society, no orderly and effective institution, in fact, no individual freedom, without the surrender by individuals of some power to central authorities who manage the courts, the police, and protect a sovereign community from others in a world where sovereignty still carries with it the potentiality of war.

And we Americans should always keep in mind that the Constitution, which has provided unity to the nation for almost two centuries, was made possible by a rather raw power deal: the deal between the large and small states that provides Delaware with the same number of senators as, say California, New York, or Texas.

The inherent dilemma between individual freedom and the organized social life was never set out more memorably than in Plato's account of the death of Socrates. Socrates could find no way but the acceptance of a death sentence to resolve his dual commitment: to his personal integrity and to the sovereign community of which he was a part.

But, as the story of Socrates also illustrates, ideas themselves are a form of power. His reflections on the relation of the individual to society—and other aspects of his heritage—have influenced the life of mankind for almost 2400 years.

As you all no doubt know, John Maynard Keynes addressed himself to the notion of ideas as a form of power, in the closing passage of his famous *General Theory.* He asserted that, in the end, ideas were more powerful than vested interests in shaping economic policy. Keynes's *General Theory* has, indeed, demonstrated the validity of that view over the forty-one years since its publication. And, as you will see, I would now regard the success of that demonstration as somewhat excessive—or, at least, excessively prolonged.

I begin with these general observations because I have decided to address one dimension of the power of the United States. Paraphrasing the definition of power in Webster's dictionary, I shall pose the question: Does the United States possess "control, authority, or influence over others" sufficient to shape its own destiny in the economic environment that has emerged on the world scene since the close of 1972 and to influece significantly and constructively the destiny of the world economy as a whole? Although conventional dimensions of power enter into the answer I shall give to his question, I shall also argue that the most important determinant of the outcome lies in the world of ideas.

I begin, in fact, with an idea—an idea that has emerged from a rather pure academic exercise. Since 1972 I have been bringing to fruition some forty years of study and teaching in the form of a history of the world economy over the past two centuries. Out of that effort I have concluded that the world economy entered, in the closing months of 1972, a fifth Kondratieff upswing.

Now, who was Kondratieff and what is a Kondratieff cycle?

N.D. Kondratieff was a Russian economist. Writing in the 1920's, he suggested that capitalist economies were subject to long cycles, some forty to fifty years in length. His views were published in the United States in summary in the mid-1930s. They generated considerable professional discussion and debate, but dropped from view in the great boom after the Second World War. Most contemporary economists vaguely remember having run across his name and ideas in graduate school, but have forgotten precisely what it was he said.

Looking back from the mid-1920s, Kondratieff saw two and one-half cycles in various statistical series covering prices, wages, interest rates, and other data expressed in monetary terms. He sought, but failed, to find concurrent long cycles in production indexes. Kondratieff did not develop a theory of long cycles; but he asserted that a coherent explanation must exist. Since he wrote, the cycles he described have continued down to the present.

My own explanation for the phenomena Kondratieff identified centers on shifts in the prices of food and raw materials relative to the prices of manufacturers.

The period since the end of 1972 is the fifth time in the past two hundred years a rise in the relative prices of basic commodities has occured; and on each of the other four occasions it has been accompanied by manifestations similar to those we have experienced over the past four years: an accelerated general inflation; high range of interest rates; pressure on the real wages of industrial labor; pressure on those with relatively fixed incomes; and shifts of income favorable to producers of basic commodities—in our time, most notably, producers of energy. The other four occasions occurred in the 1970s, the early 1850s, the second half of the 1890s, and the late 1930s. On each occasion, food and raw material prices then fluctuated in a relatively high range for about a quarter century. Approximately another quarter century followed in which the trends reversed; that is, the prices of basic commodities were relatively cheap, as they were from 1951 to 1972. Each of these periods was, in an important sense, unique, and the trends did not unfold smoothly; but the fact is that the world economy for almost two centuries has been subject to a rough and irregular pattern of long cycles in which periods of about twenty to twenty-five years of high relative prices for food and raw materials gave way to approximately equal phases of relatively cheap food and raw materials.

I am not wedded to the notion that these cycles will continue in the future. But I would guess that the inexorable pressure of excessive population increase in the developing world, the tendency of the poor to spend increases in income disproportionately on food, the rising demand for grain-expensive proteins among the rich, the raw material requirements of a world economy where industrialization is spreading in the southern continents, and the high marginal cost of expanding the non-OPEC energy supply will persist for some time. Given these powerful and sustained forces operating on food, energy, and raw material prices and the costs we shall have to incur to achieve and maintain clean air and water, I believe we are in for a long period when the prices of these basic inputs to the world economy will remain relatively high. Indeed, I would guess that we shall only have a fifth Kondratieff downswing if and when we create a new, cheap (hopefully infinite and non-polluting) energy source. As we all know, energy is a critical factor not only in its own right but also because of its role in agriculture and in the extraction of raw materials and, potentially, in rendering the conversion of salt water into fresh water economical.

Down to 1914 the classic response to a Kondratieff upswing was to open new agricultural and raw material producing areas: the American West, Canada, Australia, Argentina, and the Unkraine. The great movements of international capital during this era were, in substantial part, induced by the price system, combined with new technologies of transport and production, to bring new supplies into the market and to restore balance in the world economy. In the fourth Kondratieff upswing (say, 1933-51), the diffusion of new agricultural technologies, rather than the opening of new physical frontiers, reestablished a tolerable balance in food production without much conscious government intervention; although the exploitation of Middle East oil after 1945 ranks, in the field of energy, with the opening up of the American West to agriculture a century earlier. But in the 1970s and beyond we confront the fifth Kondratieff upswing period in a setting quite different from that of the past. I wish we could, but we cannot realistically rely to the same extent on the automatic workings of the price system and private capital markets to restore and maintain balance. All over the world, in one way or another, policy toward resources is in the hands of governments or is strongly influenced by governments. At every stage in the effort to restore balance, therefore, public policy will be involved. We shall have to think and consciously act our way through the fifth Kondratieff upswing.

If I am roughly correct in my assessment of where we now stand in the sweep of economic history, the key tasks we shall face over the next generation in the world economy and our own are quite different from those confronted in the 1950s and 1960s. In those two decades, the world economy expanded at a rate never before experienced over the past two centuries. Global industrial production increased at an annual rate of 5.6 pecent from 1958 to 1971, the volume of trade at 7.3 percent. The highest previous figures were 4.2 percent (1900-1913), respectively. This majestic expansion depended, in part, on relatively low prices for energy, raw materials, and food. These relatively low prices facilitated the rapid diffusion of the automobile, durable consumer goods, and the migration to suburbia in Western Europe and Japan as well as in North America. They helped raise real incomes and permitted an expansion in higher education, health services, and welfare programs to proceed concurrently with a rise in outlays for private purposes. These increased expenditures for consumers goods and services induced high levels of private investment. The industrialized world experienced a quarter century of low unemployment and prosperity. The low relative prices for basic commodities had a depressing effect on some of the economies in Latin America and the other developing continents, notably in the 1950s; but, on balance, the developing world benefited greatly from the good markets provided by the momentum of North America, Western Europe, and Japan; and they benefited also from the relatively low energy prices and the food surpluses the United States made available on concessional terms, as well as from a flow of foreign aid. The rate of growth of industrial production was, in fact, higher in the developing nations than in the advanced industrial world—over 7 percent per annum. And, although many difficult problems evidently remained as the 1970s began, by historical standards the developing countries had made much more rapid progress since 1950 than had Western Europe and the United States during their early stages of growth in the nineteenth century.

But now, of course, a great deal has changed. The growth rates of the advanced industrial countries have slowed down; unemployment has risen; idle industrial plant is endemic; *Business Week,* in its October 17, 1977 edition, ran a special report on the major industrialized nations entitled "The Slow-Investment Economy"; and, except for the oil-exporting countries of OPEC, the growth of most of the developing economies has dangerously decelerated. I say dangerously because the rate of population increase, while beginning to slow down, is still extremely high in most of the developing countries; and high growth rates are required to avoid even larger numbers of unemployed and semiemployed workers than there were even in the 1960s.

Now, how could the notion that we are in the midst of the fifth Kondratieff upswing help the world community deal with this rather dismal set of circumstances; and what role in correcting things can American economic power—the American capacity to influence the course of economic events—play in resolving our problems? Evidently, the key tasks of the world economy are to regain its lost momentum and, simultaneously, to deal with the problems of energy, food, pollution control, and the other supply problems that have moved so disconcertingly to the center of the stage in the 1970s. What the notion of a Kondratieff upswing suggests is that the two tasks are linked; that the route back to full employment and rapid growth is through enlarged investment to solve our resource and supply problems. We must, in our time, perform the equivalent of opening up the American West, as was done in the third quarter of the nineteenth century; or opening up Western Canada, Australia, and Argentina, as was done in the decades before the First World War. But this time there are no vast, empty, physical frontiers, with the possible exception of the seabeds. Nevertheless, I don't believe we can reachieve both rapid growth and make the necessary structural adjustments our situation requires by diverting the flows of investment to expansion and conservation of basic resources.

Let me illustrate this central proposition with respect to the United States.

Where are the nation's great problems that require large investments? The answer is, surely, in these fields:

—energy production and conservation;
—water development, conservation, and transfer;

—investment in our transport system to deal with energy problems to provide cost-effective urban mass transit systems, and to rehabilitate obsolescent parts of the transport network;

—land rehabilitation and forestry development (including development for biomass energy) and the modernization of rural life, especially in the impoverished rural regions of the South;

—the reduction of air and water pollution;

—and expanded research and development in energy and other resource fields, for reasearch and development are the equivalent in our time for the open physical frontiers of the past.

I have tried, but failed, to generate from Washington estimates of the orders of magnitude of the investment required to meet the nation's palpable needs in these basic resource fields; although the work of the U.S. Water Resources Council and the National Transportation Policy Study Commission should yield such estimates in time. But in energy we have a pretty good feel, at least, for the answer as a result of work done at the University of Texas at Austin.

To fulfill the targets of President Carter's National Energy Plan will require some $700 billion in investments in 1976 dollars between now and 1985. This would constitute a jump in the proportion of fixed private investment in energy-related fields from 18 percent in 1974 to an average of more than 30 percent over the period 1977–85. This is a very large shift, indeed; and, if accomplished, would provide powerful stimulus to the economy. It requires energy investment to expand at over 7 percent per annum. We have also calculated the regions in which this investment would have to take place. It is not evenly spread, but enlarged energy-related investment is required in all the regions of the United States for new energy production, conservation, and the switch of the utilities to the use of coal. As you all know, there is considerable skepticism that the provisions of the energy bill that emerged from the House of Representatives will, in fact, achieve the administration's production and conservation targets. But it is obvious that an all-out national effort to fulfill those targets would take us a long way back to full employment and rapid growth. I should add that the energy investment estimate I gave you excludes transport, housing, and other infrastructure that would be associated with an effective national energy plan.

In surveying the information now available on investment requirements for water, transport rehabilitation and development, pollution control, and research and development, I could not derive equivalent approximate figures. But from what we do know, they also require large additions to current investment levels if the nation's needs are to be met.

From surveying these fields and the nation's authentic requirements in them, I, at least, emerge with confidence that the means to full employment are at hand, if we address vigorously resource problems that will become progressively more serious with neglect.

If the route to full employment is all that obvious, why are we still wallowing along with 7.5 percent unemployment and a weak recovery? Why is the problem of reachieving high growth rates and full employment difficult? It is difficult for related intellectual and institutional reasons. Intellectually, our leading economists, be they Republican or Democratic, are experts on manipulating effective demand. Children or grandchildren of John Maynard Keynes, they are awkward in handling resources and supply problems. Keynes's doctrines were formulated at a time of cheap food, raw materials, and energy, during the third Kondratieff downswing. Keynes's theoretical structure virtually ruled out changes in technology or the supply of basic commodities to permit his system to focus on the level of effective demand. Keynesians tend to think these supply problems will take care of themselves if the level of effective demand is high enough. This is simply not the case with respect to energy, agriculture, raw materials, or the environment. A theory of demand will no longer suffice. We need a theoretical framework that embraces problems of supply, as well as demand.

I said we also have an institutional problem. Institutionally, we do not yet have the tools to mount large investment programs in those resource fields. We know how to raise or lower the Federal Reserve discount rate and the rate of expansion of the money supply. We know how to enlarge or diminish the federal budget deficit. Since the 1930s, we have learned how to carry out public service job programs. But we lack the institutions for mounting the kind of public-private sector collaboration required to increase investment in the directions required by this particular Kondratieff upswing.

That is why the leadership of the governors of the northeastern states in pressing forward a northeast energy development corporation is so important, as was the generalization of the concept by the Midwestern Governors' Conference and the National Conference of Lieutenant Governors in August. They extended the role of regional banks beyond energy to water, transport, and other urgent needs.

It now appears that we shall have hearings in the Senate this autumn on regional development banks.

Before we're fully geared to the tasks of the 1970s and 1980s we may also need a national equivalent of the old Reconstruction Finance Corporation; a new way of organizing our federal and state budgets that would separate investment in resources from conventional expenditures; and we shall certainly need a new spirit of public-private cooporation.

A return to high and sustained growth rates in the United States is not simply a matter of worshiping material growth for its own sake. It is a matter of social as well as economic importance at home and it is of major international significance.

It is of social importance because only in an environment of rapid growth and high demand for labor are we likely to make a serious dent on the hard core unemployment of our northern central cities and the hard core rural underemployment in the South and all the social costs that accompany these dislocations. I would not deprecate the measures being taken or envisaged to deal with urban and rural unemployment; but if we continue to experience high average unemployment and a weak demand for labor, we shall be pushing on a string in trying to solve these deeply rooted problems. In a high employment economy, businessmen cease to look on these pools of potential labor as a sad social phenomenon and begin to view them as a badly needed part of the working force. That happened to a significant degree in the 1960s when we got average unemployment in the United States down to 4 percent or less. When average unemployment was under 4 percent, minority unemployment came down under 7 percent. Right now it is twice that level—much higher, as we know, for teenagers.

Much the same is to be said about President Carter's proposed welfare reforms. They are quite explicitly geared to the provision of more jobs. But if present high average unemployment continues, we shall have difficulty sustaining our present welfare system, let alone expanding it.

Internationally, an America that had regained steady momentum via the route I have described would make three major contributions to the world economy as a whole:

—Our recovery would stimulate directly the economies of Western Europe and Japan as well as Canada; and, indirectly, by our example, we would demonstrate how advanced industrial economies can regain their momentum in the new environment of the fifth Kondratieff upswing.

—A sustained revival of the advanced industrial economies would provide enlarged markets to the developing economies of Latin America, Africa, the Middle East, and Asia whose momentum depends heavily on their capacity to earn foreign exchange.

—A sustained revival of the advanced industrial economies is the only setting in which their legislative bodies—including our Congress—are likely to grant the developing nations the increased aid and liberalized trade arrangements they seek. Indeed, there is now considerable danger that chronic stagflation will yield a costly revival of protectionism in the world economy.

Now, let me illustrate the linkage between the American economic preformance and the prospects for the world economy more narrowly by outlining briefly the challenge we face in energy.

The situation we confront can be summarized in three propositions.

Proposition One Is International. The best energy analyses we have tell us that OPEC's production capacity in the 1980s will not be able to meet the oil import requirements of the United States, Western Europe, and Japan. Some oil exporters will begin to experience by the early 1980s an absolute decline of their oil reserves. Those who would still command substantial reserves—notably Saudi Arabia—will not find it in their interest to expand production capacity fast enough to meet the world's requirements. Saudi Arabia is already two years behind schedule in expanding its oil production schedule; and that schedule was not geared to the level of oil import requirements now envisaged for the 1980s. The CIA report, released by President Carter, on the oil supply-demand balance in the 1980s puts the date of crisis as early as 1983—only six years away.

This is also the ominous judgment of the MIT study, directed by Carroll Wilson, entitled *Energy Global Prospects, 1985-2000.* This report, developed by experts from every part of the world, concludes that it is necessary "that energy resources be developed with utmost vigor . . . Failure to act could lead to substantially higher energy prices . . . with the depressant effects on the economies of the world and the consequent frustrations of the aspirations of the less developed countries. The major economic and social difficulties that might arise could cause energy to become a focus for confrontation and conflict."

The grim global prospect for the 1980s is why President Carter's energy balance sheet calls for the United States to conserve energy and to increase energy production in such a way as to reduce our 1985 imports below the level of 1976. President Carter's target is imports of about six million barrels per day by 1985 as opposed to about seven and a half in 1976, and about nine in 1977. The OECD in Paris calls on the United States to achieve an even lower import figure for 1985, four million barrels per day. Our allies know that the United States is the only OECD country that contains a large potential energy reserve. It is, therefore, quite understandable that Western Europe and Japan would expect the United States to develop that reserve promptly and avoid competing for limited OPEC supplies six or so years from now.

Proposition Two. The best objective analyses we have tell us that the plan laid before the Congress and passed by the House of Represent atives will fall radically short of its targets. Those analyses come from universities, think-tanks like Resources for the Future, and Congressional Research Service, the Office of Technology Assessment of the Congress, the Congressional Budget Office, and the General Accounting Office.

If these experts are roughly correct, the United States could confront an import requirement of something like fifteen million barrels per day as opposed to the six called for in President Carter's plan or the four which the OECD assigned to us.

Energy experts—like all other kinds of experts—differ among themselves. But I can tell you that every objective energy expert of whom I am aware shares the view that the legislative and administrative arrangements of President Carter's plan will not achieve its production goals; there will be a large shortfall; and this shortfall is potentially disastrous for the United States, Western Europe, and Japan.

Why this shortfall? Why the gap between the administration's production figures and its implementing arrangements? Frankly, I don't know. But if you study the administration's energy proposals, you will find that, for whatever reasons, the administration drew back from an all-out energy production effort in the United States. The plan simply does not face up to what it will take by way of incentives, capital, and the prompt settlement of the environmental issues if its own production targets are to be fulfilled. And there is good reason to believe that the target for decelerated consumption will fall short as well.

Proposition Three. The lead times between energy investment and energy production are so long that an all-out production effort cannot wait.

One might take the view that it was quite rational for the United States to rely on increased imports from OPEC until the situation got tight in the 1980s and then go into a massive all-out production effort. After all, Alaska oil should buy us a year or so of respite in the rise of oil imports. The North Sea oil will do the same for Western Europe. Why the urgency? The answer lies in the long lead times between the decision to produce energy and energy coming on line. As I go through those lead times, recall the six years, until 1983, the CIA gave us before the global supply and demand curves cross. It took us eight years to begin to get a trickle of Alaska North Slope oil; ten years to begin to get a flow from the North Sea; it will take between six and twelve years to open up and get supplies from offshore Atlantic and Pacific sources once they are firmly established, and right now earlier leasing schedules have been significantly delayed. To establish new coal mines, even, requires four to eight years. It is estimated that from six to nine years will be required to generate usable energy from tar sands, and ten years for shale and synthetics from coal. In Europe and Japan it takes six to ten years to put a nuclear power plant on line once the decision is made to build it; it requires ten to twelve years in the United States. If we provide the incentives and capital, we can get some additional gas and oil from the lower forty-eight states more quickly—say two to three years; and about four years are required to generate additional offshore oil in the Gulf of Mexico.

Looked at overall, there is no doubt in my mind, at least, that if we do not wish to run a mortal risk with our own economy, with the economies of Western Europe and Japan, with the momentum of the developing nations, and with the strategic position of the United States and our allies, we ought to launch right now an all-out energy production as well as conservation effort in the United States. If we do so, there is a fair chance we can contain our oil imports, help avoid a crisis a few years down the road as dangerous as that of the 1930s, and, as I indicated earlier, take a long step back to full employment and rapid growth.

I could present other specific examples of how the nation's success or failure in handling our domestic resources will shape the destiny of the world economy; for example, our policy towards agriculture. But let me draw back now and generalize what I have to say about the economic power of the United States.

Since the late 1950s I have argued that the central phenomenon at work in the world arena has been the diffusion of power away from both Washington and Moscow. The process can be arbitrarily dated from 1948 when the Marshall Plan was accepted by the Congress, launching the revival of Western Europe. That was also the year Tito split with Stalin, launching a diffusion of power within the Communist world, which now includes the confrontation on the inner frontiers of Asia between the Soviet Union and China. The primacy of the United States in the immediate post-1945 years was the product of inherently transient circumstances: the war-induced weaknesses of Western Europe and Japan; and the full recovery of the United States during the Second World War from the depression of the 1930s. Putting aside nuclear matters, there is every reason to believe that the diffusion of economic and political power will continue over the long term. The trends in world production and trade foreshadow a relative decline in the American position in the world economy as the latecomers to industrialization move forward, gaining command of increasingly sophisticated technologies.

But the special character of the economic issues that have emerged on the world agenda since the end of 1972 has increased, for a time at least, the capacity of the United States to influence how well and promptly those issues are dealt with.

First, as I have indicated, the United States alone commands sufficient alternative energy resources to reduce sharply global dependence on OPEC oil and, thereby, permit the world economy to transit the next decade or so without a grave crisis. Our resources include vast amounts of coal and shale as well as the capacity to build nuclear power plants on a large scale. We also have unexploited possibilities even with present technologies for using solar and geothermal energy.

Second, the United States, if it continues to nurture its agricultural base, should remain the dominant source of food exports, including exports to certain developing nations until their own production can be expanded at a higher pace. The United States agricultural export capacity is also a significant cushioning factor in our balance of payments, strengthening the relative position of the dollar among the major currencies.

Third, as I argued earlier, the energy and energy-related investment requirements in the United States are so large that it should be easier for the United States than for others to return quickly to full employment and thereby help lead the OECD world in that direction.

Fourth, the United States has special advantages in research and development that will play a critical role over coming decades in agriculture, raw materials, and pollution control, as well as in energy. The proportion of GNP spent on R & D has fallen in the United States since the 1960s; but the absolute level of our R & D resources still towers over that of the other major industrial nations.

Finally, the United States has a special responsibility and capacity for political leadership. This is not a matter of higher virtue. It is the case because, if the United States fails to lead, there is, as yet, no nation to fill the gap: Western Europe is insufficiently unified; Japan too vulnerable; the Soviet Union too constricted by its ideological commitments to lead comfortably a heterogenous mixture of politics; China is similarly inhibited and at a stage of development when its inner problems and border anxieties dominate its energies. Leadership in this context in no way implies dominance. It requires a mixture of three elements: a national capacity to act significantly with respect to the major issues; a capacity to define common objectives in ways that are not excessively self-serving; and, then, the capacity to help translate those objectives into a working agenda, and to help move it forward with dogged stubbornness. These are assets the United States potentially commands.

To return to Webster's definition, the economic power of the United States does not involve much control or authority, as those terms are normally used; but we do command a very considerable potential influence over the course of events. Although our power is a good deal less than it was thirty years ago, we remain, I believe, the critical margin in the world economy and the global political community.

Our power to influence constuctively the course of events does not lie merely in the scale of our potential energy, agricultural, and R & D resources. It lies in our ability to work together as a national community, once common purposes have been defined and accepted. But I don't believe we can define those common purposes effectively until we escape from one set of ideas and create another. Right now we are trying to live in a post-Keynesian era with Keynesian concepts and policies. The key to the future of American economic power may lie, therefore, in the world of ideas: in creating a coherent conception of where we are, what we face, and building on those concepts some new institutions to do what must be done. But, as I said at the beginning, there would be nothing particularly new about a situation where the effective exercise of power depended, ultimately, on ideas.

Let me try to drive this point home because it is, perhaps, the major general contribution I can make to this course.

In the 1930s, the United States experienced unemployment that rose over 25 percent. That was not because we lacked the economic power to correct the situation. We lacked the necessary ideas and concepts.

In the 1930s, the military weakness of the United States encouraged the Japanese and German militarists and certainly helped bring on the Second World War. That was not because we lacked military potential, it was because we lacked a national consensus on our interests in the world.

Starting in the immediate postwar years, France, under the leadership of Jean Monnet, launched a plan to modernize its economy. Starting with considerable war destruction and much obsolescent plant, France moved forward to a point where its income per head is now perhaps 30 percent higher than that of Great Britain. That did not happen because France has more resources or other forms of economic power than Britain. France developed an idea—a concept—of what needed to be done; Britain, for complex reasons, did not. As Monnet has written, "modernization is not a state of affairs, it is a state of mind (esprit)."

Obviously, to a degree, resources matter in assessing a nation's potential power; but the critical factors are ideas, a sense of communal purpose, and morale.

Or, as it is to be found in Proverbs (29:18): "Where there is no vision, the people perish."

That bit of ancient wisdom has never been more true than in contemporary America facing the tasks of the fifth Kondratieff upswing.

Copyright © 1979 by W.W. Rostow.

Brian M. Jenkins

Terrorism—A New Dimension of Power

One of the first analysts to report on urban guerrilla warfare and international terrorism, Brian Jenkins is currently engaged in directing research on political conspiracy and violence, guerrilla warfare and international terrorism for The Rand Corporation. He is also a consultant on nuclear terrorism to the Nuclear Regulatory Commission.

Mr. Jenkins began his career as an artist, earning a B.S. in fine arts from the University of California, Los Angeles. While studying painting at the University of Guanajuato, Mexico, he switched career plans and returned to UCLA for a master's degree in history (1964). A Fulbright Fellowship enabled Mr. Jenkins to attend the University of San Carlos, Guatemala, where he researched the history of antigovernment consipiracies, remaining a second year on a research grant from the Organization of American States.

Comissioned in the Army Reserves upon graduation from UCLA, Lieutenant Jenkins went on active duty as a paratrooper shortly after his return from Guatemala. He volunteered for the Green Berets in early 1966 and served with the Seventh Special Forces Group in the Dominican Republic as part of the Inter-American Peace Force of the OAS. In late 1966, he went to the Defense Language Institute, Monterey, to learn Vietnamese, then was assigned to the Fifth Special Forces Group in Vietnam. Captain Jenkins won two Bronze Stars and a Vietnamese Cross of Gallantry.

Mr. Jenkins returned to UCLA in 1968 to work on a Ph.D. in history, specializing in the study of conspiracy and revolution, and became a Rand consultant that year. He went back to Vietnam in 1968 as a civilian member of the Long Range Planning Task Group in Saigon, staying in Southeast Asia until mid-1969 and returning later that year and again in 1971. He was the first person in Vietnam to receive the Department of the Army's highest award for Outstanding Civilian Service, awarded for his service on the Planning Group.

In 1972, Mr. Jenkins became an employee at Rand. His reports and articles have been published and quoted in numerous publications, including the Encylopedia Britannica, Time, The New Yorker, Newsweek, *the* New York Times, *the* Los Angeles Times, *among others. He is the author of* International Terrorism: A New Mode of Conflict *and* Will Terrorists Go Nuclear?

I want you to think about some recent headlines, perhaps some things you saw when you turned on your television sets in the recent past. In New York, 100,000 people evacuate major office buildings, trading on one of the commodities exchanges is interrupted. The costs of the disruption for the episode are put in the tens of millions of dollars. In West Germany, state visits are cancelled, the entire cabinet meets, representatives of all political parties and the prime ministers of several German states attend. The prime minister of the Federal Republic takes personal command of the special crisis team. Meanwhile barbed wire, sentry boxes, and sandbag gun replacements are thrown up around government buildings, and the homes of political leaders; armored cars and police armed with submachine guns take up positions at street corners around the capital. For a while the government is virtually paralyzed. Its success or failure in dealing with the crisis, political observers say, will determine the future political climate of the country. In Japan the cabinet also meets in crisis. Here, too, the government is temporarily paralyzed. A decision is made to yield; this has happened before; released prisoners are flown to the scene. Although the incident ends without fatalities, many criticize the Japanese government for capitulating. Japan's minister of justice resigns.

In each of these three cases the crisis I have described was caused not by a national emergency of some sort, not by a state of imminent war, not by a coup d'etat nor an insurrection, but rather by incidents of terrorism. In the first case a series of bombings and bomb threats in New York. In the second case by the kidnapping of a prominent business executive, and susequently the hijacking of a West German airliner. And in the third by the hijacking of a Japan Airlines plane.

Such incidents have become common in recent years. Repeatedly during the last few years small groups have demonstrated that by using terrorist tactics they can achieve disproportionate effects. They can attract worldwide attention to themselves and to their causes. They arouse worldwide alarm, they create international incidents that national governments are compelled to deal with—often before a worldwide audience. To protect against their attacks, or to respond to the crisis situations they create, governments are forced to expend resources vastly out of scale with the magnitude of the actual threat. This increased use of terrorist tactics over the past decade, in my view, reflects fundamental changes in the nature of political power that will have important consequences for society and government. And it is these I would like to address.

There are numerous definitions of terrorism. Let me describe terrorism here simply as the use of actual or threatened violence to gain attention and to create an atmosphere of fear and alarm that in turn will cause people to exaggerate the strength of the terrorists and the importance of their cause. And since most terrorist groups, most groups that use terrorist tactics, are typically small and weak, the violence they practice must be deliberately shocking.

Terrorism is thus violence for effect, but not necessarily for the physical effect on the target itself. Indeed the targets of the terrorist's attack, the actual victims of the terrorist attack, may be incidental, may be secondary in the objectives they seek. The people watching are the primary targets of the terrorists' attack. We might say that terrorist attacks are almost choreographed to achieve maximum publicity. Terrorists often take hostages, for example, to deliberately increase the drama by putting human life in the balance. Terrorism is a form of theater. To describe how the theory works, I'll describe an episode in a play I saw several years ago in New York. The play was put on by a small radical underground theatre group.

I don't remember what most of the play was about, but I do recall this episode. All of the actors and actresses, dressed in black leotards, lined up on the stage in front of the audience. The first actor took out a glass mason jar, unscrewed the lid, took out a live butterfly, held it up for the audience to see, released it, and the butterfly flew off somewhere into the stage lights. The second actor in the row did the same thing; took out a glass mason jar, unscrewed the lid, reached in, took out a live butterfly, held it up, and released it. And this one flew out into the audience. The third actor began to do the same thing, took out a glass jar, reached in, took out a live butterfly, lit a match and burned the butterfly in front of the audience. Now think about that for a moment. Imagine the shock, the revulsion at the senseless act of violence, a trivial act of violence to be sure—the life of one insect—but choreographed in such a way, to cause shock among the audience. It worked. The people in the front row were ready to leap up on the stage and strangle the actor who had burned the butterfly. Had they passed a hat in the audience that night to take up a collection for the butterfly's life, I have no doubt they could have raised a sizable amount. If you keep that story in mind, you begin to get at the fundamental theory of how terrorism works. Instead of the lives of insects, the lives of human beings are placed in the balance in a deliberately choreographed, deliberately dramatized situation; demands are placed upon the audience watching, designed to achieve shock. This effect expands the importance of the whole event.

The concept of terrorism itself is an old one. The actual term "terrorism" entered the political lexicon almost two centuries ago during the French Revolution, but the idea and the practice are much older than that. But international terrorism as we see it today is a relatively recent invention, the product of a confluence of recent political and technological developments. Contemporary technology has provided terrorists with new targets and new capabilities. Jet air travel, for example, gives them both dramatic targets and unprecedented mobility, allowing them to strike almost anywhere in the world.

Recall the Tel Aviv Airport massacre of May 1972, in which Japanese terrorists recruited in Japan [met Palestinian terrorists in North Korea, formed an alliance] flew to the Middle East to receive training, went to one European country to pick up their weapons, went to another European country to board an aircraft, flew on that aircraft to Tel Aviv Airport in Israel, got off that plane and began machine gunning passengers, most of whom were Puerto Rican pilgrims on their way to the Holy Land. Such actions are made possible by the tremendous mobility that we have in the world today.

The second important technological development is the development in communications in recent years: radio, television, communication satellites—the media that make it possible to broadcast to a worldwide audience the dramatic incidents of violence terrorists are capable of creating. And if you think of terrorism, as I tend to do, as a form of theater, a violent form of theater to be sure, then the ability to reach an audience of several hundred million provides the terrorist with a tremendous amount of leverage and seeming power.

A third development is modern society's increasing dependence on technology, new forms of technology, in some cases fragile systems, in some cases quite vulnerable systems. I have mentioned one already—civil aviation. Looking at it from one point of view, a modern 747 jet is a masterpiece of modern technology, a flying theater. Looking at it from the terrorists' point of view, it is a tin can filled with 350 hostages at 39,000 feet. Other vulnerabilities that recently have come in for a great deal of discussion in this country are the vulnerabilities inherent as the country becomes more dependent on nuclear power, with increasing traffic in fissionable material and radioactive waste material and the possibilites that this may afford political extremeties in the future.

A fourth development is the appearance of new weapons that increase a small group's capacity for violence. When I refer to weapons development here, I am not talking about the weapons development we have seen since World War II: major weapons systems such as intercontinental ballistic missiles, nuclear weapons, nuclear submarines, things of this sort. I'm talking about the perhaps less dramatic, but no less important, developments that have taken place in the area of individual weaponry—small packages of explosives with minaturized detonating devices, the kinds of things that make a letter bomb possible, the small handheld precision guilded weapons, which I'll discuss later. These things increase an individual's capacity for violence. These are the *technological* developments that have provided terrorists with these new capabilities. The *political* circumstances that led to the development of the tactics of international terrorism are three.

First, I would mention the failure of the rural guerrilla movements in Latin America in the late 1960s. Following the victory of Fidel Castro in Cuba, there was a proliferation throughout Latin America of rural guerrilla movements in Guatemala, in Brazil, in Bolivia, and in other countries of Latin America. But by the end of the 1960s, it was quite apparent that the Cuban model of revolution could not easily be duplicated elsewhere. As a result, the revolutionary groups began to turn their attention to the cities—the cities where they could be assured of attracting worldwide attention. They quite naturally turned to the dramatic tactics of certain bank robberies, seizing hostages—first their own government officials and later foreign diplomats.

The second event was the stunning military victory of the Israelis in the six-day war in 1967, which caused the Palestinians to abandon their dependence on Arab military power to achieve their aims and to rely more heavily on the tactics of terrorism with the approval and support of Arab governments.

The third political route of modern terrorism would be the widespread anti-Vietnam War and antigovernment demonstrations in the universities of Western Europe, Japan, and the United States. To be sure, by no stretch of the imagination could the antigovernment or antiwar protests be called acts of terrorism. People were exercising their rights to protest. But historically, these mass protest movements spawned extremist fringes, small groups that were dedicated to carrying on a struggle by violence even after the student movements had subsided. And so emerging from the demonstrations of West Germany in the late 1960s were the Baader-Meinhoff group and the June 2nd group. Emerging from the mass demonstrations in Tokyo in the late 1960s was the United Red Army in Japan. Emerging from the protest movement in this country were our own small groups, the Weather Undergound,

The New World Liberation Front, the Red Dawn, the Red Guerrilla Family, and others.

Once the tactics of terrorism were developed, of course, and their utility demonstrated and displayed worldwide by means of mass communications, they in turn provide inspiration and instruction for other groups and terrorism, becoming self-perpetuating phenomena.

Let's think about that for a moment. What really are the major sources of terrorist power today? First, it is the high value that most societies place on human life. Governments are extremely reluctant to allow hostages to be killed (particularly hostages of another nationality) despite many cases of popular pressure that a line must be drawn, that capitulation must stop. Governments are extremely reluctant to have people killed, to have the blood on their hands. So the tremendous value we place on human life, and certainly I would not argue for the contrary, is one of the vulnerabilities in our society and a vulnerability that terrorists can exploit and one that gives them tremendous power. That terrorists recognize and exploit this can even be seen in the frequency with which terrorists use the tactic of seizing hostages. Indeed approximately a third of all incidents of international terrorism involve taking hostages by hijacking airliners, taking over embassies, or kidnapping individuals. Terrorists seize hostages, whether diplomats, corporate executives, tourists, sometimes just anybody handy, to deliberately heighten the drama of the episode by placing human life in the balance and thereby increasing their own leverage. In return for the release of hostages, terrorists have received millions of dollars in cash. In one single episode in Argentina they received sixty million U.S. dollars. I want to point out that that is equivalent to one-third of that country's national defense budget. They have gotten military aid in return for hostages; they've gotten financing for various philanthropic enterprises such as distributions of food and clothing to the poor. They've obtained the release of imprisoned comrades, safe passage for themselves to other countries, and compelled governments to denounce treaties.

A second source of terrorist power, and one to which I have alluded already, is free access to the media, which does enable them to reach a worldwide audience, thus magnifying the importance of their actions. This statement is by no means an argument for censorship. It's the price we pay for having a free press and is a recognition of a vulnerability in a free society. I tend to regard the media, particularly the electronic media, as a vulnerability in the same way that I regard civil aviation as a vulnerability. We certainly can stop airline hijackings by grounding all airliners. So we can still stop terrorist access to the media by censoring all the media, but that is not the point. The media are an extremely useful and beneficial tool for our society. Access must be unlimited at both ends, both for the people making the news and the people in the audience. But it is a vulnerability.

A third source of power, particularly for those terrorists who operate internationally, is the historically unprecedented respect shown in the world today for the concept of national sovereignty, even for the sovereignty of those nations that provide sanctuary and aid to terrorists. In another era, I suppose, nations victimized by terrorists operating from abroad probably would have reacted militarily. Again, this is not a call for the return of the gunboat diplomacy of the nineteenth century, but simply a recognition that gunboats and punitive expeditions no longer have any place in the world. And groups can take advantage of this decision of national governments to abide by the rules.

While it is easy to become somewhat overly alarmed about terrorism, I think it is important to point out that the actual amount of terrorist violence has been greatly exaggerated; indeed, that is proof of its success in gaining worldwide attention. But measured against the world volume of violence, the number of casualties from terrorist violence is trivial. I don't meant to say that any death is not tragic and shocking, but let's look at the statistics. About a thousand persons have died in international terrorist incidents since 1968. Over two thousand or so have been injured. If we add the casualties of domestic political violence in places such as Belfast and Buenos Aires, then the total number of deaths may ascend to about 10,000 at the most. More than twice that number of people are murdered every year in the United States. The annual homicide rate in this country is approximately 20,000 people. And indeed since 1968, six million people in the world have died in thirteen wars. Six million. So when we take those thousand deaths and we measure them against the world volume of violence, without sounding callous, it is trivial. The important fact is not to keep in mind that it is trivial violence, but to keep this in perspective when talking about some of the draconian countermeasures that are demanded for dealing with the terrorists—some of the final solutions that are more dangerous than the threat the terrorists themselves pose to society.

Of course, it can be argued that terrorism is not appropriately measured by body counts, by property damage, but rather by the amount of attention it receives, by its ability to create these national and international crises by the cost of protection against terrorist attacks, which are enormous, by the amount of alarm that terrorists create, and by the consequences that these have for society. Terrorist tactics are calculated to rivet attention and to create alarm, and in this they succeed. The fundamental issue here is fear, and perhaps the biggest danger posed by a terrorist is not in the physical damage they do, but in the atmosphere of alarm they create that corrodes democracy, breeds repression, and contributes to the sense of insecurity of an era of changes.

Fortunately, thus far the world has not responded in overly repressive ways, at least not in most nations. Legislation has produced a growing corpus of law to deal with politically motivated crimes, specifically acts of terrorism. In many cases, terrorism has been identified as a crime, different from, and in most cases more serious than, the traditional crimes that terrorists commit: murder, kidnapping, arson. New criminal offenses, such as air piracy, have been identified. Many countries have extended their penal codes to cover crimes committed outside of the national territory, such as crimes aboard airliners. Legislation has broadened police power. In some countries, trial procedures have been changed generally to the accused's disadvantage. Often measures adopted as temporary have become permanent, or at least have prevailed for far longer than their drafters had originally anticipated. Several nations have created committees or coordinating groups at the national level to coordinate national efforts against terror. New special antiterrorist organizations have come into being within police departments or within internal security organizations. Military participation in police functions has increased. Private security forces have grown tremendously. Special military units for possible use in antiterrorist operations abroad have also been organized and trained.

But while the measures enacted to combat terrorism have impeded free movement to a certain degree, subjected travelers to more scrutiny, and on occasion created a nuisance, we cannot say without some exaggeration that democracy has been imperiled by them. Authoritarian regimes have characteristically reacted with repressive measures. Nations with strong democratic traditions have cautiously limited certain liberties as the price of security. Civil libertarians argue, however, that these infringements, however small, are too high a price for tranquility. And it is true that such measures tend to have a cumulative effect; and indeed our society quickly accustoms itself to them. If just ten years ago, I had told you, or indeed someone had told me, that before boarding the airplane my baggage would be X-rayed, my hand luggage would be searched, and I personally might be frisked, I would have been outraged. I would have called my lawyer, I would be talking about unlawful search and seizure. And yet today this is something we not only put up with it is something we even welcome as a guarantee that the plane is going to the destination for which we bought the ticket. We have ample reminders on our television screen that this is not always the case.

But we don't live in airports and we wouldn't particularly like to live in airports. Yet in Belfast, the entire downtown area, a depressing place, has been turned into a huge airport: the city has been surrounded with fencing and checkpoints and, if one goes into downtown Belfast, one is searched; metal detectors are there, one is frisked, and packages are examined. This, in a free society! So the consequences can be quite severe. Historically, terrorism has bred repression.

While the use of terrorist tactics has proved useful, as I have been emphasizing here, in getting publicity and occasionally in obtaining some political concessions, few terrorist groups can claim to have achieved any of their long-range political objectives by such means. In that respect, terrorism is a failure. Indeed it is hard to see how assassinations, bombings, kidnappings, and how hijackings can be translated into the achievement of the terrorist objectives. Do Palestinians seriously expect Israel to accede to the creation of a Palestinian homeland because its planes have been hijacked? Do South Moluccan terrorists think that the Dutch government can deliver them an independent Molucca? The answer is probably no. As I say, it does work for publicity and by evidence of that how many of you honestly had ever heard of South Molucca before the incidents that took place in the Netherlands? I had some idea that South Molucca must be somewhere south of North Molucca, which exhausted my entire knowledge of the subject. As I say, the answer is probably no. They don't really believe that the Dutch government can deliver them an independent Molucca, but it is important from their point of view. Terrorists often see themselves as the victims of solutions that the world has imposed upon them. The Palestinians in their view are dispossessed by a decision of the British to create a homeland for the Jews, by decisions made in the United Nations, by continued U.S. support for Israel, in sum by a series of decision made elsewhere. And thus the terrorist approach is to create, through the use of terrorist tactics, an intolerable situation that will compel the world to intervene and impose another solution that will be favorable to them.

Terrorists fighting on behalf of independence movements or separatists causes hope to produce sufficient pain and expense to compel the central authority to give up and withdraw from the contested territory. They do not win, but they simply prolong the struggle and hope that the other side will give up and go home. Revolutionary terrorists hope to create a situation that will simply make it impossible to govern. Thus, terrorists don't expect to defeat their opponents, they expect their opponent to eventually quit or wear out or some external power to come in and impose a solution on their opponent, or society to collapse. All they have to do is prolong the struggle.

But what about the future? What trends are discernable now? I believe that the use of terrorist tactics will persist as a mode of political expression. All terrorists have to do is prolong the struggle; it doesn't necessarily achieve for them their long-range goals, but terrorists are typically shortsighted and those who use or would use terrorist tactics are sufficiently encouraged by the occasional publicity, the occasional tactical victories, to preclude their abandonment of terrorist tactics. They see their goals in terms of short-range goals and these have been met. Among the other trends, I think it's safe to say that terrorists appear to be getting more sophisticated in their tactics, their weapons, and their exploitation of the media. Terrorists will remain highly mobile, able to strike targets anywhere in the world. Some of the new weapons being developed for military arsenals, such as shoulder-fired surface-to-air missiles may find their way into the hands of terrorists. Indeed this is perhaps one of the most frightening new developments.

We are currently in the process—that is the United States, the countries of Western Europe, the Soviet block countries—of developing and deploying a whole new range of weapons called man-portable precision guided munitions or PGMs. Now what is a precision guided munition? It is simply a weapon that enables you to correct the course of the projectile after it has left the barrel of the gun. In other words, hitting the target does not depend on how good of a shot you are. You can correct the course after firing, or the projectile itself may have in its nose a T.V. screen or perhaps an infrared heat-seeking device that allows it to correct its own course. There's nothing particularly new about this technology. It's the same technology that enables us to land rocketships on the moon. What is new is a result of the developments in the electronics industry; the components of these systems are becoming more and more miniaturized and what could be put in an intercontinental ballistic missile can now be put in a weapon that is three and one-half feet long, weighs thirty pounds, has a range of one to three kilometers, and a hit probability approaching one. That means, if you can see it, you can hit it.

Now it's not conjecture that such weapons will find their way into the hands of terrorists; indeed they already have. At the Rome airport several years ago, several Arab terrorists were arrested. They had in their possession the Soviet Strela missile the SA-7. This has an infrared heat-seeking device. An infrared heat-seeking missile, shoulder fired, tracks the heat of an aircraft engine and literally flies right up the tail pipe and explodes inside the aircraft. These are now deployed by the military in the hundreds of thousands. By the end of the decade, these weapons will be available not only to the developed countries of the world, but to as many as thirty or forty of the Third World nations. If we postulate even a conservative loss rate by diversion, by illegal sales, by theft, of one-tenth of one percent, then these weapons will be loose in the hundreds by the end of the decade. That may be insignificant militarily, but we're not talking about the use against military targets. We're not talking about weapons being used against tanks or against tactical aircraft. We're talking about their use against civilian aircraft, or moving cars in a presidential motorcade, or a speakers' podium from a distance of one to three kilometers.

Terrorist groups appear to be strengthening their links with each other. One result is the emergence of multinational free-lance terrorist groups willing to carry out attacks on behalf of causes they are sympathetic with or to undertake specific operations or campaigns of terrorism on commission from client groups of governments. We see that nations that are unwilling or unable to mount a conventional military challenge on the battlefield may adopt terrorist tactics or employ terrorist groups as a mode of surrogate warfare against other nations. Other trends include the emergence, particularly in Western Europe, of a semipermanent terrorist subculture—composed of several generations of terrorists, plus their supporters, their sympathizers, their lawyers, their propagandists, their chroniclers, their groupies—all of whom are in some way dependent upon continued terrorist activity. One West German official has called it the "terrorist scene." Within this subculture, terrorism is evolving from a set of tactics used to support an ideology into the ideology itself. Now this is a terribly significant development in terms of what terrorists may do in the future, because previously terroristic action has always been, to a degree, constrained by the political considerations of not doing something that would alienate the terrorists' constituents of the terrorists. You don't poison the water supply in the name of the popular front and expect to remain popular for very long. And if we don't expect terrorists to make moral judgments, they do at least, we hope, make practical political judgments. There are upper limits, we hope, even on terrorism. But if we begin to think of a terrorist subculture, if we begin to think not of an external constituency, whether that is "the people" or "the workers" or some other perceived constituency and instead, think of the constituency as the terrorists' subculture itself, then constraints on actions are seriously eroded; and terrorists may do things to demonstrate that they can do them, or do things to see if they can be done. Terrorist actors play before an audience of other terrorists, and the possiblities for more serious violence are increased as constraints are eroded and the competition for the world's attention heats up.

Another trend is the evolution of politically motivated terrorist groups into a more traditional form of criminal organization that still maintains a political veneer. In many countries the business of terrorism is becoming a business itself. The IRA, for example, is heavily into extortion, runs protection rackets, participates in defrauding insurance companies, and is also acquiring legitimate businesses, such as pubs and taxicab companies. One of Argentina's largest terrorist groups is reported to have built up a large stock portfolio with the ransoms it has collected. Today's terrorist groups may become tomorrow's Mafia. Perhaps with the evolution from politically motivated activities into the more traditional areas of crime, there may come a certain conservatism. In the first case we see a terrorist subculture carrying out actions for the sake of carrying out those actions. In this case, we see actions carried out with a profit motive. And if there isn't any profit motive, one doesn't carry out the actions. One sees considerations of not alienating the public too much so as not to bring too much heat down on the organization. As they evolve into more criminal organizations, like Mafias, they may dissuade themselves from undertaking some of the more serious acts that might otherwise be considered.

Still another trend is the appearance of a new generation of "Luddites" out to destroy the machinery of Western Industrial Society in the name of a vaguely leftist anticapitalist, humanist, antitechnology ideology. We'll see this in certain areas, particularly in Europe, where the purely environmental antinuclear power movement has in a sense merged with the unenvironmental political radical movement: political radicals fastening themselves on the mass demonstrations against nuclear power and operating according to their own agendas to use this enthusiasm and this protest as an instrument against the state. Nuclear power becomes a symbol of the state, a symbol of modern technology that, in their view, is not wanted by everyone.

We see it also in Italy in the number of bombing attacks in the past twelve months on data processing centers—another symbol of modern society. What better symbols of modern industrial society than the nuclear reactor and the computer. Attacks on the computer centers, bombing attacks with messages left behind that this computer center is training the tools of the capitalist state and must be destroyed, or that the computers themselves are the instruments of a capitalist state. We see it also in terms of some conflicts between French university students and the government on the issue of curriculum, where the students are objecting to the increased emphasis being given business administration and scientific educational courses in the universities—and, in their view, the consequent devaluing of the humanities degree. I share some sympathy with this attitude, holding as I do a humanities degree myself, but the point is that the French government sought to bring about these changes in order to reduce the number of graduates every year who graduate into the ranks of the unemployed with their humanities degrees. The government attempted to move more people into the sciences, provoking a tremendous reaction, violent demonstrations, even some bombings. In the antinuclear movement, and I'm not talking about the environmentalist anticuclear opposition, I'm talking about a political antinuclear movement, in that and other confrontations involving the rejection of a more scientific world, a more business-oriented university curriculum, there is the shared judgment that modern industrial society and modern government are becoming increasingly technological and increasingly inhuman and, as a result, people are being dehumanized. And that the only way to fight back against this is to destroy the technology. The idea of terrorism in the name of humanism may strike some as novel and incongruous, but we do have some examples of this as a third trend.

International terrorism is still a comparatively minor problem in the world. I think the societal consequences of terrorism go far beyond anything yet accomplished by the terrorists themselves, or even contemplated by the terrorists. The developments that have made international terrorism possible could eventually redefine war and compel us to alter our present concepts of security, of defense, and eventually of government itself. It seems that the equations of power are changing. Put terrorism into its historical perspective and we see that as a result of new weapons, as a result of the invention and demonstration of these new tactics, power—defined here in its most primitive sense as simply the capacity to destroy or to disrupt—is descending to smaller and smaller groups. Or to put it another way, that the small bands of political extremists, the irreconcilables, the fanatics, the lunatics that have always existed in society have become an increasingly potent force to be reckoned with. The capacity for violence affecting large numbers of people, once possessed only by organized military forces, is coming into the hands of gangs, whose grievances, whether real or imaginary, it will not always be possible to satisfy. And that is going to have some important effects.

One immediate effect we have already seen is the major diversion of resources into internal security functions. The protections of political leaders, diplomats, airports, nuclear facilities, and other vital systems is going to demand increasing manpower and money. I foresee the continuing growth of what we might call an internal defense budget. It won't appear as an internal defense budget, but it will be dispersed among the budgets of various government agencies as well as the security expenditures of private business. It seems to be part of a major shift in society from viewing security traditionally in terms of secure national frontiers, clearly a national responsibility, to the defense of what we might call interperimeters, guarded facilities, airport perimeters, privately patrolled communities, security buildings, alarmed homes, where the burden of this kind of defense is increasingly placed upon local government, the private sector, and the individual citizen.

Should terrorism persist, we may anticipate that some of the security measures of a kind that are now enforced at airports will be extended to other areas. The nature of this course will depend on the future course of terrorist tactics. Continued placing of bombs aboard aircraft or in an airline terminal could result in routine X-raying of all baggage, not just a portion of it. Bombs in public buildings could bring about some sort of screening process at entrances, similar to, but certainly more elaborate than, the present routine identification and cursory search of briefcases at certain federal office buildings. Increasingly, employees and visitors may be compelled to pass by metal and explosives detectors and to have all parcels examined. Identity cards will become more prevalent in our society. Various forms of clearances may become routine for an increasing portion of society. Armed private security guards may become ubiquitous. Buildings themselves may become more fortified. A friend of mine, who is an architect, recently participated in the designing of a major bank in the city of San Francisco. He said, "You know that this building is designed without any windows below the third floor." The San Francisco area has 25 percent of all the bombings in this country. But think of it, this bank is designed like a fortress, with no windows to be blown out below the third floor. We're talking about a building being turned into a medieval castle. Indeed geographically, society in the future may become a series of separated or overlapping perimeters that people move through to work, travel, or visit—in a sense a more medieval society. The only difference is that the moats and the drawbridges and the portcullises are in a more electronic form.

The second consequence is that national sovereignty seems to be eroding. This is not simply the result of terrorism; it's happening anyway. International financial organizations, multilateral economic institutions such as the EEC and OPEC and the multinational corporations have diminished the economic prerogatives of the state. The global dimension of the world's major problems—population growth, food, energy, pollution—makes them seem beyond the capacity of any single nation to solve. Ethnic separatist movements, proliferating around the world, many of them fielding small terrorist groups, are rejecting central authority. The earth itself is increasingly being subdivided. Do you know that since the end of World War II, the number of independent nations has tripled. By 1990, there will be 200, perhaps 250, independent nations in the world, many of them politically unstable and economically nonviable. Nation-states are still the primary unit for fighting wars, and they still possess the indefinable magic of sovereignty once considered the divine rights of kings. But they are being stripped of this power, as governments are compelled to yield in front of a public audience to small bands of extremists. What magical sovereignty is there left?

As for being the primary unit for fighting wars, that also is changing. Nations do maintain their credentials in the last resort by monopolizing the means of major violence. But as the balance of military, that is destructive power, shifts away from national armies toward smaller armies that do not necessarily represent or confine their destructive activities to any particular nation, national governments may indeed lose their monopoly over the means of large-scale violence and we may see the emergence, semipermanent or permanent, of subnational and transnational entities. The world then becomes an unstable collection of nations, ministates, autonomous ethnic substate governments in exile, national liberation fronts, guerrilla groups aspiring to international recognition and legitimacy, and a collection of emphemeral but disruptive terrorist organizations, some of which are linked together in vague alliances, some perhaps the protégés of foreign states. It may be a world of formal peace between nations, free except for brief periods of open warfare, but with a higher level of political violence. Looking at it historically, a world not unlike the late Middle Ages or perhaps Renaissance Italy, in which we had kingdoms and various duchies and condottiere and cities going to war with other cities in a style of diplomacy and warfare that was far more fluid than that today.

The questions remain: How will society reckon with violent little groups that are trying to make it impossible to govern? How will the world deal with several hundred sovereign and semisovereign political entities? As political extremists invent new tactics and acquire new weapons, as society acquires new vulnerabilities, as extremists are able to project exaggerated power through mass communications, these developments pose a unique challenge to democratic governments that try to govern by peaceful consensus.

Copyright © 1979 by Brian M. Jenkins.

Theme 3
Power and Politics

James MacGregor Burns

Power and Politics—An Overview

James MacGregor Burns is Woodrow Wilson Professor of Government at Williams College, where he has taught since 1941. Professor Burns received a B.A. from Williams College and an M.A. and Ph.D. from Harvard University. He also attended the London School of Economics.

He is author of Congress on Trial, Roosevelt: The Lion and the Fox, Kennedy: A Political Profile, The Deadlock of Democracy: Four Party Politics in America, Presidential Government: The Crucible of Leadership, Roosevelt: The Soldier of Freedom, Uncommon Sense, *and* Edward Kennedy and the Camelot Legacy. *For his second volume on Roosevelt he was awarded the Pulitzer Prize in history, the National Book Award, and the Francis Parkman Prize for 1971.*

Dr. Burns has served as president of the American Political Science Association and has recently published a major study, Leadership *(1978).*

> *We must, under modern conditions, reassess the old idea that the main governmental protection of civil liberty, social and economic rights, and due process of law lies in the legislature or the courts or state and local government. The main protection lies today in the national executive branch. As a general proposition the Presidency has become the chief protector of our procedural and substantive liberties; as a general proposition, the stronger we make the Presidency, the more we strengthen democratic procedures and can hope to realize modern liberal democratic goals.*
>
> *The danger of presidential dominance lies in a different and more subtle tendency. It lies not in presidential failure but in presidential success. It lies not in the failure to achieve our essential contemporary goals of freedom and equality but in their substantial realization and in the incapacity of presidential government to turn to new human purposes.*
>
> (*From* Presidential Government.)

I am enormously impressed that the University of Delaware is sponsoring a program on the toughest and most central question in American politics and political science, and that's the question of power. It's the most badly understood, it's the most superficially treated subject, in my view, in political sicence. It should be a cutting edge of theory in political science; it's not. When I think of how the physicists have developed their central concept of energy (and to think with both happiness and horror of how the physicists have *applied* that central concept of energy), and contrast how little we political scientists have done with our subject of power, it seemed to me that if this university was willing to sponsor a series of programs on that subject, I would like to be present! This subject is so serious and so difficult there is no way for me to trivialize it, there is no way for me to glamorize it, there is no point in my telling anecdotes about it; but it would simply divert us from the toughest job that political scientists and all social scientists, and I must say all practitioners—and particularly all of us who are the subjects of power, the *targets* of power—must undertake. It would take time away from the kind of analysis that I would like to offer, with the hope that you will stay with me while we go through some difficult material not because it's gobbledygook but because it is a tough subject. And I make a point of this because there are countless treatments of power that make it into a simple subject, and my point is that it is *not*.

Just as we search for leadership we also seek to cage and tame it. We recoil from power even as we are bewitched and titillated by it. It's a kind of fad, power is, and it's too bad we can't put as much analysis into it as we devote attention to it. We devour books on power—power in the office, power in the bedroom, power in the corridors. People proport to teach about power, what it is, how to get it, how to use it, how to "gain total control over everyone around you." That's the title of a book, a very popular book. We think up new terms for power: "clout," "wallop," "muscle." We measure the power of the aides of great men by the number of yards between their offices and that of number one. And far more serious, in this age we cannot escape the horror of naked power. Stalin controlled an apparatus that year after year and in prison after prison quietly put to death millions of persons, some of them old comrades, with hardly a ripple of protest. Between teatime and dinner Adolf Hitler could decide whether to release a holocaust of terror and death in an easterly or in a westerly direction, with stupendous impact on the fate of a continent and the world. On smaller planes of horror, American soldiers slaughter women and children cowering in ditches, village tyrants oppress serfs and slaves, revolutionary leaders disperse whole populations into the countryside where they dig or die. The daughter of Nehru jails her political adversaries and is jailed in turn. So we of this century and of this generation may be forgiven our preoccupation with power, but I contend we are paying a steep intellectual as well as psychological price for this mere obsession.

Viewing politics *as* power has blinded us to the role of power *in* politics, and hence to the pivitol role of leadership. Two world wars, the murder of entire cities, scores of revolutions, the rise of men of transcending power like Ghandi and Mao, and the unleashing of the atom, have distorted our perception of the terms on which, I argue, most human relationships are conducted. These terms are not naked power, or even manipulation. The terms on which we conduct most of our relationships, unless we are terrorists in Germany, is face-to-face persuasion, exortation, reciprocity, morality—in short what I call leadership. Now perhaps I, in my own person, exemplify the problem, for I have shared this distorted perception of power. I was born in the last year of World War I, I grew up in the aftermath of that war, which took its toll in my own family. I took part in World War II. I have spent a lot of time studying the records of these and other wars and I have been struck by the sheer physical impact of men's armaments. Yes, I did watch the invasion of Okinawa, the unleashing of massive power over the beaches of that one-time tranquil island. I have lived, as many of you have, in the age of political titans and, hence, I too have assumed that their actual power equaled their reputed power. As a political scientist, I have belonged to a power school that analyzed the interrelationships of persons on the basis only of power. We political scientists have desparately tried to find the central unifying concept; and, I think, I at least exaggerated the role of power. In studying leaders, too, we have vastly overrated the power factor. And I believe that naked power as we define it will be an analytical tool of dwindling importance in the years ahead because power as coercion will be less significant than power as *transaction* and power as *transformation*.

Now it's very natural that we would have this obsession with power. One reason is that striking displays of power like the ones I've mentioned stick in our memories. They stick in our memories while the more subtle interplays of leaders and followers elude us. Just a couple of examples. I've long been haunted by a tale that John Speke brought back from Africa when he was undertaking his very early exploration of the source of the Nile. He came upon a tiny kingdom which, interestingly, was the kingdom of Uganda. He was briefed when he got there by the outer guards as to court decorum. He was told that while the king's subjects groveled before the throne, their faces plastered with dirt, he, this visiting Englishman Speke, would be allowed to sit on a bundle of grass while minstrels played on the tambera for him, and then he would be summoned to the court where rats, porcupines, goats, cows, and women would be arrayed for presentation to him.

While all of this happened, amid much decorum, Speke was holding something he knew would be useful and of interest to the king of Uganda; and that was a gun. The king showed an avid interest in the gun that Speke showed him, and indeed the king invited Speke to take some potshots at the cows that were assembled there. Amid great applause Speke dropped five cows in a row with this fantastic weapon that he had brought. Speke goes on, "The king now loaded one of the carbines I had given him with his own hands, and giving it full cock to a page told the page to go out and shoot a man in the outer court, which was no sooner accomplished than the little urchin returned to announce the success with a look of glee such as one would see in the face of a boy who had robbed a bird's nest, caught a trout, or done any other boyish trick. The King said to him, 'and did you do it well?' 'Oh, yes,' the little boy said." Speke says that the affair created little interest in the court and no one inquired about the man who had been killed. It's a story to make one pause. Metesa was an absolute monarch, but could a man be randomly shot by the whim of a tyrant, indeed by the whim of a boy? Did the victim have no mother or father, no protective brothers, no lover, no comrades with whom he had played and hunted? But then I think one must not suspend disbelief. One has to ask, did Speke actually *know* what happened in the outer court? Was the king staging an act for him to impress him? If a man did die was he an already doomed man? If not, would Metesa later pay a terrible price at the hands of his subjects?

Or take the case of the nurse of the children of Frederick William, king of Prussia. Frederick William despised the mildly bohemian ways of his older son. I know it's very hard to think that once upon a time that fathers despised the bohemian ways of their sons, but so he did. But this father heaped humiliations on his son, had him flogged in public, and when his son, the crowned prince, fled with a male companion, the king had them arrested. He falsely told his wife that their son had been executed. He beat his children when they intervened in their brother's behalf. He dealt with the companion, who was a son and grandson of high-ranking generals, by setting aside a life imprisonment sentence imposed by a military court in favor of the death penalty. The king then forced his son to watch out a window while his companion was beheaded. One of the few persons in this whole thing to stand up to the king was the younger children's nurse, who barred his way when he tried to drag his cowering children out from under a table. She got away with it.

So shocking are such acts of tyrants, so rarely reported the courageous acts of defiance, that we have tended to exaggerate the role of naked power to minimize that of moral leadership. We forget that even the most despotic are continually frustrated by foot dragging, quiet sabotage, communications failure, stupidity, even aside from moral resistance and sheer physical circumstance. We forget that not all human influence is necessarily coersive or even exploitative. We forget that most influence consists of deeply human relationships in which two or more persons *engage* with one another. They engage for self-interest and because they have—or at least they achieve—mutual values, motives, and goals.

The question I raise is whether we can disenthral ourselves from our preoccupation with naked power, with coercion and despotism. Can we consider the far more complex, but more consequential exercise of mutual persuasion, exchange, and transformation? Perhaps not, because brute power and sheer evil are always more fascinating than frailty and virtue. Sinners usually outsell saints, at least in Western cultures, and the ruthless exercise of power always seems more sophisticated while moral influence always seems more naive. Still I believe that if we can grapple with the real nature of power we can overcome this preoccupation.

Let me take up what seems to me the two essentials of power, one of which will be very obvious to you, and the other much less obvious—and that's where we have trouble with the concept. We all have power to do acts that we lack the motive to do. I define power as embracing (1) resources and (2) motives. It's *motives* that we usually ignore as we look at the resources. We all have power to do acts that we lack the *motive* to do. We have the power to buy a gun and slaughter people. We have power to crush the feelings of a loved one who cannot defend herself or himself. We have power to drive a car down a crowded city sidewalk. We have power to torture an animal. On the other hand, we all have the *motives* to do things that we do not have the *resources* to do. We have the motive to be president or senator or a judge, to buy a big yacht, to give away millions to charity, to travel on beautiful ships and yachts for months on end, to right injustices, to tell off the boss.

These two essentials of power—motive and resources—are interrelated. Lacking either one, power collapses. Lacking motive, resource diminishes; lacking resource, motive lies idle because both resource and motive are needed and because both may be in short supply. Power is an illusive and limited thing. No one has mastered the secrets of personal power as physicists have penetrated the atom, and of course it's probably just as well that we have not.

To understand the nature of leadership does require understanding of the essence of power, for leadership is a special form of power. Human beings for two thousand years or more have tried to penetrate the mysteries of power, but it remains illusive. Forty years ago Bertrand Russell called power the fundamental concept in social science, in the same sense, he said, in which energy is a fundamental concept in physics. This is a compelling metaphor because it suggests that perhaps the source of human power may lie in immense reserves consisting of the wants and needs of the wielders and targets of power, just as the winds and the tides, oil and coal, the atom and sun have been harnessed to supply physical energy.

What is power? We are told, in one well-known definition by a political scientist, that the power of A over B is equal to the maximum force that A can induce on B minus the maximum resisting force that B can mobilize in the opposite direction. If you are bewildered by that, I am too. And no only that, but one wonders about the A's and the B's, the X's and the Y's in that kind of equation of power. Are these A's and B's mere croquet balls knocking other balls and being knocked in some game of the gods? Or do these A's and B's and X's and Y's and others have their own wants and needs, ambitions and aspirations? And what if a ball does not obey a god just as Frederick William's children's nurse stood in the autocrat's way? Is this formula more a metaphor of physics than one of human power? No wonder some would banish the concept of power!

Still, that formula that I just recited does make one important point that is fundamental to an understanding of power. It makes the point that power is a *relationship among persons*. Power is not just a gun, it is not just a baton, it is not just a hundred dollar bill that can be passed from hand to hand as a kind of entity of power. Power is a relationship among human beings. Max Weber defines "power" (he uses the term *macht*) as the probability that one actor within a social relationship will be in a position to carry out his own will, despite resistance. This formula is rather simplistic, but advances our study since it reminds us that there is no certain relationship between what the power holder does and how the power target responds. Those who have pressed a button and found no light turned on, those of us who have admonished a child with no palpable effect, rather welcome this factor of probability, or shall I say improbability. But what controls the degree of probability? Motive, intention, power resources, skill? Are the power wielders acting on their own or are they agents of other power wielders? And what if a power wielder orders a target to do something to somebody else? Who then is the real power target? To answer such questions, power wielder and power target and all the other croquet players, mallets and balls must be put into a broader universe of power relationships. *Power and leadership are part of a social causation.*

A second question relates to purpose, and this is often overlooked by the people who talk about power. They see somebody exercising power and maybe having some effect; they rarely stop to ask whether the effect had anything to do with what the power wielder *wanted* to do. I think one of the best definitions of "power"—one of the best short definitions of "power"—is the "production of intended effects." The cardinal question though is the ambiguity of intention, or purpose. What is the nature, the intensity, the persistence, the scope of purpose? How is the power wielder's intent communicated to the target? Assuming an intent or purpose of the power wielder, to what extent is there a power relation if the power wielder's intent is influenced by the power wielder's prior knowledge and anticipation of the target's response? That's perhaps a rather heavy-handed way of saying if I tell you what to do, but I am influenced in what I tell you to do by my prior knowledge of your reaction, presumably that influences what I tell you to do—in which case who is the power wielder? Am I the power wielder or are you the power wielder? And if you start to examine that question of motive and intent it becomes extremely complicated, especially if you're thinking in terms of the relationships of many people. To what extent then is intent or purpose part of a wider interaction among the wants, needs, and values of the power wielder and the power recipient?

My answer to these terribly difficult questions is that here we call on the disciplines not of political science or of history or of philosophy, or theology, but the discipline of psychology. I believe that a psychological conception of power will help us cut through some of the complexities and provide a basis for understanding the relations of power to everyday events. This approach is based on the assumptions that I have suggested: that power is first of all a relationship, and not merely an entity; that it involves the intention or purpose of both power holder and power recipient; and hence that it is collective and not merely the behavior of one person. On these assumptions I offer the following definition of "power," and I'm sorry to give you a heavy definition, but all my thought is incorporated in this definition, which you may find useful in your own thinking. I view the power process as one in which *power holders possessing certain motives and goals have the capacity to secure changes in the behavior of respondents and in the environment by using resources in their power base that relate to the targets and to the motivations of those targets.* In short, instead of setting up the simple relationship of power wielder and power recipient, or looking simply at the gun that the power wielder may have, and the fact that the power target has no gun, I would look immediately at the motivation of both the power wielder and the target. And if you say that this does not sound very sensational, I would have to say to you that in most studies of power these motivational, these psychological aspects, are left out.

With that definition I would like again to try to correct the traditional picture of single-minded power wielders simply exerting control over respondents. Their main motive, the main motive of power wielders, may incidentally not be to control somebody else, it may be to control *themselves.* In fact, power holders themselves may have just as varied motives, wants, needs, expectations, and so on, as their targets. Some people who seem to be pursuing power are not really pursuing power, they are pursuing *status, recognition, prestige, glory,* and some may even be seeking power as a way of achieving even loftier goals. I had a very good friend once in Massachusetts politics who got to be governor of Massachusetts. I used to watch him as governor. He was a man very concerned about policy and program and being a good governor, but if you ask me what gave him the most gut satisfaction, and the thing that he secretly hankered for when he went through many, many years of trying to be governor, was to be ushered into a beautiful black cadillac by a state trooper and then driven around the State of Massachusetts by that state trooper. I think that really represented to him the most marvelous aspect of his job and it was not particularly a power-related motive.

Once into the field of motivation, we have to think of the varied motivations that go into the search for power. Some use power not only for status, but to collect possessions, such as paintings, cars or jewelry, or they may collect wives or mistresses, less to dominate them than to love them, possibly, or at least display them. Others will use power to seek novelty and excitement. Still others may enjoy the exercise of power mainly because it enables them to exihibit—if only to themselves—their skill and knowledge, their ability to stimulate their own capacities, and to master their environment. Those skilled in athletics may enjoy riding horseback or skiing, even solitary pastimes with nobody admiring them. I'm sure many of us have gone through this experience in various athletic contests where nobody may be around. But you can't tell me that we don't take great pleasure out of a particularly nice tennis stroke against a backboard or particularly nice piece of writing or a nice piece of skiing when nobody else may be on the ski slope. Indeed, the psychologists have a particular name for this, "effectance." Now I must grant that there are the single-minded power wielders who fit the classical images of Machievelli or Hobbes or Nietzsche, I don't want to present an unbalanced picture. Certainly there are people who expoit their external resources, their economic, social, psychological, and institutional resources, their training and skill and competence to make persons and things do what they want done. But the key factor is *what do they want done*. The motives of power wielders may or may not coincide with what the respondent wants done. Power wielders may or may not recognize respondents' wants and needs. If they do, they may recognize them only to the degree necessary to achieve their goals, and if they must make a choice between satisfying their own purposes and satisfying the needs of respondents they could choose the former.

To define power not as a property or entity or possession but as a *relationship* in which two or more persons tap the motivational basis in one another and bring varying resources to bear in the process is to perceive power as drawing a vast range of human behavior into its orbit. The arena of power is no longer the exclusive preserve of a power elite, or of an establishment, or of a person clothed with legitimacy. Rather power permeates all human relationships. It is ubiquitous. It exists whether or not it is quested for. It is to some degree the glory and the burden of humanity. But I would still argue that it must be seen in its proper context.

If you want to have a very ordinary but very poignant, graphic illustration of how power can exist between two people who don't seem to have very much power to throw around, put yourself in the position of a student who is madly in love with another student, who is the object of attention by a great number of other people—the simple, classic picture of being terribly in love with someone who is not terribly in love with you. This happens all the time. And anybody who has been in that position of being terribly in love with somebody who is not in love with him or her knows that a sense of impotence results. You try this tactic and you try that tactic. You try ignoring the other person, not writing, not talking, not phoning. You try overcoming the other person, you try tricks and so on, you try all the resources you may have. You may have a certain amount of resource one way or the other, but if you're in a fundamental system of impotence, in this sense, you're helpless and you can squirm and try all you want but you cannot overcome that motivational imbalance, if I might use a heavy term for such a relationship. On this score I recommend Somerset Maugham's *Of Human Bondage,* which is the picture of a young man who is a slave of a women he really does not love, or admire, but is infatuated with. She keeps dominating him because of that imbalance of the relationship. He needs her, she does not need him, except when she comes for him for a little financial help. It's a very aptly named book.

Robert Dahl has developed well the dimensions of power, the scope, and the intensity of the aspects of power. I would like to indicate, in a kind of autobiographical way, how I have responded to my own intellectual dilemma in dealing with power. I suggested earlier that I had been, in effect, a member of what might be called the "power school" of political science and found it inadequate. What I have done is get interested in a companion subject, on which I have just spent six years of study, something I simply call "leadership." It is a loose and popular term, but one that I have used to deal with the intellectual deficiencies of power. I would like to summarize how this has opened, for me, new intellectual vistas.

As you will gather from what I've said, I've been searching for the really meaningful aspects of these human relationships in power situations, acknowledging the role of power, but not being overcome by it. I've seen in my own life in politics many examples of the apparent naked demonstration of power. Let me just tell one other little story that I experienced very directly, to show why I think there has been an exaggeration of the role of power. The chief aide to the same governor that I mentioned earlier told me about a little episode that took place in the governor's office about 1:00 in the morning. In came the president of the state senate, who had been one of the most powerful, most influential supporters of the governor when he ran for office and since getting to be governor. He went up to the governor and said, "Now governor; I've not asked you for a single favor despite all I've done for you, but, I do now have a favor I want to ask of you. I have a cousin who is desperately in need of a job. There is, you mentioned, a job that would be available and I would like to ask you to appoint him." The governor said, "Oh I'm terribly sorry but he would not be appropriate for this job. I promised to make very good appointments and I can't do this." The president of the senate said, "Well, I can't understand this, I mean it's as though you're trying to be the perfect ingrate. I want to ask you again, man to man, would you simply help me on something that is very important to me?" The governor said, "I just cannot do it." The president of the state senate at this point said, "Governor, if I get down on my hands and knees and beg you to make this appointment, will you?" There was a long pause and the governor said, "No, I simply cannot do it." The president of the senate then got down on his hands and knees and begged the governor to make this appointment. The governor did not make the appointment. Now that's the kind of story that illustrates the power relationship that we hear about. That's the kind of story that is circulated, as it too was a very dramatic and very poignant situation. But what we often don't hear about is the moral. The moral was that the man who told me the story, the aide to the governor, ran into the president of the state senate at a function about two weeks later and said how moved he had been. The president of the state senate said, "Oh come on, that was just a great act, wasn't that a great act I put on?" I would suggest that if we are willing not to suspend disbelief, if we are willing to be rather hardheaded about these apparent demonstrations of naked power, aside from certain societies like totalitarian Germany or Russia, we would not be quite so impressed by them.

What I have tried to do in my work on leadership is to generalize about the relationship of power wielder and power target, which I will now call leader and follower, in a way that lifts it out of the episodic, lifts it out of the narrowly biographical, lifts it out of these individual little stories. Would it be possible to generalize about the leader-follower relationship, just as we try to and indeed can generalize about entities like energy? I think we can because of some remarkable work that has been done in the recent decades in the field of psychology. Again to simplify this, I would single out two men in particular; one is Abraham Maslow, and the other Professor Kohlberg, presently at Harvard. What Maslow did was to develop a theory of structure of motivations drawn from empirical data. He (not alone) developed a theory about what happens when "lower" motivations are satisfied and "extinguished" and "higher" ones created. First of all he viewed the structure of motivations as a rather commonsense heirarchy of motivations. He said certain needs come before other needs, and this is something you would expect, that is, even a starving man who is absolutely intent on food will still not go into a burning house to get food because one thing he will fear more than lack of food would be that kind of pain or death. That's a very simple example, but Maslow worked this out in a very systematic way. His main point was very interesting to me; it was that as leaders, or if you will "power wielders," satisfy or help satisfy certain motives or needs, the followers, the power recipients, those affected by that action, will escalate, will graduate up through a structure of needs from the most essential needs, like safety and security and physical survival, to a series of needs that finally, in Maslow's view, culminated in self-realization and self-actualization, in aesthetic needs far above the base needs of survival.

Other people have worked in this area and feel that they have found a rather general, perhaps even universal, tendency in this direction. Kohlberg (and anyone who is familiar with these great bodies of literature will understand that I am greatly condensing a rather complicated mass of information and ideas) applies the same kind of approach to levels of moral judgment. He is very interested in what people do in real life situations in terms of principles of judgment and standards of actions that sometimes confront them. To take one example of what he and his associates have done, they have framed a simple question and addressed it to a cross section of persons: "If it were illegal in a certain culture to rob a store, and if your children were dying of starvation, would you break into a store in order to take food to your children?" Well you can imagine the answer you typically get to this. The point is they have asked these and hundreds of other complex and subtle questions in a number of cultures around the world, in a variety of cultures, and they have isolated what they feel are levels of moral judgment, from the most self-involved, the most limited, to the "highest" level. There we find lofty principles of moral behavior that involve great selflessness and moral leadership and willingness to submerge one's own welfare for the benefit of society as a whole.

Now what I am trying to do in my own work is to make use of this in leadership theory, to develop a theory of leadership that embraces power but is much more subtle and realistic than these crude theories of power. Leaders recognize common needs. As the leaders tap those motivational basics, as the leaders reach down to the genuine and authentic needs and wants of the people, then there is a *transformation of leaders as well as a transformation of followers.* Because the great distinction between the power wielder and the leader is that the power wielder is trying to achieve his own purpose, separate from the follower, to be a governor, to make a million, to lead a movement, whatever it might be. The leader is *leading,* the leader is arousing, recognizing, and satisfying the followers' fundamental needs. In turn, the followers are being raised up to higher levels of need, to higher levels of self-fulfillment and self-realization and self-actualization and the higher levels of moral judgment—and all this rebounds back on leaders and affects them.

I have advanced a number of practical rules, which I can boil down to one that is perhaps not very far from the Golden Rule: that the power of leaders ultimately does depend on the power of followers and that the hope of leaders and the strength of leaders ultimately turns on their ability to mobilize and to transform followers who in turn transform leaders.

Hence the whole leadership-followership relationship can become the glory of a nation rather than a curse or a shame. What I am proposing actually is not all that different from what we do daily and automatically. We make approaches to people and anticipate their reaction and perhaps anticipate our own reactions to their reactions. A function of leadership is to engage followers and not merely activate them. To comingle needs and aspirations and goals in a common enterprise is the process that makes better citizens of both leaders and followers. To move from manipulation or power wielding is to move from the arithmetic of everyday contacts and collisions to the geometry of the structure and dynamics of interaction. It is like moving from checkers to chess, for in chess, the game of kings, we estimate the powers of our chessmen and the intentions and calculations and indeed motives of our adversary. But democratic leadership, I contend, moves far beyond chess because, as *leaders* instead of mere power wielders, the chessmen come alive, and bishops and knights and pawns take part on their own terms and with their own motivations, values, and goals. The game moves ahead with new momentum, direction, and possibilities. In real life, in short, the most practical advance for leaders is not to treat pawns like pawns, nor princes like princes, but persons like persons. Woodrow Wilson called for leaders who by boldly intepreting the nation's conscience could lift the people out of their everyday selves. That persons can be lifted into their better selves is the secret in my view of elevated leadership.

Copyright © 1979 by James MacGregor Burns.

Howard Baker

Political Power

Howard Baker is currently serving in the United States Senate as senator from Tennessee.

Senator Baker attended college at the University of the South in Sewanee, Tennessee, and Tulane University in New Orleans. He served in the navy in the Pacific during World War II and was discharged as a lieutenant (jg).

After returning from the service, Senator Baker enrolled in the University of Tennessee at Knoxville. He was elected student body president and graduated from the College of Law in 1949. He practiced law in Huntsville and Knoxville before being elected to the Senate in 1966.

In 1966, Baker became the first popularly elected Republican senator in Tennessee history. During his first eight years in Washington, he helped lead the fight to revitalize relations between local, state, and federal governments, improve the quality of the environment, and secure the right of full citizenship for young people.

An early advocate of full citizenship for young people, Senator Baker cosponsored voting rights legislation and a constitutional amendment to lower the voting age to eighteen. The senator also played an active roll in the successful efforts to replace the draft with an all-volunteer army and introduced legislation creating the Military Manpower Commission to provide for more effective utilization of the defense dollar.

Senator Baker is currently a member of the Senate Select Committee, which is investigating the activities of some sixty government agencies with intelligence or law enforcement responsibilities to make sure that the United States maintains an effective intelligence program without endangering the rights of citizens.

Senator Baker's work as vice chairman and ranking Republican on the Senate Select Committee on Presidential Campaign Activities (the "Watergate Committee") won him bipartisan acclaim and respect throughout Tennessee and the entire country.

I'm a devout believer in the political system in the United States. I have almost a theological reverence for the exquisite balance of powers in the three departments of government. I rather think that it is likely that the Founding Fathers, as great as they were, probably never dreamed that the system would still be as relevant 200 years later as it was when they adopted it and when the Constitution was ratified. The three departments, with partial and overlapping jurisdictions and with, in part, an intentional and part unintentional system of checks and balances and of stresses, they set up in the system, have served us well over the years. The one thing the Founding Fathers did not provide for and that has evolved, I think, was a product of our genius for self-government is the political system. I am speaking now of Republican and Democratic politics. Because in the entire range and spectrum of design of the Constitution and its several amendments, in the Declaration of Independence, the other cornerstone document of the Republic or for that matter in the statue law, there are simply no provisions for how the people of the United States communicate to that edifice and structure of government that was given us. I used to think that was an omission of rather major proportion that our otherwise very thorough Founding Fathers had perpetrated; but it appears on closer examination that the matter was considered and discarded, that is the matter of deciding how the people would express the range of their desires and dissent.

It was in that vacuum that the political system grew up in the United States. It is special; it doesn't exist anyplace else in the world—a system of two broad-base national parties, at least as they have existed for the last hundred years or so. Not conservative parties or liberal parties or labor and Socialist or Communist or whatever; not ideological confrontation, but two broad-based parties, each not only able but indeed anxious to accommodate a wide variety of viewpoints and ideas ranging from the very liberal to the very conservative within the same party. And you see in that way you have an internal debate with the parties, both the parties. It tends to attenuate, to knock the corners off the major debates in the country, before they ever reach the Congress or the public forum. The party system has served us very well; and in one respect it has become the fourth department of government.

In almost theological terms, at least terms of political theology, America has been remarkably right in the major decisions she has made in the course of these first few hundred years of her existence. Not because she has always had great leaders—she's had her share—but rather because the country has made the right decisions and has transmitted that judgment through the political system to the structure of government. Most of the major decisions have been made at the polling places.

In the course of the Watergate affair, the thing that really bothered me was that the essence of that arrangement, the fourth department of government, public participation by citizens concerned for the formulation and publication of issues, might be damaged or indeed even destroyed, that so many people might drop out of the system as a result of disillusionment or discouragement that we will no longer be able to harvest the judgment of the country and to translate it into useful public policy. But that didn't happen, and I am convinced now that the political system as we know it is just as effective and possibly even more sensitive today than it was twenty years ago and almost certainly more so than it was a hundred years ago.

A lot of things have happened to embellish and extend the virtues of representative democracy. The Republic is better served, for instance, by the fact that we have a very high literacy rate in the United States, people are more aware as a result of higher educational attainments. The Republic is better served because, as Buckminister Fuller said, the world has come to the point where it communicates instantaneously and transports almost roughly the same things at the same time. On network television, on the radio, in the mass circulation newspapers and magazines, the people in Salem, Oregon, are concerned about the same things, roughly, as the people in Dover, Delaware, at essentially the same time. So as a result of the advances in science, technology, transportation, communications—the electronic media in particular, the nation is closer to being a nation-state than it ever was.

The value and quality of representative democracy is greater now than it ever was before. I think, in terms of what I call a heightened social conscience, the country is in a better position, a superior position to make fundamental judgments than it ever was before. If America makes her greatness out on the stoop of public opinion, then the genius for self-government is what propels us to essentially right decisions and our heightened social conscience is particularly important as we face the problems before us. For instance, the recent civil rights activities in the United States represent the most profound change in the social fabric of a country ever obtained without widespread bloodshed in the history of civilization.

It didn't happen with the Civil Rights Act or the Voting Rights Act. It is the accumulation of effort and judgment of the country ranging almost back to the earliest days of the Republic, maybe since the framing of the Constitution when some people were classified as three-fifths of a person. The concern for color, the concern for equality, the concern for the reality of opportunity for the elimination of social barriers or legislative discrimination or economic maladjustment—these concerns are the product of what I believe to be a spontaneous outpouring of the heightened American social conscience. Maybe such a social conscience has existed earlier, but I rather doubt it. At least it has not existed to the extent that it would force and require the social changes and the economic readjustments that now exist in this country. I not only have a profound respect for the system, I also happen to think that the system is in pretty good shape, probably the best shape that it was ever in.

We have the brightest, the best educated, the most affluent young generation in the history of the Republic. But they are only just barely good enough because the challenges that will face them will make those that faced us in our time pale and insignificant by comparison. In my time, in my place in the Senate of the United States, I have to worry and think about the proliferation of nuclear weapons beyond the club or group of seven nations. But in the near future, almost certainly, nonproliferation will be about the controlling of enormous destructive power in the hands of not seven but say a hundred nations, or two hundred nations—if there are two hundred nations by then. In addition, destructive nuclear devices could be in the hands of groups and nonnational entities; the results could make civilization an absolute horror. So if the system is what it should be, and if the next generation is better able to serve that requirement, then they will have to make judgments in the future better than we have in the past. Providence has given them the dubious honor of trying to wrestle such questions as nuclear justification; unfortunately I have no good solutions for them.

I only have the same admonition that my father gave me to give them. As a young man I was convinced I would never be engaged in politics. There then came a time in my life when it was certain to my own satisfaction that I would, not because I felt some compelling urge to or even some ambition to fulfill a sense of accomplishment in politics, but because it seemed to me that unless I spoke my piece, someone else was going to speak it for me. The admonition my father gave me was, "You may sometimes doubt the judgment of the country, but you better never doubt the country's authority." So learn and you have the humble good sense to recognize that as smart as you are, as bright as you may seem, as relevant as your ideas may be, as infallible as your theories are, that, finally, it is the collective best judgment of this country that has served her well—the stoop of public opinion. The political parties in this country are essentially a sensing mechanism to reach out to, resonate to, and respond to the range of the desires and the dissent of the sovereign judgment of this country. As the admonishment states, "Remember that the collective judgment of the country is likely to be the better judgment in the long term."

What other issues will you have to face or do I have to face at this time with my colleagues in the House of Representatives and in the Senate?

The example of nuclear proliferation comes to mind so readily as an issue that our citizens must address and is so terrifying that it is an irresistible first example. But there are others that are almost as important. For instance, the United States, I'm convinced, is now in the process of evolving its first foreign policy since World War II. I don't know just what it is going to be; I have rather fixed ideas on what it should not be. But I also have an idea that it will not be the old foreign policy—for instance, a dependence on forward position defenses or a raid through Western Europe behind the shield of NATO or along the Asian crescent, which finally produced our standing defense against aggression in Vietnam. That's not what it's going to be. But is it going to be a massive assured destruction, a parody of terror, maybe that's what it is now. And maybe that's not bad, maybe that's the human condition—to preserve the peace by mutual assured destruction.

There ought to be something better than that; maybe mutual assurance survival would be better than mutually assured destruction. Maybe there needs to be better international order. The United Nations, as grand and as noble as its original concept and as useful as it may be today, has fallen far short of the expectations and the requirements of humanity at these times. I was a delegate to the United Nations for the United States in the General Assembly for two months in this past year. I was appalled. The most elemental form of precinct politics was being utilized by the sovereign nations of the world and in most cases against what I thought of as the best interest of the United States. They might as well have been ward politicians bargaining and trading. If the United Nations is not the route, then how do we go about trying to regularize the intercourse of nations, to lessen the tensions that tenuate the conflicts and avoid the assured destruction.

Consider the problems of the Middle East. The Middle East has been at war one way or other since the dawning of mankind, apparently; it happens now that it is more important to us than ever before because of the extraordinary array of resources in that region of oil, of gas, and because of the existence of the created state, Israel, sanctioned by the United Nations and supported by the United States—the ancient sought-after homeland for the world's Jews. But how do we reconcile that conflict? Someone asked me what do you do about the legitimate rights of Palestinians; aren't they legitimate rights? My answer was of course there are legitimate rights of Palestinians, but there are legitimate rights of Jews as well. And in a practical array of things we have to understand the legitimate rights of Palestinians has become a code word that means the establishment of a Palestinian state on the West Bank, which is a very different thing from the legitimate rights of Palestinians.

What do we do about South Africa? The Horn of Africa? The Third World? How do we go about an even-handed policy that does not condone the oppression of a minority against a majority or a majority against a minority, or the elimination of freedom of the press by the avoidance of intrusion into the internal affairs of another country. How do you make any sense out of that hodge-podge? How are we to clarify these on the stoop of public opinion?

We are fond of saying, even now, that we are the richest nation on earth, although we are not, in terms of annual per capita income; we are in terms of total gross national product. But what do we do? Do we continue to freight and burden the market system with public services and other requirements that have the inevitable effect of dampening the vitality and the energy of the productive system? Put that way, most of you will say no, we're not going to do that. On the other hand, are we going to turn our backs on legitimate aspirations of those who have suffered the persecution and indifference of discrimination for years. Are we, the richest nation on earth, going to turn our backs on those who are hungry and poor and disadvantaged, who inherited their plight? I'll bet you'll say "no" to that too. And how do you make that balancing judgment? How is government going to decide those two things? How do we vitalize and maximize the productive utility of the free market system and still engage in the most compassionate undertakings that any central government ever tried? That's a sampler of the challenges to us.

What do we do about national defense? Haven't we finally reached the point where we can devastate the Russians many times over and they us? Isn't it silly then to develop new weapons? Put that way, of course, that is true. Put the other way, how can you ever expect the United States to implement a foreign policy if it is not undoubtedly strong in the face of any threat and of any contingency? How do we make the judgment and the allocation of resources, the construction of weapons systems versus a willingness to engage in mutually arrived at disarmament of strategic arms or conventional arms? The list of the dilemmas continues. A little placard in my office says, "Someday someone will bring a question to which there is an answer." But I don't suggest these things to tell you that the Congress or the country is turned off by the complexity of the issues but rather to say this is the nature of the undertaking and the problems are rarely simple. The country has not thrived on simplistic solutions. But we'll have the right solutions only when we all participate in the forming of collective judgment. That is why I encourage everyone to involve himself in partisan political activity, according to talents and taste. Don't think of politics as something unsavory and unpleasant; it's an essential part of the system. Someone asked Will Rogers once, "Is it true that the Congress is made up, Mr. Rogers, of thieves and rascals." Will Rogers is supposed to have replied, "Why of course, but it's a pretty good cross-section of its constituency."

Controversy should swirl around a president. The president understands, as I expect all presidents before him have, that being the central focus point of the administrative responsibility of the government, conflict is inevitable. Not only inevitable but desirable, because the nature of the political system is a testing process, and it is necessary in the nature of an adversary preceeding it to put the test to the public. Don't be put off by conflict; very few things are decided without conflict, at best the conflict of ideas. Don't be put off because somebody else would do it for you, because they just might. Don't be put off by the notion that free enterprise and capitalism is old-fashioned. I happen to believe it is just the beginning and dawning of the free-market system and that if we nurture it carefully it will provide an abundance that will for the first time give us some reasonable opportunity to provide the good things of life for more and more people.

Don't think that we'll solve the real issue vicariously in the sense that we'll make in the national Senate legislative determinations and governmental regulations and policy and remove the struggle from the stoop of public decision. We won't and we can't. Contribute your own thoughts and ideas to these problems and these solutions, because that has been the genius of the American system, the only power of politics.

Copyright © 1979 by Howard Baker.

Bella Abzug

Women and Political Power

Bella Abzug is a graduate of Hunter College. She received a law degree from Columbia University and practiced law in New York City from 1944-1970. Ms. Abzug was a representative from New York in the 92nd, 93rd and 94th Congress. She is a member of the National organization for Women, National Women's Political Caucus, and the American Civil Liberties Union. She was appointed by President Carter as presiding officer of the National Commission on the Observance of International Women's Year, which held the National Women's Conference in Houston November 18 to 21, 1977 under a law introduced by Congresswoman Abzug. She has served as cochair of the President's National Advisory Committee for Women.

Ms. Abzug is author of Bella! Ms. Abzug Goes to Washington *(1972), which is an account of her experiences in her first year in Congress.*

> *It's important for me to run again so that other women will be encouraged to do the same. One thing that crystallized for me like nothing else this year is that Congress is a very* unrepresentative *institution. Not only from an economic class point of view, but from* every *point of view—sex, race, age, vocation. Some people say this is because the political system tends to homogenize everything, that a Congressman by virtue of the fact that he or she represents a half million people has to appeal to all sorts of disparate groups. I don't buy that at all. These men in Congress don't represent a homogenous pont of view. The represent their own point of view—by reason of their sex, background, and class.*
>
> (*From* Bella!)

I went into the political arena because I was a political science major and a lawyer and I believed in the Constitution. I believed in Democracy; I believed it meant what it said. And I really thought this was a great country and thought it should take care of all the people in it. Somehow or other that isn't happening. In this very recent period we're confronted with some very serious social problems. It disturbs me greatly. What are our problems? We have the need to end mass unemployment and put millions of people, jobless Americans, to work. We need to restore our cities. We need to guarantee adequate low cost health care to all Americans. We have to provide dignity and security for millions of older Americans. We have to open the doors of genuine opportunity to women and minorities. We have to develop rational policies to protect the environment and conserve energy. We have to slow down the arms race and work for peaceful settlement in the Middle East and other places where there is conflict.

No matter how sincere and well-intentioned our government leaders may be, programs for real change in this country historically have been achieved only as a result of movements by people from the grassroots and only by involving more people in power and in decision-making. We have to remember that our nation began its life as a flawed democracy, and that continued. Our Declaration of Independence spoke of the inalienable rights of man to life, liberty, and the pursuit of happiness. It didn't speak of women. They had no rights. It didn't speak of slaves. They had no rights, whether they were men or women.

I was privileged to be present at the United Nations when President Carter came to sign the new declarations that we had never before agreed to sign, including a human rights declaration. He talked about the historical commitment of the United States to human rights and he started to quote very proudly from our Declaration of Independence, which spoke of the inalienable rights of men to life, liberty, and the pursuit of happiness. At that point, he looked up and happened to look right into my face. On the receiving line after the signing of the delcaration, he said, "You know, Bella, I was thinking when I quoted that line from the Declaration of Independence and looked up and saw you that, had you been there, it probably would have been written and read differently."

The truth is that our forefathers didn't give a hoot about our foremothers. I'm sure many of you, particularly those of you interested in women and history of this country, know the story about Abigail Adams, who was as great a first lady as any we've every had. She wrote to her husband, John Adams, as he was writing our great charter of liberty. It was probably the first "Dear John" letter in the history of this country. In her letter, she beseeched him to "remember the ladies" in the Constitution that was being drafted. The future president replied, "Depend upon it, we know better than to repeal our masculine systems."

And so it was that in the beginning of our nation, only men of property could vote, white men. Gradually, the franchise was extended to more and more white men. The Civil War brought the right to vote to black men, at least technically, although, for generations thereafter, the lynch rope and poll taxes effectively disenfranchised most of them. The decision was made not to extend the franchise to black women or white women or any women.

It took a century of struggle to win the vote for women, and we are now in the process of trying to make democracy more inclusive by bringing women and young people and minorities into places of government where choices and decisions are made. That has been one kind of struggle.

While our foremothers were trying to expand the base of democracy, we have also been engaged in other kinds of struggle. I think it's worth recalling or noting that every notable advance in American democracy, every notable piece of social legislation, whether it was the elimination of child labor, or whether it was the enactment of social security, employment insurance, environmental protection, or the votes in the Congress to cut off funds for the war in Vietnam, all of these were products of organized movements by people; and women were involved in each of them. They may not have been recognized as leaders, but they were in there doing the work.

I have often pointed out to people who ask me about myself that I have been personally active in movements for change most of my lifetime. I fought as a young lawyer against the McCarthy witch-hunts in the fifties. I fought for justice for blacks in the courts both in the South and the North in the fifties. It was in the women's movement to end nuclear testing. I was in the movement to stop the war in Vietnam. I've been involved in a major effort to reform my own party, the Democratic party, so that it would be more inclusive and more representative of the total spectrum of the population. I was involved in Congress in the struggle to expose Watergate and impeach Nixon. I am in the movement in and out of Congress to make our government more open and more responsive to the needs of people. These issues have all been terribly important in the life of our nation, but the movement that I think has the capability of making the profoundest changes in our society is the women's movement.

You may have read various articles claiming that the women's movement is dead or dying. I can assure you that is not true. We're alive and kicking. We've had setbacks. I believe the campaign to get final ratification of the Equal Rights Amendment will now get an enormous boost. In my opinion we will continued to have a women's movement as long as women are denied equal opportunities in social, economic, and political life. As long as we have a state of affairs in which an all-male U.S. Supreme Court denies disability pay to pregnant women when it provides disability pay to men who get a vasectomy; as long as a Congress of the United States insists upon two laws when we believe that there should be one law for all people in this country; so long as the Congress of the United States had the audacity to say that there shall be one law for poor women and one law for rich women, when it denies Medicaid funds for abortion even though the right to abortion has been decided to be a fundamental right of privacy protected by the Constitution of the United States; that is how long we will continue to have a women's movement.

I would be the last one to suggest that all women have identical needs or that we look alike, think alike, or act alike. The irony is that we have to get together as women, as a sex, in order to win the right to act and live as individuals and not as stereotypes. That means the right to be a doctor, not only a nurse; the right to be a school principal, not only a teacher; the right to be an executive, not only a bookkeeper; the right to be a president, not only a first lady. I remember hearing our president say that he looked forward to the day when his daughter, Amy, could be not only a president's daughter but a president. I assume he was talking about equality politics, not dynasty politics.

It reminds me of some of my own experiences when I first came to the Congress of the United States. We got an invitation to go to the White House. I called my husband, Martin Abzug, and said, "Well, we got this invitation to go to the White House but I don't think we can go." He said, "Why not?" I said, "Well, I've been saying some pretty nasty things about the President, 'Let's impeach him.' " Martin said, "Well, of course, we're going to go to the White House because I want to see the place that I'm going to live when I'm going to be the 'first man.' "

We have made some progress. I think we have raised the national sensitivity to issues of discrimination that concerns women. But the fact is that women are still among the last hired and the first fired; the fact is that women have been hit harder than men by skyrocketing unemployment. Most women work not to fulfill themselves or to gratify their egos but simply because they need the money to support themselves, their families, their elderly parents. Most women work today because they have to work to support their families and themselves: single women, widowed women, separated women, divorced women, women whose husbands are unemployed. Yet despite the passage of the Equal Pay Act, the gap between earnings of women and men has actually gotten wider in the past twenty years. In 1955, women workers earned a salary that was nearly 64 percent of that earned by men; now they earn just 57 percent.

That means that a woman working today averages a little more than half of what a man earns and it is also a fact that a woman with a college education earns a little less than a man with a high school education. These are some of the discriminatory conditions that have produced the women's movement and have also impelled more and more women into political activity and public life. We realize that change is not handed to anyone by those who have the power. You have to fight for it and in order to do that you have to get political power. Our foremothers spent their lives working for women's suffrage, and after we won the vote, we used our power to elect men and to do what I call the housework of a political campaign, the drudge work.

There have been about seven thousand women elected to local, state, and national office around the country, which is twice as many as we had in 1970, before there was a women's political caucus; but it's still only 8 percent of all elective positions. We have two elected women governors. There are three women lieutenant governors. In the U.S. House of Representatives, we have only 18 women out of 435 members. The United States Senate remains a virtual male preserve. I have always said that a stag Senate means a stagnation. This is a great country and one reason for our greatness is that we are a very diverse land. We come from many different places and it's the dynamic of this country that we do. Yet the power structures in this country do not reflect the great diversity and variety of Americans that have moved this country forward and made it one of the most important nations in the world. If you look at the United States Senate, you will find men not very diverse in terms of where they come from or what economic levels, racial or national origins they represent. There are only two women, appointed as temporary replacements for their dead husbands.

You have to know that the major decisions of life and death are made by a very exclusive few: the United States Supreme Court. The Supreme Court has been handing out justice in this land to men and women and never once has that bench had on it one woman, not one woman in the two hundred-year history of this country. If you watch those decisions they indicate quite clearly that the woman's touch is missing. When President Nixon had the opportunity to appoint people to that Court, despite the fact that there were pressures from bar associations of men and women and other politicans and so on to appoint a woman to the bench, he was constantly suggesting that he couldn't find a woman who was good enough. I used to say that he couldn't find a woman who was bad enough, and that's why he never appointed a woman to the United States Supreme Court. This is a tremendous distortion of democracy. I believe that the failure to have women at the heads of the major structures and institutions of our country has really injured the capacity of this country. I believe that women should be at the head of corporations. Women should be at the head of labor unions; they constitute 41 percent of the work force. In the AFL-CIO executive council there is not one woman. I don't think it's natural. When God flooded the world and was recreating it through Noah, everybody was brought onto the ark in pairs. We do most things in pairs. It's just not natural, it seems to me, to have the structures of our nation that make the decision that affect every single one of us exclude not only women, but exclude young people, exclude minorities, exclude people who are not among the wealthiest people in our society. I believe that our society has been terribly handicapped and its priorities have been distorted by the submerging of the talents and the skills and the energy of more than half of our population.

Remember, when we talk about women and their freedom and their liberation, we are also talking about males and their freedom and their liberation, because men too have been locked into roles that do not necessarily represent what they want. Women in our movement understand one thing. They know that our struggle is not merely a struggle against sexism, but it is basically a struggle to create a society that has a soul. Women know that we're not going to get child care centers in a society that still spends $120 billion on armaments. We're not going to get equal pay for equal work while there are other priorities to provide more profits for large monopolies like the oil industry. Therefore, the people who are involved in the women's efforts today know that we not only have to fight sexism, but we have to fight poverty, fight racism, and fight institutional violence both at home and abroad.

Until recently there weren't many history books written about women in America. We were underecorded and unrepresented. Occasionally, there would be a reference to the first women's rights meetings in America in 1848; 250 women and 40 men, including the great abolitionist, Frederick Douglas, met in Seneca Falls, New York. It was the first time these women had dared to speak in public. But they did speak, and they spoke for the right of women to go to school, to engage in business, to own property, to act as guardians of their children and finally, with much fear and wonderment at their own daring, they even spoke out for the right of women to vote. I mentioned before that it took us a century of struggle to win the right to vote for women. It was a very long, tough, and at times heartbreaking struggle. Women were ridiculed. They were patronized and scorned and jailed and beaten. They were told they were too pure and too good to get involved in sordid politics. There were many women who declared that they would never, never think of voting. It was unwomanly, they said. It was a sin to vote, they said. It would destroy religion. It would destroy God, it would destroy the country. Interesting, isn't it, that we hear those same words in connection with the Equal Rights Amendment. The funny part of it is you'd have to look very far and wide to find any woman today who will say she opposes equality in the voting booth. The day will come, soon I believe, when equal rights for women in all aspects of our lives will be the law of the land and I predict that our children's children will be amazed to read in the history books that there was a time in this land when women were denied equality and denied the right to control their own bodies.

It's important that we understand what is really taking place in this country. In states throughout our nation thousands of outmoded laws remain on the books. Laws denying married women the right to own property, or make a contract, or establish legal residence; laws requiring married women to obtain court approval to engage in business; law prohibiting women from signing death certificates; laws prohibiting women from working on high paid night shift jobs but allowing them to work as low paid cleaning women in office buildings after the men have gone home. At the very top of the power structure of this land is the kind of male power structure I have described to you: a male White House, a male Senate, a predominantly male House of Representative, an all-male Supreme Court. These are some of the inequities that we have to change. These are some of the inequities that we will change.

It is a particularly exciting time to be a woman. Women are a majority of the population, 51.3 percent, who have been treated like a minority. I am talking about majority power, not minority power. Our present journey started more than a century and a half ago when American women began organizing to win the rights of citizenship. Our journey to the Houston National Women's Conference started with a bill, Public Law 94167, that I had the honor to introduce in the Congress as a follow-up to Internation Woman's Year in 1975. It was passed by Congress. A small number of congressmen were disturbed at the idea of so many women getting together to discuss and to act on our common concerns and problems. I had a lot of fun with it. Someone came up to me and said, "Oh, Bella, you just want to get this money appropriated so you women can go down somewhere and booze and have a good time together." I said, "Listen, I don't drink, as you all know, not that women don't have an equal right to booze, but the fact is I've attended many, many conferences of women all over this country and not once did I ever hear any woman ask for 'call boys.' " It's quite clear that God created man in his own image and men created conventions in their own image. But we were to have a different kind of convention. Some congressmen objected to spending money on us even though the cost averaged out to be about a nickle for each women in this country. But we persisted. Our bill passed overwhelmingly. It was signed by the president and then the women took over.

Our conference was a great success. It was inspiring and it was a first in many ways. It was the first time that the federal government has sponsored a National Woman's Conference and the fifty state meetings and six territorial meetings that preceded this event. It was the first time that the Congress and the president had mandated American women to identify and help remove the barriers that stand between us and full equality with men. The mandate under which we met did not tell us to consider whether women *should* seek to end discrimination or *should* seek full equality, full citizenship, and full participation in society. Instead, it took a stand *for* equality, a position that I believe has the support of a majority of Americans.

The Congress of the United States has a policy on women. It did pass overwhelmingly the Equal Rights Amendment, which requires ratification by three more states to become an amendment to the Constitution. Congress has passed many other laws, which provide for equal pay for equal work and for eliminating discrimination against women in employment and education, as it has passed laws for eliminating discrimination against minorities and others.

The Congress, mandating our Houston conference, was saying, in effect, for some reason our laws have not been implemented. The fact is that women are still unequal in this country and what we are saying for the women in this country is, here, have conferences in every single state and the territories of this nation, elect delegates to a nation conference, and at this nation conference as well as at these state conferences, consider what the barriers to the accomplishment of full equality are and come back and make recommendations to the Congress and the president as to how we can eliminate or tear down the barriers that have prevented women from achieving full equality, because that is what the law does mandate.

The law under which we met was therefore rooted in the belief that men and women should share equally in the rights and opportunities that our democracy offers. How could it be otherwise? Two hundred years after our nation was born in the great struggle for the rights of the individual, the law directed us to examine the past and the present. It directed us to examine the status of American women, our needs, our problems, and the diversity of our lives. It directed us to seek changes and improvements in the lives of women who have been held back by discriminatory practices. That was our mission and I believe we accomplished it. Overwhelmingly, we adopted a national Plan of Action that includes twenty-five major recommendations on ways in which equality between men and women can be made a living reality.

Many of us see a future in which women will be free to live and work as individuals, as members of families, as members of society without the constraints of narrow customs and prejudices that demean our self-worth and without laws that treat us as inferiors or weaklings. Some women may prefer a future that simply continues the past. Our purpose is not to tell women how to live or what to do. It's simply to say that women must be free to choose what they would do. The National Plan of Action that we adopted reflects the breadth of concerns and needs and interests of the multitude of American women—homemakers, older women, disabled women, battered women, rural women, women in prison, women on welfare, women in business and the media, and in the arts and the humanities. Our resolutions proposed ways to increase the number of women in elective and appointive office and to strengthen the roles of women in the continuing struggle for world peace and disarmament. We have resolutions that deal with child care, child abuse, rape, the right to reproductive freedom, the rights of minority women, the rights of disabled women, the right to sexual preference, and overwhelmingly we call for final ratification of the Equal Rights Amendment.

Our National Plan of Action reflects the changing status of women in our society, particularly as it affects the two largest groups of women—homemakers and working women. We know, in fact, that most women will fill both of those roles at some time in their lives. Throughout the history of our nation women have worked, but today more women have been working than ever before. Many are housewives, or homemakers who work part-time or on night shifts to help pay the mortgage and the grocery bills. Many, however, support themselves. It's important that we make the point that this conference makes, that we understand that our concern is for *every* woman. No objective value is placed on the labor of homemakers and the result is that these women are placed at a serious disadvantage in inheritance and social security laws, in divorce and separation laws. In some states, a widow loses all right to any share of the family estate if her husband leaves her out of his will. In another state, a husband can still control his wife's earnings. In practically all states women have no way to enforce support laws when husbands refuse to take financial responsibility for their families. Contrary to popular belief, divorce settlements are meager and short-lived.

If so many women are concerned today about our status in the family, on the job, and in our educational system, it is because more and more women have begun to examine their lives and themselves. Women are speaking for themselves. The whole nation will have to listen to what we say. What we did in Houston was to create a grassroots network of women that will become part of an irreversible worldwide movement in which women are speaking out for our needs. We are trying to create a better world in which men and women do not victimize each other but work together for a decent life for all people. There can never be any turning back to a time when women were segregated in auxiliaries and prevented from using their skills and abilities, barred from places of power. We can no longer accept the condition in which men rule the nation and the world, excluding half the human race from effective economic and political power.

Now we can argue about whether women, if we arrive at that stage where we do share power with men, will create a better world. Personally, I believe we will. Personally, I believe that women will change power. (It isn't that I think women are superior to men, it's just that we've had so little opportunity to be corrupted by power.) But I also believe that the woman who goes into politics is a very different kind of person from the average politician. I served in the Congress of the United States with eighteen fine women. I have met and worked with women all over this country, as I have with some very fine men in the political arena. The women in Congress and the other political offices, whom I know, particularly those who are feminists, are more serious, they're more committed to social conditions, they spend a lot more time on their work, they are less involved in personal advancement and more involved in the issues. Because we have a commitment to changing conditions in society, we can improve and change our own lives, and indeed we will change power. I believe we will not allow ourselves to be corrupted by power and we will not become the spokespersons of the special interests and the lobbyists who dominate too much of the power structures of this country. If we had the opportunity, we could figure out ways to spend some of the $370 billion the world spends on armaments each year for more rational and humane purposes, like feeding the hungry and housing the homeless and creating jobs and preventing disease, ignorance, and illiteracy. Personally, I'm not interested in seeing women get an equal chance to push the nuclear button. What I want to see is women and men working equally together for a peaceful world in which the young sons and daughters of this country can live without fear.

But whatever women choose to do with equality, I think it must be ours as a matter of simple justice. The struggle for women and men in this country to secure meaningful democracy is far from over. Women have much to do. We have to see that our National Plan of Action becomes a reality. We have to create a major national network that will reach out to millions more women and men to enlist them in our cause.

We have to win real political power for women because as long as the power structures of this country are dominated by one part of the population, women will be limited to roles as supplicants, rather than decisionmakers.

The women's movement has become an indestructible part of American life. It is not one organization. It is not one set of ideas. It is not one particular life-style. It is millions of women deciding individually and together that we are determined to move history forward, for ourselves and for others. we are a dynamic moving force that will make political changes in this country. Because as we fight for jobs, we're going to fight for jobs not only for ourselves but for men who are excluded from the employment market. As we fight for the rights of minorities who have been excluded by reason of their skin, we're going to fight not only for women of color, but men of color. As we fight for the right to have a national health insurance program that will provide for women, we are fighting for a national health program for the whole country.

The women's movement is the homemaker deciding that raising children and cleaning and cooking and all the other things she does for her family is work that should be accorded respect and value. It is the young women student asserting that she wants to play baseball, major in physics, or become a brain surgeon. It is the working woman demanding that she get the same pay and promotion opportunities as a man. It is the divorced woman fighting for social security benefits in her own right. It is the widow embarking on a new career. It is the mother organizing a day care center. It is the battered wife seeking help. It is the woman running for public office. It is the disabled woman who wants to be treated as a total human being who has the same needs as other women.

The time for equal rights has come. I think about American democracy a lot. Women after all have been here from the beginning of this nation. We have fought on its frontiers, we have raised the children of America, we have worked in its factories, its fields and offices and homes, we have fought for America. America cannot be a full democracy without the dignity and the full participation of its women.

But I think mostly of what a Southern woman named Nell Battee-Lewis wrote after the suffrage amendment to the Constitution was finally ratified. This is what she said, "The pedistal has crashed. There are many even now who would patch the idol together. It was only an image after all. In its place is a woman of flesh and blood, not a queen or a saint nor a symbol, but a human being with human faults and human virtues, a woman still only slowly-rising to full stature but with the sun of freedom on her face." We want freedom not only for ourselves but we want freedom to realize the real potential of America. We believe the power that women have to give to this country can make a difference in the lives of ourselves and the generations that we create and those that will come after us. And in that sense, I think the women's movement leads in the effort to create meaningful social change and to create a change in the relationship of forces that will bring power not only to women but to the whole country. Join us in that effort.

Copyright © 1979 by Bella Abzug.

Noam Chomsky

Intellectuals and the State

Noam Chomsky was born in Philadelphia, Pennsylvania, in 1928. He attended the University of Pennsylvania, where he studied linguistics, mathematics, and philosophy. He was a Junior Fellow of the Society of Fellows at Harvard University from 1951 to 1955. His Ph.D. was awarded by the University of Pennsylvania. Since 1955, Professor Chomsky has taught at the Massachusetts Institute of Technology, where he is now Institute Professor in the Department of Linguistics and Philosophy.

Chomsky's work has received wide recognition in academic circles and he has lectured in a number of different countries. He was awarded honorary doctorates by the University of Chicago and by the University of London. In 1967 he gave the Beckman Lectures at the University of California at Berkeley; in 1969 he delivered the John Locke Lectures at the University of Oxford as well as the Shearman Memorial Lectures at the University of London.

Professor Chomsky's reputation began with his work in the field of linguistics. ". . . man, for Chomsky, is essentially a syntactical animal. The structure of his brain determines the structure of his syntax, and for this reason the study of syntax is one of the keys, perhaps the most important key to the study of the human mind." ("Chomsky's Revolution in Linguistics," by John Searle in the New York Review, *June 29, 1977). Thus, language is defined by syntactical structures and those structures are determined by innate properties of the human mind. Linguistics becomes an interesting study of the belief that one can argue from syntax to the structure of the human mind.*

Chomsky is also well known for his political views and writing. Since 1965 he has been one of the leading critics of American foreign policy. American Power and the New Mandarins (which is dedicated "to the brave young men who refuse to serve in a criminal war") is one of the strongest indictments of American involvement in Vietnam to appear to date. In it he attacks American imperialism and those who have continually deceived the American public about the nature of our activities in Cuba, Vietnam, and other areas.

The topic that was suggested was "Limits of Power." I will discuss some aspects of that question, though it's much too broad to try to cover. When we discuss the nature and exercise of power and its limits we are considering certain relations among individuals and institutions whereby some are in a position to make decisions to which others may conform or suffer a penalty for failing to do so. There are many such relations of power. I am going to be concerned here only with specific ones, those that are realized in the social institutions of advanced industrial society, in particular our own; and even more specifically, I want to consider the problem that constantly arises of ensuring that no serious challenge is raised to the free exercise of power within these social institutions. I want to consider how this problem is faced in a society like ours, in an advanced industrial society.

There are two basic questions that I would like to consider in these remarks, the first rather abstract, the second more topical.

First, I would like to discuss the roles that intellectuals often tend to play in modern industrial society, a topic that has been a lively one at least since the Dreyfus affair, when the term "intellectual" came into common usage as a committed group of intellectuals took a prominent stand on an issue of justice. In this context I also want to comment on the engagement of American intellectuals in the ideological battles relating to World War I, when a prominent group of liberal intellectuals including John Dewey, Walter Lippmann, and others described themselves as a new class, engaged for the first time in applying intelligence to the design of national policy.

Second, I want to turn to some of the contemporary contributions of the "new class"—specifically, their contribution to constructing the moral and ideological framework that will be appropriate to the tasks of the American state in the "post-Vietnam era." I will try to show that some rather striking features of contemporary ideology can be understood in the terms suggested in the preliminary, more general discussion.

Before proceeding, I would like to enter several *caveats*. In the second part of this talk I will concentrate on the United States, in part, because I know it better, but also because it is more important in terms of global influence. But much of what I have to say has direct bearing, I think, on other industrial democracies. Furthermore, time being short, I am going to omit many important nuances and draw lines more sharply than the full range of complexity warrants, trying to isolate some "ideal cases" that can serve to organize and facilitate our understanding of more complex phenomena, much as one does in the natural science, for example. Though such an effort carries risks, it is indispensable if we hope to proceed beyond a kind of "natural history" to some understanding of what lies behind a confusing range of events, acts, and pronouncements. Finally, I will, reluctantly, have to omit the documentation that is certainly required to make a case that I will only sketch in outline. I have tried to do this elsewhere in books and articles.

What are the typical roles of the intelligentia in modern industrial society? There is a classic analysis of this question in the works of Bakunin, about a century ago. It was he, to my knowledge, who coined the phrase "new class" in reference to those who were coming to control technical knowledge. In a series of analyses and predictions that may be among the most remarkable within the social sciences, Bakunin warned that the "new class" will attempt to convert their access to knowledge into power over economic and social life. They will try to create

> the reign of scientific intelligence, the most aristocratic, despotic, arrogant and elitist of all regimes. There will be a new class, a new hierarchy of real and counterfeit scientists and scholars, and the world will be divided into a minority ruling in the name of knowledge, and an immense ignorant majority. And then, woe unto the mass of ignorant ones.

Though a passionately committed socialist himself, Bakunin did not spare the socialist movement the force of his critique: "the organization and the rule of the society by socialist savants," he wrote, "is the worst of all despotic governments." The leaders of the Communist party "will proceed to liberate [mankind] in their own way," concentrating "the reins of government in a strong hand, because the ignorant people require an exceedingly firm guardianship . . . [the masses will be] under the direct command of the state engineers, who will constitute a new privileged scientific-political estate." They will institute a "barracks regime for the proletariat" under the control of a Red bureaucracy. But surely it is "an outrage against common sense and historical experience" to believe that "even the most intelligent and best-intentioned group of individuals will be capable of becoming the mind, soul and guiding and unifying will of the revolutionary movement and economic organization of the proletariat of every land."

As for liberal democracy, though preferable to absolutism, still it "serves to conceal the domination of the masses by a handful of privileged elite." Capitalism will develop in the direction of increased state centralization, while the "sovereign people" will submit to the "intellectual-governing minority, who, while claiming to represent the people, unfailingly exploits them." "The people," Bakunin wrote, "will feel no better if the stick with which they are being beaten is labelled 'the people's stick.'" Under either evolving system of governance—state socialist or state capitalist—"the shrewd and educated" will gain privileges, "the mercenary-minded . . . will find a vast field for lucrative, underhanded dealings," and "regimented workingmen and women will sleep, wake, work, and live to the beat of a drum."

A century later, Bakunin's "new class" has become a grim cliché. State centralization has indeed proceeded in capitalist society, along with and always closely linked to centralization of ownership and control in the central economic institutions that set the basic conditions for social life. By the turn of the century there were already close links in the United States between corporate ownership and control on the one hand, and university-based programs in technology and industrial management on the other, a development studied in a recent work by David Noble (*America by Design*). And in more recent times there has been an increasing flow of technical intelligentsia through universities, government, foundations, management, major law firms that represent broad interests of corporate capitalism, and in general through the tightly linked network of planning and social control. Spokesmen for the new class never tire of telling us how the people rule, while concealing the real workings of power. The real and counterfeit scientists have been responsible for innumerable atrocities themselves and for the legitimation of many others, while wielding the people's stick.

I need not dwell on the performance of Bakunin's Red bureaucracy when they have succeeded in centralizing state power in their hands, riding to power on a wave of popular movements that they have proceeded to dismantle and finally destroy.

I might also mention in this connection the penetrating studies of the Dutch Marxist scientist Anton Pannekoek. Writing in the late 1930s and then under the German occupation, he discussed "the social ideals growing up in the minds of the intellectual class now that it feels its increasing importance in the process of production: a well-ordered organization of production for use under the direction of technical and scientific experts." These ideals, he pointed out, are shared by the intelligentsia in capitalist societies and by Communist intellectuals, whose aim is "to bring to power, by means of the fighting force of the workers, a layer of leaders who then establish planned production by means of State-Power." They develop the theory that "the talented energetic minority takes the lead and the incapable majority follows and obeys." Their natural social ideology is some version of state socialism, "a design for reconstructing society on the basis of a working class such as the middle class sees it and knows it under capitalism"—tools of production, submissive, incapable of rational decision. To this mentality, "an economic system where the workers are themselves masters and leaders of their work . . . is identical with anarchy and chaos." But state socialism, as conceived by the intellectuals, is a plan of social organization "entirely different from a true disposal by the producers over production," true socialism, a system in which workers are "masters of the factories, masters of their own labor, to conduct it at their own will."

The emergence of a new class of scientific intelligentsia has been extensively discussed—though with a very different attitude toward the phenomenon described—by Western analysts of "post-industrial society"; for example, Daniel Bell, who believes that "the entire complex of social prestige and social status will be rooted in the intellectual and scientific communities," or John Kenneth Galbraith, who holds that "Power in economic life has over time passed from its ancient association with land to association with capital and then on, in recent times, to the composite of knowledge and skills which comprises the technostructure." Both have expressed high hopes for the new "educational and scientific estate," Bakunin's "new class," ruling in the name of knowledge. But I must emphasize that Pannekoek did not conclude that since the technical intelligentsia make decisions on behalf of others in capitalist democracy, they therefore hold power.

One may, I think, note a kind of convergence, in this regard at least, between so-called "socialist" and capitalist societies. Lenin proclaimed in 1918 that "*Unquestioning submission* to a single will is absolutely necessary for the success of labour processes that are based on large-scale machine-industry . . . today the Revolution demands, in the interests of socialism, that the masses *unquestioningly obey the single will* of the leaders of the labour process" (emphasis in original); "there is not the least contradiction between soviet (i.e., socialist) democracy and the use of dictatorial power by a few persons." And two years later: "The transition to practical work is connected with individual authority. This is the system which more than any other assures the best utilization of human resources."

Consider, in comparison, the following dictum:

> Vital decision-making, particularly in policy matters, must remain at the top. God—the Communist commentators to the contrary—is clearly democratic. He distributes brain power

> universally, but He quite justifiably expects us to do
> something efficient and constructive with that priceless gift.
> That is what management is all about. Its medium is human
> capacity, and its most fundamental task is to deal with
> change. It is the gate through which social, political,
> economic, technological change, indeed change in every
> dimension, is rationally spread through society . . . the real
> threat to democracy comes not from overmanagement, but
> from undermangagement. To undermangage reality is not to
> keep it free. It is simply to let some force other than reason
> shape reality . . . if it is not reason that rules man, then man
> falls short of his potential.

In short, reason demands submission to centralized management—this is true freedom, the realization of democracy. Apart from the reference to God, it would be hard to tell whether the quote is from Lenin, or—as indeed is the case—Robert McNamara, a typical example of the scientific and educational estate in state capitalist democracy.

Science has also been called upon to explain the need for submission to the talented leadership of those whom Isaiah Berlin has called "the secular priesthood." For example, Edward Thorndike, one of the founders of experimental psychology and a person with great influence on American schools, solemnly explained in 1939 the following grand discovery of modern science:

> It is the great good fortune of mankind that there is a
> substantial positive correlation between intelligence and
> morality, including good will toward one's fellows.
> Consequently our superiors in ability are on the average
> our benefactors, and it is often safer to trust our interest to
> them than to ourselves. No group of men can be expected to
> act one-hundred percent in the interest of mankind, but this
> group of the ablest men will come nearest to the ideal.

Earlier he had explained that "the argument for democracy is not that it gives power to men without distinction, but that it gives greater freedom for ability and character to attain power."

Think what this means in capitalist democracy. Some complex of characteristics tends to enhance wealth and power (it also doesn't hurt to have rich parents), including political power, which is closely linked to success in the private economy. This collection of characteristics—some combination of avarice, lack of concern for one's fellows, energy and determination, a certain style of cleverness, etc.—is "nearest to the ideal," and democracy permits the people so endowed to rise to power, which is good, because they are our benefactors, given the correlation between intelligence and morality.

Suppose we add a standard assumption that is central to many of the modern justificatons for meritocracy, and to much of economic theory as well: people labor only for reward—the natural state for humans is to vegetate. It then follows that talent should be rewarded, for the benefit of all, since otherwise the talented and moral (recall the correlation) will not bestir themselves to act as our benefactors. The message, for the great mass of the population, is straightforward: "You are better off if you are poor—accept powerlessness and poverty, for your own good." One might note the importance of this lesson when other techniques of social control fail, for example, the promise of endless growth, which has served for a long period to induce conformity and obedience.

The secular priesthood has noticed that democracy poses some problems for the realization of the rule of reason, in which everyone submits willingly to his benefactors. One problem is that in a democracy, the voice of the people is heard. Therefore it is necessary to find ways to ensure that the people's voice speaks the right words. The problem was faced in an interesting essay by the well-known political scientist Harold Lasswell in the early 1930s. He wrote that the rise of democracy—or, as he put it, "the displacement of cults of simple obedience by democratic assertiveness"—"complicated the problem of eliciting concerted action," a problem perceived early by "military writers." The spread of schooling "did not release the masses from ignorance and superstition but altered the nature of both and compelled the development of a whole new technique of control, largely through propaganda." With the rise of democracy, "propaganda attains eminence as the one means of mass mobilization which is cheaper than violence, bribery or other possible control techniques." Propaganda, he explained "as a mere tool is no more moral or immoral than a pump handle." It may be employed for good ends or bad. "Propaganda is surely here to stay; the modern world is peculiarly dependent upon it for the coordination of atomized components in times of crisis and for the conduct of large scale 'normal operations.' " It is "certain that propaganda will in time be viewed with fewer misgivings." He went on to point out that "the modern conception of social management is profoundly affected by the propagandist outlook" in its task of eliciting "concerted action for public ends." The propagandist outlook respects individuality, but

> this regard for men in the mass rests upon no democratic dogmatisms about men being the best judges of their own

> interests. The modern propagandist, like the modern psychologist, recognizes that men are often poor judges of their own interests . . . With respect to those adjustments which do require mass action the task of the propagandist is that of inventing goal symbols which serve the double function of facilitating adoption and adaptation.

Management must cultivate "sensitiveness to those concentrations of motives which are implicit and available for rapid mobilization when the appropriate symbol is offered." The modern propagandist "is able and anxious to apply the methods of scientific observation and analysis to the processes of society" and "to direct his creative flashes to final guidance in action," since in creating symbols he is "no phrasemonger but a promoter of overt acts."

It would seem to follow that no moral issue is posed by a benevolent dictatorship, manipulating "men in the mass" by appropriate forms of propaganda. This Leninist idea is a typical doctrine of the "new class" and an example of the convergence of which I spoke earlier.

In fact, in capitalist democracy the pump handle will be operated by those who control the economy, and it comes as little surprise to learn that they have fully comprehended this message, most notably, in the "public relations" industry which has flourished ever since the potential for regimentation was discovered during the first World War. "Public relations," we learn from a leading spokesman for industry, James Selvage, "is nothing more than the mass production of personal good manners and good morals." And a vast effort has been expended to ensure that Americans have both—as these are defined by our benefactors, a development that Alex Carey has discussed in important and insightful work.

The leading figure in the public relations field, Edward Bernays, has had interesting things to say about these matters. "Leaders . . . of major organized groups, . . . with the aid of technicians . . . who have specialized in utilizing the channels of communications, have been able to accomplish . . . scientifically what we have termed 'the engineering of consent,' " he explained in the *Annals of the American Academy of Political and Social Science* in 1947—at a time when a vast propaganda campaign was undertaken by government and industry, which has not flagged since. The phrase "engineering of consent," Bernays continues,

> quite simply means the application of scientific principles and tried practices to the task of getting people to support ideas and programs . . . The engineering of consent is the very essence of the democratic process, the freedom to persuade

and suggest . . . A leader frequently cannot wait for the people to arrive at even general understanding . . . democratic leaders must play their part in . . . engineering . . . consent to socially constructive goals and values.

Once again, it is buisiness and its representatives in government who will, in practice, judge what is "socially constructive." Bernays was honored a few years later by the American Psychological Association for his contributions to science and society.

Who has this freedom to persuade and to suggest, which is the essence of the democratic process? Evidently, it is not evenly distributed—nor should it be, given the correlation between intelligence and morality. An estmate of how the freedom to persuade is distributed appears in the leading business journal *Fortune* in 1949, where it is claimed that "nearly half of the contents of the best newspapers is derived from publicity releases; nearly all the contents of the lesser papers . . . are directly or indirectly the work of [Public relations] departments." The editors go on to make the now familiar point that "It is as impossible to imagine a genuine democracy without the science of persuasion as it is to think of a totalitarian state without coercion." Indoctrination is to democracy what coercion is to dictatorship—naturally, since the stick that beats the people is labeled "the people's stick."

With such insights as these we begin to gain a better picture of one major role of the intelligentsia in capitalist democracy. Contrary to the illustions of the postindustrial theorists, power is not shifting into their hands—though one should not underestimate the significance of the flow of trained manpower from university to government and management for many decades. But the more significant function of the intelligentsia is ideological control. They are, in Gramsci's phrase, "experts on legitimation." They must ensure that beliefs are properly inculcated, beliefs that serve the interests of those with objective power, based ultimately on control of capital, in the state capitalist societies. The well-bred intelligentsia operate the pump handle, conducting mass mobilization in a way that is, as Lasswell observed, cheaper than violence or bribery, and much better suited to the image of democracy.

I have been speaking so far only of those who are sometimes call the "responsible intellectuals," those who associate themselves with external power or even try to share in it or capture it. There are, of course, those who combat it, try to limit it, to undermine and dissolve it, or to clear the way for an effective democracy which, in my view at least, must incorporate the leading principles that Pannekoek outlined. There is a revealing analysis of these several roles in the major publication of the

Trilateral Commission, a private organization of elites of the United States, Western Europe, and Japan founded at David Rockefeller's initiative in 1973, which achieved some notoriety when its members captured the posts of president, vice-president, national security adviser, secretary of state, defense and treasure, and a host of lesser offices in the latest U.S. presidential elections.

This study, called *The Crisis of Democracy*, is the work of scholars from the three trilateral regions. The crisis of democracy to which they refer arises from the fact that, during the 1960s, segments of the normally quiescent masses of the population became politically mobilized and began to press their demands, thus creating a crisis, since naturally these demands cannot be met, at least without significant redistribution of wealth and power, which is not to be contemplated. The trilateral scholars, quite consistently, therefore urge more "moderation in democracy."

The lesson is similar to one offered to the underdeveloped world by another distinguished political scientist, Ithiel de Sola Pool, who explained in 1967 that

> In the Congo, in Vietnam, in the Dominican Republic, it is clear that order depends on somehow compelling newly mobilized strata to return to a measure of passivity and defeatism from which they have recently been aroused by the process of modernization. At least temporarily, the maintenance of order requires a lowering of newly acquired aspirations and levels of political activity.

This is not mere dogma, but what "we have learned in the past thirty years of intensive empirical study of contemporary societies." The trilateral scholars are proposing, in essence, that the same lesson be applied at the center of industrial capitalism as well.

Earlier precedents come to mind at once, for example, medieval attitudes toward the third estate. The "qualities which bring credit to 'this low estate of Frenchmen' " are "humility, diligence, obedience to the king, and docility in bowing 'voluntarily to the pleasure of the lords' "— Huizinga's characterization, citing the chronicler Chastellain. Correspondingly, on the underdeveloped periphery of modern civilization the natural state of passivity and defeatism must be restored. And at home, in the version of democracy expounded by the Trilateral analysts, the commoners may petition the state, but with moderation. It is unnecessary for these scholars to stress that other social groups, somewhat better placed, will not temper their demands, though the American contributor does recall, with a trace of nostalgia perhaps, that before the crisis of democracy had erupted "Truman had been able to govern the country with the cooperation of a relatively small number of Wall Street lawyers and bankers," a happy state to which we may return if the commoners cease their indecent clamor.

It is in this context that the Trilateral Commission study turns to the intelligentsia, who, according to their analysis, come in the familiar two varieties (1) the "technocratic and policy-oriented intellectuals," responsible, serious, and constructive; (2) the "value-oriented intellectuals," a sinister grouping who pose a serious danger to democracy as they "devote themselves to the derogation of leadership, the challenging of authority, and the unmasking and deligitimation of established institutions"—even going so far as to delegitimate the institutions that are responsible for "the indoctrination of the young"—while sowing confusion and stirring dissatisfaction in the minds of the populace.

Speaking of our enemies, we despise the technocratic and policy-oriented intellectuals as "commissars" and "apparatchiks," and honor the value-oriented intellectuals as the "democratic dissidents." At home, the values are reversed. Ways must be found to control the value-oriented intellectuals so that democracy can survive, with the citizenry reduced to the apathy and obedience that becomes them, and with the commissars free to conduct the serious work of social management. The intellectual backgrounds of all of this, I have already discussed.

It is interesting that the term "value-oriented" should be used to refer to those who challenge the structure of authority, with the implication that it is improper, offensive, and dangerous to be guided by such values as truth and honesty—the trilateral scholars nowhere attempt to show that the value-oriented intellectuals they so fear and disdain are wrong or misguided in their conclusions. It is also striking that subservience to the state and its doctrines is not regarded as "a value," but merely the natural commitment of the intelligentsia, or at least their more honorable representatives.

At the outset I mentioned the Dreyfusards and the liberal American intellectuals who rallied to the state during the First World War. It is fair, I think, to regard these two groups as early variants of the two categories of intellectuals distinguished in the Trilateral Commission study.

Those who denounced the injustice of the state at the time of the Dreyfus affair by no means dominated French intellectual life, as H.F. Wesseling reminds us in a recent study. They typify the "value-oriented intellectuals" who have always been such a trial to their more sober colleagues.

Consider, in contrast, the group of liberal pragmatists in John Dewey's circle during World War I. In December 1916, the editor of the

New Republic wrote to President Wilson's leading adviser, Colonel House, that their most fervent wish was "to back the President up in this work" and "be faithful and helpful interpreters of what seems to be one of the greatest enterprises ever undertaken by an American president." At the time, Wilson was calling for "peace without victory"—and a few months later, for a victory without peace. By then, his leading enterprise was to guide a divided nation into the European war. The intellectuals proved to be faithful and helpful interpreters of this great enterprise. According to their own estimate, which may be exaggerated, "the effective and decisive work on behalf of the war has been accomplished by . . . a class which must be comprehensively but loosely described as the 'intellectuals' " (*New Republic*). The nation entered the war "under the influence of a moral verdict reached after the utmost deliberation by the more thoughtful members of the community"—the secular priesthood, the technocratic and policy-oriented intellectuals, the commissars. The latter term is in fact rather apt. The techniques of propaganda described by later scholars were largely developed and applied with much success during World War I and led to the explosive growth of the public relations field shortly after—though for accuracy, I should add that "the more thoughtful members of the community" were as much the victims of the highly effective British propaganda machine, with its manufacture of "Hun atrocities," as they were purveyors of war propaganda, proceeding (in their own words) to "impose their will upon a reluctant or indifferent majority."

It would only be fair to commend the BBC for returning the favor in October and November of this year, with its presentation on the Third Programme of a series entitled "Many Reasons Why: The American Involvement in Vietnam" (see *The Listener* for excerpts). Demonstrating its taste for symmetry, the BBC has concocted an account that is certain to delight the American propaganda services no less than the response of the more thoughtful members of the American intellectual community must have warmed the hearts of such men as Sir Gilbert Parker, who headed the American section of the British propaganda bureau in World War I, and who was able to gloat about "the permeation of the American Press by British influence" in his secret reports to the British cabinet.

The services rendered to the state by the academic professions during World War I are surveyed in a recent work by Carol S. Gruber (*Mars and Minerva*). Historians were particularly keen to be mobilized. A National Board for Historical Service (NBHS) was founded by a group of historians "to bring into useful operation, in the present emergency, the intelligence and skill of the historical workers of the country," so one of them (A.C. McLaughlin) wrote in *The Dial* in May 1917. One of the founders of the NBHS, Frederic L. Paxson, later described its activity as "historical engineering, explaining the issues of the war that we might the better win it"—an early example of "the engineering of consent." The press was also mobilized. An NBHS study of the German press concluded that the "voluntary co-operation of the newspaper publishers of America resulted in a more effective standardization of the information and arguments presented to the American people, than existed under the nominally strict military control exercised in Germany." The main government commission (Creel Commission) established to direct wartime propaganda made effective use of the services of American scholars. Among its achievements was a pamphlet entitled *The German-Bolshevik Consipiracy,* which employed documents generally regarded as forgeries in Europe (and later shown to be forgeries by George Kennan) to "demonstrate" that the Bolsheviks were paid agents of the German General Staff, who had materially aided them in coming to power. In later years too historians were to persist in "historical engineering," in the war against the Bolshevik menace. In his Presidential Address to the American Historical Association in 1949, Conyers Read explained that

> we must clearly assume a militant attitude if we are to survive . . . Discipline is the essential prerequisite of every effective army whether it march under the Stars and Stripes or under the Hammer and Sickle . . . Total war, whether it be hot or cold, enlists everyone and calls upon everyone to assume his part. The historian is no freer from this obligation than the physicist . . . This sounds like the advocacy of one form of social control as against another. In short, it is.

The long sorry record has been surveyed, to the present, in an important unread monograph by Jesse Lemisch, entitled *On Active Service in War and Peace.*

Not all of the scholars who lent their services during World War I were acclaimed. Thorstein Veblen, for example, "prepared a report demonstrating that the shortage of farm labor in the Midwest could be met by ending the harassment and persecution of the members of the Industrial Workers of the World (IWW)," Carol Gruber points out, but "he also, however, together with his assistant, was fired for his pains" from his position as statistical expert for the Food Administration.

Then too there were "value-oriented intellectuals" who did not see the light. Randolph Bourne is the best-known case. We may recall how he was dropped by the *New Republic,* and forced out of an editorial position on *The Dial* by John Dewey, one indication of his displeasure over

Bourne's penetrating criticism of the liberal intellectuals who were working to sell the war, Bourne felt, in the interests of "an opportunist progamme of state-socialism at home"—with the secular priesthood in command—"and a league of benevolently-imperialistic nations abroad."

Clarence Karier, who has discussed this period in very illuminating work, goes on to observe that John Dewey had much contempt for the "pacifists" who, in his words, "wasted rather than invested their potentialities when they turned so vigorously to opposing entrance" into the war instead of working for attainable goals within the growing chauvinist consensus (July 1917). In a more abstract discussion of "force and coercion," Dewey had expressed his view that if pacifists "would change their tune from the intrinsic immorality of the use of coercive force to the comparative inefficiency and stupidity of existing methods of using force, their good intentions would be more fruitful." Continuing, Dewey explained:

> Squeamishness about force is the mark not of idealistic but of moonstruck morals . . . The criterion of value lies in the relative efficiency and economy of the expenditure of force as a means to an end. With advance of knowledge, refined, subtle and indirect use of force is always replacing coarse, obvious and direct methods of applying it. This is the explanation to the ordinary feeling against the use of force. What is thought of as brutal, violent, immoral, is a use of physical agencies which are gross, sensational and evident on their own account, in cases where it is possible to employ with greater economy and less waste means which are comparatively imperceptible and refined.

His general point was that "the only question which can be raised about the justification of force is that of comparative efficiency and economy in its use." This in April 1916. A good, sober, pragmatic evaluation, which we have heard in other contexts since, without Dewey's qualifications.

Not surprisingly, Dewey felt that the war had taught valuable lessons in this regard. He wrote that "the one great thing that the war has accomplished, it seems to me, of a permanent sort, is the enforcement of a psychological and educational lesson . . . It has proved not that it is possible for human beings to take hold of human affairs and manage them, to see an end which has to be gained, a purpose which must be fulfilled, and deliberately and intelligently to go to work to organize the means, the resources and the methods of accomplishing those results."

Now that this lesson had been learned, "The real question with us will be one of effectively discerning whether the intelligent men of the community really want to bring about a better reorganized social order." The war had revealed the possibilities of intelligent administration, and it is now the responsibility of the intelligent men of the community to rise to the occasion, organizing intelligence to the design of a more benign state capitalist social order, with the economical and refined use of force to achieve socially desirable ends.

I have so far been discussing the first of my two topics, the roles played by intellectuals, focusing on the role of commissar versus dissident, technocratic and policy-oriented versus value-oriented intellectuals. Now I would like to apply these remarks to the contemporary world. First, however, a few general comments, to set the stage, as I see it.

The United States emerged from World War II with unparalleled wealth and power. Quite naturally, state power was employed to construct an international order—extensive, though not all-encompassing—that would satisfy the needs of the masters of the domestic economy. Equally naturally, this is not what one reads in most history books, though the basic facts are, I believe, well-established and the business press is often quite straightforward about the matter. For example, as the Vietnam war came to an end, *Business Week* commented editorially on "the fearful drift of foreign policy": "the international economic structure, under which U.S. companies have flourished since the end of World War II, is in jeopardy," this leading journal of the business community observed. Within this internation economic structure, "fueled initially by the dollars of the Marshall Plan, American business prospered and expanded . . . No matter how negative a development, there was always the umbrella of American power to contain it . . . The rise of the multinational corporation was the economic expression of this political framework." But now, they fear, "this stable world order for business operations is falling apart," in part because of the American failure in Indochina. I should mention, parenthetically, that analyses along these lines, which are quite accurate, are generally dismissed as "Marxist" under the conventions of American academic scholarship, though not when they appear in business publications.

In general, the postwar global enterprise was a stunning success, though there were reversals, the most dramatic in Southeast Asia. In the course of a "limited war," which proved quite costly, U.S. power declined somewhat relative to its industrial rivals. A major task of the state and its propagandists has been and remains to reconstruct the domestic and international order that was bruised, though never undermined, by the bloody events in Indochina. I will concentrate here only on the reconstruction of the ideological system, since that is the province of the intelligentsia; more central tasks are delegated elsewhere.

Ruling groups throughout the "First World" of industrial capitalism also have a stake in the reconstitution of American power, and particularly, in ensuring that underdeveloped countries do not strike an independent course but remain subordinated to the needs of the industrial democracies. The rich and powerful of the world require a system of beliefs to justify their dominance, as they enter into "North-South dialogue." To construct and promulgate such a system is the task of the intellectuals—again, the sober and serious among them.

In the United States, the prevailing version of the "White Man's Burden" has been the doctrine, carefully nurtured by the intelligentsia, that the United States, alone among the powers of modern history, is not guided in its international affairs by the perceived material interests of those with domestic power, but rather wanders aimlessly, merely reacting to the initiatives of others, while pursuing abstract moral principles: The Wilsonian principles of freedom and self-determination, democracy, equality, and so on. Responsible controversy proceeds within a narrow spectrum: at one extreme, there are those who laud the United States for its unique benevolence; at the other extreme, we find the "realist" critics—George Kennan and Hans Morgenthau, for example—who deplore the foolishness of American policy and believe that we should not be so obsessively moralistic but should pursue the national interest in a rational way.

The work of the realist critics gives the deepest insight into the dominant ideology, and reveals dramatically the extent of its penetration. In the early 1960s, Hans Morgenthau—who is near the outer limits of responsible criticism, and to his credit, passed beyond them a few years later—could write that the United States has a "transcendent purpose," namely, "the establishment of equality in freedom in America," and indeed throughout the world, since "The arena within which the United States must defend and promote its purpose has become world-wide." "America has become the Rome and Athens of the Western world, the foundation of its lawful order and the fountainhead of its culture," though "America does not know this."

To be sure, Morgenthau recognizes certain defects both at home and abroad—in Central America and the Phillippines, for example, But he chides those critics who rely on the ample historical record to deny the "transcendent purpose" of America and who claim that the United States is very much like every other power—what is often described (though not by Morgenthau) as a "radical critique," a revealing choice of words. Such critics, according to Morgenthau, are guilty of a simple error of logic: "to reason thus is to confound the abuse of reality with reality itself." It is the unachieved "national purpose," revealed by "the evidence of history as our minds reflect it," which is the reality; the actual historical record is merely the abuse of reality.

The theological overtones are apparent, and Morgenthau is not unaware of them. He remarks that the critics, who mistake the real world for reality, have fallen into "the error of atheism, which denies the validity of religion on similar grounds." The comment is apt. There is indeed something truly religious in the fervor with which responsible American intellectuals have sought to deny plain fact and to secure their dogmas concerning American benevolence, the contemporary version of the "civilizing mission."

But the doctrines of the state religion were not able to survive the war in Vietnam, at least among large parts of the population. The result is an ideological crisis. The institutional foundations for the repeated counterrevolutionary intervention of the postwar years remain unshaken. But the doctrinal system that has served to gain popular support for the crusade against independent development has collapsed. The problem of the day is to reconstruct it. It is a serious problem, since imperial intervention carries costs, both material and moral, which must be borne by the population. I would now like to survey some of the methods by which this problem is being faced by the secular priesthood.

The first task is to rewrite the history of the American war in Vietnam. This is relatively easy, since the press and academic scholarship have consistently held to the required mythical history. According to the myth, the United Stated intervened, unwisely perhaps, to defend South Vietnam from aggression. Our good motives were transmuted, somehow, into bad policies. Scholars tell us that the United States did not realize that Vietnamese communism was a nationalist movement—planners thought that Ho Chi Minh was an agent of Moscow, or perhaps "Peiping." The fault lies in error, misunderstanding, ignorance, or perhaps an excess of benevolence in undertaking a costly defense of a nation that was unwilling to save itself. This is not the place to review the documentary record, which establishes that top-level planners undertook, consciously and knowingly, to destroy the forces of Vietnamese nationalism, and did so on the basis of calculated and rational imperial strategy. Unable to restore French rule, they launched a war against the largely peasant population of South Vietnam, later extending the aggression to the rest of Indochina, conducting military operations and "nation-building" programs of indescribable barbarism. But we can be quite sure that the custodians of history will present a different story, and since their position in the propaganda institutions is virtually unchallenged, they will succeed in this endeavor—and indeed, already have, substantially.

A more difficult task is to shift the moral onus of the war to its victims. This seems a rather unpromising enterprise—rather as if the Nazis had attempted to blame the Jews for the crematoria. But undaunted, American propagandists are pursuing this effort too, and with some success. Things have reached the point where an American president can appear on national television and state that we owe no debt to the Vietnamese, because "the destruction was mutual." And there is not a whisper of protest when this monstrous statement, worthy of Hitler or Stalin, is blandly produced in the midst of a discourse on human rights. Not only do we owe them no debt for having murdered and destroyed and ravaged their land, but we now may stand back and sanctimoniously blame them for dying of disease and malnutrition, deploring their cruelty when hundreds die trying to clear unexploded ordnance by hand from fields laid waste by the violence of the American state. The only unresolved issue is the remains of American pilots missing-in-action, not American responsibility to help rebuild what they destroyed. Worse yet, we refuse to allow others to aid them. Recently India tried to send 100 buffalos to Vietnam to help replenish the herds decimated by American terror. This tiny gift had to be channeled through the Red Cross to avoid American retribution—cancellation of "Food for Peace" aid, in this case. Peasants in Indochina pull plows, because the animal herds were destroyed by American bombardment. And the *Washington Post,* which concealed and supported that aggression, publishes photographs of Cambodian peasants pulling plows as an illustration of Communist atrocities. In fact, the photographs in this case are probable fabrications of Thai intelligence, so clumsy that they were rejected even by the right-wing English language Thai press—though the European press has been less discriminating in this regard. The *Post* knows this, and knows its account of the source of the photographs to be a falsehood, but will not so much as publish a letter giving the documented facts that it knows to be true, let alone publicly retract its fabrications—one small example of the stream of misrepresentation now disfiguring the American (indeed Western) press with regard to postwar developments in Indochina. I have documented a good deal of this elsewhere (see N. Chmosky and E. Herman, *The Nation,* June 25, 1977) and will not review it here. The crucial point is the truly obscene character of the attempt to blame the victims, the denial of American responsibility, and the startling success of this campaign.

Another task for the intelligentsia is to reduce the "lessons of the war" to the narrowest possible terms. Again, this is not very difficult, since the intellectuals always tended to construe the issues in an entirely unprincipled fashion. There is a study by a Columbia University sociologist, Charles Kadushin, that gives a good deal of insight into the facts, which are rather different from what is generally assumed. He conducted a careful study of attitudes of a group that he called "the American intellectual elite" in 1970, at the very peak of active opposition to the war, when colleges were closed down in opposition to the invasion of Cambodia and demonstrations swept the country. Much of his study was devoted to the war in Vietnam. The "intellectual elite" opposed the war, almost to a man. But the grounds for their opposition deserves careful attention. Kadushin identified three categories of opposition, on what he called "ideological," "moral," and "pragmatic" grounds. Under "ideological" opposition to the war he includes the belief that aggression is wrong, even when conducted by the United States. Opposition on "moral" grounds is based on deaths and atrocities: the war is too bloody. "Pragmatic" opposition to the war is grounded on the feeling that we probably can't get away with it: the war is too costly; the enterprise should be liquidated as no longer worthwhile.

There are two points of interest about this analysis. First, the terminology itself. No doubt the group surveyed would have been unanimous in deploring Russian aggression in Czechoslovakia. But on what grounds? Not on "pragmatic" grounds, since it was quite successful and not very costly. Not on "moral" grounds, since casualties were few. Rather, on "ideological" grounds: that is, on grounds that aggression is wrong, even if it is relatively bloodless, costless, and successful. But would we ever refer to this as objection on "ideological grounds"? Surely not. It is only when one challenges the divine right of the United States to intervene by force in the internal affairs of others that such sinister terms as "ideological" are invoked.

More interesting, however, is the distribution of responses. Opposition to aggression on "ideological" grounds was very limited. More objected on "moral" grounds. But to an overwhelming degree, objections were "pragmatic." Recall that this survey was taken at the height of popular opposition to the war, when, in contrast to the "intellectual elite," substantial segments of the unwashed masses had come to oppose the war on grounds of principle and even to act on their beliefs, much to the horror of more delicate souls who now explain that their sense of irony and the complexities of history kept them removed from such vulgar display. As for the survey itself, my guess would be that a similar study in Germany in 1944 might have produced comparable results.

Similar attitudes are revealed in the debate over "amnesty" for those referred to as "draft dodgers." The more compassionate feel that they should be granted absolution for their crimes, though others sternly object that they must bear some punishment at least. That the real question is the granting of "amnesty" to those who conducted the war, or the intellectual claque that supported them until it became too costly, is an observation that far transcends the limits of "responsibility," within the reigning doctrinal system. It is commonly alleged that the "draft dodgers," and the student movement on the whole, opposed the war out of fear. They were unwilling to face the terrors of the war. In fact, the leading initiative in the American resistance, which was unprecedented in scale and character, was taken by young men who could have easily escaped combat—not very difficult at the time for privileged groups—but who chose to face great risk, long imprisonment or exile, out of simple moral commitment. Similar comments apply rather generally to desertion, the resistance of the underprivileged. The common claim that student opposition to the war collapsed because of the termination of the draft, though comforting to ideologues, is also false. In fact, certain more "politicized" elements in the student movement had (foolishly in my view) come to regard opposition to the war as relatively unimportant long before the draft was ended; and mass opposition to the war quite closely reflected the degree of overt American involvement, independently of the draft. But the ideological system cannot tolerate the fact that there was a principled opposition to the war, primarily among the young, conducted with great courage, conviction, and considerable effectiveness. Therefore it is necessary to pretend that the serious and meaningful opposition was led by sober-minded intellectuals and heroic politicians, those "thoughtful members of the community" who, like their predecessors, reached a verdict "after the utmost deliberation" and acted with dispatch to restore national policy to its proper channels.

The rewriting of this history too deserves serious attention, more than I can give it here. To illustrate with just one case, consider the current (December 10, 1977) issue of the *New Republic,* still more or less the official journal of the liberal intelligentsia. The lead editorial, entitled "The McCarthy Decade," is an ode to Eugene McCarthy, who "changed the landscape of American politics" when he challenged Lyndon Johnson in the 1968 presidential campaign. The McCarthy campaign, the editors allege, "seeded the political system with men and women schooled in dissent" and introduced "a streak of unpredictable idealism" into American political life. "The most obvious postscript to the McCarthy campaign was the ending of the Vietnam war," as McCarthy "and his cohort established a consensus on the need to end that war." The editors quote with approval John Kenneth Galbraith's statement on the aforementioned BBC program that McCarthy is "the man who deserves more credit than anybody else for bringing our involvement in the war to an end," and they proceed to laud McCarthy for his modesty in refusing the mantle of hero. McCarthy, they conclude, "has insured that no President ever will feel again that he can carry on a war unaffected by the moral judgment of the people."

Compare this analysis with the facts. By late 1967, the mass popular movement against the war had reached a remarkable scale. Its great success was that the government had been unable to declare a national mobilization. The costs of the war were concealed, contributing to an economic crisis which, by 1968, had brought leading business and conservative circles to insist that the effort to subdue the Vietnamese be limited. The *Pentagon Papers* revealed that by late 1967, the scale and character of popular opposition was causing great concern to planners. The Tet offensive, which shortly after undermined government propaganda claims, enhanced these fears. A Defense Department memorandum expressed the concern that increased force levels would lead to "increased defiance of the draft and growing unrest in the cities," running the risk of "provoking a domestic crisis of unprecedented proportions." Mass popular demonstrations and civil disobedience were a particular concern, so much so that the Joint Chiefs of Staff had to consider whether "sufficient forces would still be available for civil disorder control" if more troops were sent to crush the Vietnamese.

The unanticipated growth of protest and resistance was largely spontaneous. It took place against a background of considerable hostility in the media and the political system, and occasional violence and disruption. One can identify deepy-committed activists—Dave Dellinger, for example—who worked with tireless devotion to arouse and organize the public to oppose American aggression, with its mounting and ever more visible atrocities. There were some, like Benjamin Spock, who supported the young resistors, and even a few who joined them; for example, Father Daniel Berrigan, who offered "our apologies, good friends, for the fracture of good order, the burning of paper instead of children," when he and six others destroyed draft files in Catonsville, Maryland. But one will search in vain for the contribution of Eugene McCarthy to "establishing a consensus" against the war or arousing opposition to it. In the difficult early period, he did not even rise to the level of insignificance. There were a few political figures—Ernest Gruening and Wayne Morse, for example—who condemned the escalation of the American war. McCarthy never joined them.

After the Tet offensive in January 1968, it was generally recognized that the United States must shift to a more "capital-intensive" effort, relying on technology rather than manpower. The American expeditionary force was beginning to collapse from within. The American command was coming to learn a familiar lesson of colonial war: a citizen's army cannot be trusted to conduct the inevitable atrocities; such a war must be waged by professional killers. After 1968, the war dragged on for seven long years, with mounting barbarism and major massacres, such as Operation SPEEDY EXPRESS in the Mekong Delta in 1969. Popular opposition peaked in the early 1970s, and continued, despite press efforts to conceal U.S. initiatives, until the very end. Throughout this period too, there was barely a whisper from Eugene McCarthy.

Why then has McCarthy been elevated to the liberal pantheon? The reason is simple. His brief appearance in 1968 symbolizes quite accurately the opposition to the war on the part of the liberal intelligentsia. Riding to national prominence on the wave of mass opposition to the war, McCarthy slipped silently away after failing to gain the Democratic nomination at Chicago in August 1968. He did succeed, briefly, in diverting popular energies to political channels, and came close to gaining political power by exploiting the forces of a movement that he had played no part whatsoever in mobilizing. His utter cynicism was revealed with great clarity by his behavior after he lost the nomination. Had he been even minimally serious, he would have made use of his undeserved prestige as a "spokesman" for the peace movement that he had so shamelessly exploited, to press for an end to the American war. But nothing more was heard from McCarthy, who demonstrated by his silence that he cared as little for the issue of the American war as he did for his youthful supporters who were bloodied by police riots in the streets of Chicago as he was attempting to win the Democratic candidacy, through their efforts on his behalf. He is, in short, a proper figure for canonization by the liberal intelligentsia.

The general attitudes of this group are reflected in the material now being produced on the "lessons of the war." To cite again just one of many examples, the well-known Asian specialist Edwin Reischauer of Harvard writes that

> The real lesson of the Vietnam war is the tremendous cost of attempting to control the destiny of a Southeast Asian country against the cross-currents of nationalism. Southeast Asia simply is not open to external control at a cost that would make this a feasible proposition for any outside power.

The clear implication is that if the costs were less, the effort to impose "external control" would be quite legitimate—if exercised by the United

States, that is; obviously not by China or Russia. The United States, in short, is once again unique: the obligations of the U.N. Charter, though part of "the supreme law of the land," do not apply to a state devoted with such selflessness and honor to the Wilsonian principles of freedom and independence.

Reischauer proceeds as well to repeat familiar fantasies about the origins of the American intervention in the alleged belief that Ho Chi Minh was the "front-line agent" of a unified international communism. To him, "the tragedy of the U.S. involvement in Vietnam is that this picture was never really correct," not the consequences of this "involvement" for the people of Indochina, a lesser tragedy. As is standard, he chooses to ignore the substantial documentary record which reveals that top-level planners had full awareness of the nationalist commitment of the Viet Minh and that after they had decided on intervention, they sought long and hard, without success, for some evidence to establish what they needed to justify that decision: that Ho Chi Minh was a puppet of outside forces. This documentary record is plainly unacceptable, therefore eliminated from the record of sober scholarship. "Error" and "ignorance," however, are socially neutral categories, and are available for use by critics among the secular priesthood.

The basic ideological institutions are the university-based academic professions and the mass media. I have mentioned the interpretation of the "lessons of the war"—and it is the standard one—in respectable academic scholarship. Consider now just one, again quite typical example from the mass media. The *New York Times,* in its retrospective editorial assessment of the war, observed that there has been "a decade of fierce polemics" in the United States which has "failed to resolve this ongoing quarrel" between two opposed groups: the hawks, who believe that the war could have been waged differently and more successfully, and the doves, "who believe that a viable, non-Communist South Vietnam was always a myth"—that is, that the American intervention was bound to fail. It is too early to settle this profound question, the *Times* sagely observes. We must not "try to pre-empt history's role." Rather, "this is a time for humility and for silence and for prayer."

Note that there is a third logically possible position: regardless of the judgment of history on the tactical issue to which the *Times* limits attention, the United States simply had no legal or moral right to intervene by force in the internal affairs of Vietnam (or Laos, or Cambodia) in the first place. The "complex disagreement" between the hawks and doves, as presented by the *Times,* is a debate over tactics and their efficacy. It carefully skirts the only question of principle. The "decade of fierce polemics" that the *Times* surveys—and which it leaves to the judgment of "Clio, the goddess of history, [who] is cool and slow and elusive in her ways"—happens to exclude the authentic mass-based peace movement, which rejected the basic assumption of all participants in the debate that the *Times* surveys.

There is method in this restriction of what is "thinkable": it leaves beyond challenge the basic principle of the state religion, the American right of forceful intervention if only it can succeed. So committed is the *Times* to preserving doctrinal purity on this issue that it refused even to print a letter noting that this "spectrum" was rather limited, though it did see fit to publish quite a range of opinion in response to its editorial, including a proposal that we undertake nuclear bombardment. But there must, after all, be some limits in a civilized journal.

As I have documented elsewhere, the position of the *Times* in this regard was quite typical of the national press. It is a fair generalization that among the organized and articulate intelligentsia, the war was considered to be a mistake by the 1970s at least. The war was generally opposed, but on quite narrow grounds, and within a framework of thinking that tacitly accepted the legitimacy of the exercise of American force. It is interesting, again, that those who advocated obedience to "the supreme law of the land," which clearly excludes such use of force, were regarded as dangerous radicals who must be excluded, as far as possible, from the "fierce polemics" tolerated within the ideological institutions.

These examples illustrate some rather interesting points about propaganda and the intelligentsia. In a totalitarian society, the mechanisms of indoctrination are simple and transparent. The state determines official truth. The technocratic and policy-oriented intellectuals parrot official doctrine, which is easily identified. In a curious way, this practice frees the mind. Internally, at least, one can identify the propaganda message and reject it. Overt expression of such rejection carries a risk—how serious the risk, and over how broad a range, depends on just how totalitarian and violent the state actually is.

Under capitalist democracy, the situation is considerably more complex. The press and the intellectuals are held to be fiercely independent, hypercritical, antagonistic to the "establishment," in an adversary relation to the state. The Trilateral analysts, for example, describe the press as a new source of national power, dangerously opposed to state authority. Reality is a little different. True, there is criticism, but a careful look will show that it remains within narrow bounds. Basic principles of the state propaganda system are assumed by the critics. In contrast to the totalitarian system, the propaganda apparatus does not merely stake out a position to which all must conform—or which they may privately oppose. Rather, it seeks to determine and limit the entire spectrum of thought: the official doctrine at one extreme, and the position of its most vocal adversaries, at the other. Over the entire spectrum, the same fundamental assumptions are insinuated, though rarely expressed. They are presupposed, but not asserted. I have already given a few examples. Thus according to the *New York Times,* the hawks and doves share a commitment to the fundamental unspoken principle that the United States has a legitimate right to exercise force and violence, where it chooses to do so. And the "realist" criticism of American foreign policy, which marked the outer limits of respectable controversy until the impact of the student movement forced the doors of academia to open slightly, adopts the basic assumption that U.S. foreign policy is one of benevolence—misplaced benevolence, the critics say. Across the entire spectrum of debate it is presupposed that the United States, alone in modern history, does act out of a commitment to abstract moral principles rather than rational calculation by ruling groups, concerned for their material interests.

There are many other examples. The democratic system of thought control is seductive and compelling. The more vigorous the debate, the better the system of propaganda is served, since the tacit unspoken assumptions are more forcefully implanted. An independent mind must seek to separate itself from official doctrine—and from the criticism advanced by its alleged opponents. Not just from the assertions of the propaganda system, but from its tacit presuppositions as well, as expressed by critic and defender. This is a far more difficult task. Any expert in indoctrination will confirm, no doubt, that it is far more effective to constrain all possible thought within a framework of tacit assumption than to try to impose a particular explicit belief with a bludgeon. It may be that some of the spectacular achievements of the American propaganda system, where all of this has been elevated to a high art, are attributable to the method of feigned dissent practiced by the responsible intelligentsia.

A final task of the propaganda system is to restore the faith in our transcendent purpose. It is not enough to demonstrate the evil of our enemies, and to transfer to them the responsibility for the atrocities committed against them. It is also necessary to reestablish our own moral purity. Here, events have proceeded with an almost mythic quality. I do not suggest that it was planned; merely that the propaganda system rose magnificently to the presented occasion.

The drama has unfolded in two acts: Act One may be entitled "Cartharsis," Act Two, "Rebirth," or "Spiritual Regeneration."

In Act One the evil was personalized, expelled. Richard Nixon had a point when he claimed that the press was mounting an unfair campaign against him, but he failed to comprehend the role that he was playing in the unfolding drama. In fact, the charges against Nixon were for behavior not too far out of the ordinary, though he erred in choosing his victims among the powerful, a significant deviation from established practice. He was never charged with the serious crimes of his administration: the "secret bombing" of Cambodia, for example. The issue was indeed raised, but it was the secrecy of the bombing, not the bombing itself, that was held to be the crime. Again the crucial tacit assumption: the United States, in its majesty, has the right to bomb a defenseless peasant society—but it is wrong to mislead Congress about the matter. The secrecy of the bombing was indeed remarkable. I have been privately informed by a high military officer who was involved in planning the Cambodian "incursion" in April 1970 that even top commanders were denied photo-reconnaissance intelligence, apparently because the government was unwilling to reveal to these officers the devastation from American bombing in the countryside that they would soon traverse. But any criticism of the Nixon administration on these grounds remains within the permissible bounds of tactical debate.

We might ask, incidentally, in what sense the bombing was "secret." Actually the bombing was "secret" because the press refused to expose it. Like the bombing of Laos before it, the American attack on neutral Cambodia must have been known to the press. A few days after the Nixon-Kissinger "secret bombing" began, Prince Sihanouk—whose government was recognized by the United States—called upon the international press to denounce the American attack on peaceful villages and the murder of defenseless peasants. There was no outcry, because the press was committed to secrecy, exactly as in earlier years, when the peasants of Northern Laos were mercilessly bombed, hundreds of miles from the nearest zone of combat or even supply routes. It was years later, when open season was declared on President Nixon, that the press had the gall to accuse him of having imposed a veil of secrecy over these atrocities—which are rarely recognized as atrocities, since even now the press prefers to believe that the attacks were directed against North Vietnamese and Vietcong military targets.

In these and other ways, Act One was successfully completed and the evil, now identified and localized, was expunged. Next the curtain rose on Act Two: Rebirth, the discovery of Human Rights, our new transcendent purpose. As historian Arthur Schlesinger explained in the *Wall Street Journal,* "In effect, human rights is replacing self-determination as the guiding value in American foreign policy."

In a perverse sense he is right. That is, to the exact extent that self-determination was the guiding value in the past—in the era of Nicaragua and Cuba, Guatemala and Iran, Vietnam and Laos and Cambodia, the Dominican Republic and Chile—to exactly that extent human rights will be our guiding value tomorrow. The fact that such sentiments can be seriously expressed, and greeted with respect, is itself a remarkable indication of the intellectual and moral degeneration that accompanies the triumph of the awesome propaganda system.

There is much more to say about these achievements, and I have not even mentioned domestic analogs that are certainly required to complete the story. But I think it is fair to say that the secular priesthood, relying on the method of feigned dissent characteristic of democratic propaganda systems, has very largely succeeded, within only a few years, to destroy the historical record and supplant it with a more comfortable story, transferring the moral onus of American aggression to its victims, reducing the "lessons" of the war to the socially neutral categories of error, ignorance, and cost, and reconstructing a suitable doctrine of the civilizing mission of the West, America in the lead.

To appreciate fully the range of these accomplishments, we may conduct a simple *Gedankenexperiment* along lines already suggested. Imagine that World War II had ended in a stalemate, with the Nazis driven from France and the Low Countries, but remaining a major world power, intact among the ruins. Imagine that a stratum of dissenting intellectuals had emerged, who criticized Hitler for his errors in attempting to wage a two-front war, destroying a valuable source of labor power with the death camps, reacting with too much brutality to the intolerable burdens placed on Germany at Versailles, and so on. How might they have proceeded to reinterpet the contemporary scene? Perhaps like this.

First, they would have explained the historic need for German power to be resurrected, perhaps invoking Martin Heidegger's theory that Germany alone can defend the classic values of humanistic civilization from the barbarians of East and West, not to speak of the hordes of Asia and Africa. They might then have turned to the situation in what they would have called "occupied Europe"; say France, calm and peaceful until the Anglo-American invasion of 1944 abetted by Communist-led terrorists within, and now under American occupation—recall that Eisenhower had "supreme authority" and the "ultimate determination of where, when and how civil administration . . . shall be exercised by French citizens" under a directive from Roosevelt issued with Churchill's approval. They would have observed with horror that before and during this occupation the terrorists of the resistance carried out a great massacre of collaborators, amounting to a minimum of 30-40,000 murders within a few months according to the assessment of the French historian of the resistance, Robert Aron, basing himself on a detailed analysis of the French Gendarmerie, and amounting to no less than seven million killed according to the detailed studies of Pleyber-Gradjeah, whom Aron calls a "victim of the Liberation." Appalled by these monstrous events, the German dissidents might even have produced a judgment not unlike that of the editor of the *New Republic*, who explained recently that "the American collapse [in Indochina] will read in history as among the ugliest of national crimes" (June 11, 1977)—not what the U.S. did, but its failure to persist, is criminal. Comparably, the Nazi failure to withstand the Anglo-American invasion—a foreign invasion from abroad, not a general uprising within—will read in history as the ugliest of crimes, as attested by the millions of helpless victims; we may assume that the "seven million victims" story would have prevailed within the domains of Nazi influence. Continuing, these analysts might have observed with dismay the terrible suffering of the people of France and England—not to speak of Russia—in the fierce winter of 1946-47, with production stagnating and the United States unwilling even to grant a loan except under conditions that reduce Britain to American vassalage. And so on. Perhaps, as moral men, they might have objected to an annual reenactment of the events at Auschwitz, as indecent, much as some Americans feebly protest the annual reenactment of the Hiroshima bombing by the pilot of the Enola Gay, most recently, in October 1977 in an Texas air show, before an audience of 20,000 admiring spectators.

What we have witnessed in the United States and the West generally in the past few years is in some ways a grim parody, in the real world, of this invented nightmare. It has proceeded with little articulate protest—again, a testimony to the effectiveness of the institutions of propaganda and ideology and the notable commitment of large segments of the intelligentsia to established power, even as they pretend to combat its excesses.

I mentioned before that ruling groups thorughout the First World of industrial capitalism require a system of beliefs that will justify their dominance. The "North-South" conflict will not subside, and new forms of domination will have to be devised to ensure that privileged segments of Western industrial society maintain substantial control over global resources, human and material, and benefit disproportionately from this control. Thus it comes as no suprise that the reconstitution of ideology in the United States finds echoes throughout the industrial world. To cite only one minor example, Southeast Asia correspondent Martin Woollacott of the *Manchester Guardian* expresses his dismay and astonishment that the Cambodian Marxists who studied in Paris never absorbed the "essential humaneness of French life and thought." How this "humaneness" expressed itself in Indochina under French rule I need not discuss—those interested might turn to a gripping study by Ngo Vihn Long published by MIT press in 1973. Nor is there any need to speak of the humaneness of European civilization itself, culminating in two mass slaughters. I have already mentioned the humaneness of the Paris where these Cambodian Marxists studied as World War II came to bloody end; and I could have gone on to describe its humaneness a few years before as French authorities were vigorously rounding up Jews for shipment to death camps. But it is an absolute requirement for the Western system of ideology that a vast gulf be established between the civilized West, with its traditional commitment to human dignity, liberty, and self-determination, and the barbaric brutality of those who for some reason—perhaps defective genes—fail to appreciate the depth of this historic commitment, so well revealed by America's Asian wars, for example.

Over twenty years ago, a rare study of the political economy of American foreign policy was published, under that title, by a group sponsored by the National Planning Association and the Woodrow Wilson Foundation. They observed, quite accurately, that the primary threat of communism is the economic transformation of the Communist powers "in the ways which reduce their willingness and ability to complement the industrial economies of the West." It is the recognition of this threat that has inspired American counterrevolutionary intervention in the Third World, though the spectre of Russian or Chinese aggression in Eastern Europe, Asia, the Middle East, Africa, and Latin America has been dangled before the public as a more acceptable threat. The problem remains, and will continue to evoke Western antagonism to independent development, which is often lead by a state socialist leadership that follows the model of Bakunin's Red bureaucracy. In an era of growing material shortages and resource competition, the "North-South" conflict may lead to new forms of still-unimagined horror, while stagnating economies in the industrial societies, unable to absorb a superfluous class of workers without appropriate skills, will search for ways to implement the proposals of the Trilateral analysts as to how to impose passivity and obedience, in the interests of something called "democracy."

Those who may be concerned about unemployment for intellectuals need not worry too much, I believe. Under circumstances such as these, there should be considerable need and ample opportunity for the secular priesthood.

Copyright © 1979 by Noam Chomsky.
Also appeared Internationale Vitgeversmij. Het Wereldvenster, Holland

Theme 4
The Powerful and the Powerless

Bayard Rustin

Power and Minority Groups

Baynard Rustin was born on March 17, 1910 in West Chester, Pennsylvania. After graduating from West Chester High School, where he was a member of championship football and track teams, he traveled extensively, doing odd jobs to earn money for college. In 1931, he enrolled in Wilberforce University and later attended Cheyney State College and City College of New York, where he earned his tuition by singing with Josh White and Leadbelly.

From 1941 to 1953, Mr. Rustin served as race relations secretary of the Fellowship of Reconciliation. During that period he was also a youth organizer for A. Phillip Randolph's March on Washington (1941), and became the fist field secretary of the newly formed Congress of Racial Equality (1941). In 1942, he went to California to help protect the property of Japanese-Americans who had been placed in work camps. The following year, Mr. Rustin was imprisoned in Lewisburg Penitentiary as a conscientious objector.

Upon his release in 1945, Mr. Rustin became chairman of the Free India committee and was frequently arrested for sitting-in at the British Embassy. Three years later, at the invitation of the Congress party, he made his first of several trips to India.

In 1947, Mr. Rustin participated in the first Freedom Ride—the Journey of Reconciliation designed to test enforcement of the 1946 Irene Morgan case outlawing discrimination in interstate travel. Arrested in North Carolina, he served thirty days on a chain gang. His report of this experience appeared in the New York Post *and prompted an investigation that led to the abolition of the chain gang in North Carolina.*

In 1951, Mr. Rustin went to West Africa where he worked with Azikewe and Nkrumah. He helped organize the Committee to Support South African Resistance, which in 1953 became the American Committee on Africa. Also during this time, he became director of Mr. Randolph's Committee Against Discrimination in the Armed Forces, which secured President Truman's executive order eliminating segregation in the military.

In 1953, Mr. Rustin became executive secretary of the War Resister's League, a pacifist organization. Two years later he went to Montgomery, Alabama, at the invitation of Dr. Martin Luther King to assist in the organization of the bus boycott. The following year he drew up, at Dr. King's request, the first plans for the founding of the Southern Christian Leadership Conference. For seven years Mr. Rustin served as special assistant to Dr. King.

In 1957, Mr. Rustin coordinated the 35,000-strong Prayer Pilgrimage to Washington for civil rights. The Youth Marches for Integrated Schools, which he directed, followed in 1958 and 1959. In 1960, when Dr. King was indicted on false charges of perjury in connection with his income tax returns, Mr. Rustin was appointed director of the defense committee that succeeded in winning Dr. King's case.

Mr. Rustin was deputy director of the March on Washington of August 28, 1963, which brought over 250,000 persons to the nation's capital and paved the way for passage of the 1964 Civil Rights Act. He directed the New York school boycott of February 3, 1964—the largest civil rights demonstration up to that time. He helped the striking Memphis sanitation workers raise $100,000 and organized the massive march following Dr. Kings' assassination in 1968.

Mr. Rustin has been arrested twenty-four times in the struggle for civil rights. He is currently president of the A. Phillip Randolph Institute, which, since it was founded in 1964, has conducted voter registration programs, worked to solidify relations between blacks, liberals, and unions, and worked for laws and policies that promote economic equality. He helped plan and put into operation the Recruitment and Training Program, which seeks to bring young blacks into union apprenticeship programs. Mr. Rustin also serves as chairman on civil rights, and has received a number of honorary degrees. In 1971, Down The Line, *a collection of his essays and journalism, was published.*

In 1975, Mr. Rustin helped to organize Black Americans to Support Israel Committee (BASIC), an organization of prominent black Americans that works to strengthen the relationship between the black community and the State of Israel.

> *American blacks now need to realize that there is a difference between viewing racial pride as a positive psychological attribute and attempting to build a social policy based on racism. It is, in fact, impossible to forge a creative, long-term social agenda based on racial, ethnic, or sexual goals. To*

attempt such an agenda is self-defeating and reactionary and will ultimately impede the advancement both of society and of a particular group itself.
(From Strategies For Freedom: The Changing Patterns of Black Protest, *1976, by Bayard Rustin.)*

I would like to limit my remarks to the question of power as it is concerned with minority groups. If I were to talk about other groups, the syndrome might be very different indeed. But before discussing the nature of power in minority groups, it is imperative to see the objective situation in which one chooses to exercise whatever power he can possess. And, therefore, I am going to have to consider two decidely different periods in the history of the relationship of black people to others in the United States. I would first like to talk about the Sixties, since the great period of Martin Luther King and others has no relationship whatever to the situation we face today. Let us look at the objective situation in which Martin Luther King, the NAACP, the Urban League, the National Council of Negro Women, etc., were involved.

First of all, in the sixties, we had very limited objectives. We were interested in three things that all white people had that we did not then possess. The right to send your child to a school of your choice, the right to vote, and the right to use public accommodations: theatres, hotels, libraries, etc. I would like you to note that the nation delivered its promise for those three things largely to us, with absolutely no cost to the taxpayer. I would like you to note that there was a tremendous amount of guilt in regard to black people at that period. And guilt is a fairly useless instrument for social change except as an imaginative leader can find action that raises sheer guilt to a social responsibility, and that is precisely what the movement did. Furthermore, the great vast number of Americans recognized that the treatment of black people in the sixties was extremely difficult, a burden to them, a burden to democracy, and a burden to our image in the world. Beyond that, in regard to public accommodations, in regard to a school of your choice, or voting, there were creative methods of social dislocation that could be immediately applied. All right, you don't want us to eat in that restaurant, then we shall come in and sit; when you have felt the economic pinch of not being able to serve people, as we are arrested over and over again, sooner or later the aristocratic business establishment will come to the conclusion that it is not worth this. And we did not win the Montgomery bus protest until the bus company was almost out of money. There is a strange way in which social dislocation is connected with money in this country. It speaks with an extremely loud voice. There is also the fact that the mass media had to concentrate on us not because they chose, but because the mass media, and particularly television, has so short a time to explain anything that to the degree that it is contentious and democratic you can be assured of extraordinary coverage. I would say that the mass media was perhaps the most fundamental element in the change that brought about the new legislation of the sixties. Because, for the first time, it brought into the homes of every American the brutality of bombing churches, of killing children, of lynching, of cattle prods, and as I once said to Martin Luther King, "Martin you are not a leader in the normal sense of the word; the fact is, I do not know if you could lead vampires to a blood bank. But what I do know is that Bull Conner and company are mobilizing the nation for you by what Americans see on television."

Now as important as anything else, the progress was made at the only times you can make progress in a democracy, and that is when the economy is opening up, and in the sixties, the economy was profoundly opening up. There was great economic growth during that period. As important as anything else in that period there was hope and expectation. There was the pre-Vietnam period when Americans really felt they could solve almost any problem on earth. Now I come to my major point. Power for religious and ethnic groups does not reside in themselves for change. It resides in their ability to convince the majority of the majority. They must convince them that their cause is just, that what they are asking for is sane. Thus, the great majority of Americans were won over to believe that when Martin Luther King said not one hair of one head on one white person is to be harmed, that that was meaningful to them. In fact, the black people behaved with such nobility under stress that people were won over. And let no black person believe that our ability to get that legislation and the money to activate blacks (as well as whites) came fundamentally from black people. Most of it came from the great majority of white citizens; about 50 percent of it from our Jewish brothers.

It is also clear that the power of a minority depends strictly on the limitations of ethnic and racial assertion that does not go beyond the bounds of reasonableness. Thus, people will say, you are not pushing me out of the way to get into the bus and the restaurant. And therefore, you are not straining ethnic assertion. But those same people in our time, if you insist on quotas, will feel very definitely that you are pushing beyond because they do not see it the way the minority see it. They see it as saying: "You roll over; I am not going to roll over in order that you are to get in."

In other words, the sixties was a period when what we were asking for was clearly what everyone else had but we did not have. Now the seventies are a quite different period.

First, our objectives cannot be limited. You cannot lift the great masses of poor or black in this country with a three point, no cost to the public, program. Hospital beds are needed, jobs are needed, the means of production must be changed. Whatever you name, it goes deeply into our social and economic structure. Our objectives cannot be limited. It costs the United States only a few hundred dollars for police protection to give us the three things we were asking for in the sixties. If the government is to put people back to work, find medical care, find decent housing (which is to name only three of fifty things) that will cost the American taxpayer millions and billions and billions of dollars. At present, there is not the clear racial situation there was in the sixties. You either had the right to school or the right to vote or the right to go into public accommodations. Now the picture is more profoundly an issue of class rather than race. For every black who needs a home there are four or five whites who need a home. For every black who needs a job there are five or six whites who need a job. For every black who needs a hospital bed there are four or five whites who need a hospital bed. Thus, to interpret the present situation fundamentally in racial terms is to divert blacks' attention from what the problem really is and to split the coalition that could indeed deal with the class problem.

There is no mechanism for putting people into the job problem that relieves their guilt in the way that somebody could take a trip and join Martin Luther King in the bus in Mississippi. Furthermore, there is no nonviolent way to demonstrate the nature of the problem. How do you dramatically illustrate the fact that as white people are getting less and less tuberculosis, blacks in this country are getting more and more. There is now no nonviolent mechanism for drawing people into a place under a given circumstance. The media do not any longer find drama in the black or poor condition. We are in a period not of economic growth but of economic decline. Furthermore, the great numbers of people who are brutalized by the economic decline are in despair. No movement has ever grown out of despair. All movements, the French Revolution, the American Revolution, Russian Revolution, you name it, all revolutionary movements must spring from hope that things are in fact getting better, causing a demand for them to get better faster. And as you all know, every political phiolorspher on earth has told you that the powerless, the outcast, simply are unorganizable.

Another factor has simply taken over our interest; in our jitterbug concerns for social progress, we Americans simply hop from one movement to another. Now when white people say I don't want to hear any more about blacks, you know I have a certain degree of sympathy with them, because, you can't have heard on television for fifteen years about the black problem without getting a little unconcerned. I shall never forget that when I was in India there were scores of people dropping dead in Calcutta at the railway station. For the first four months when I was picking these people up I had a terrible agony of soul knowing that these people were starving, they had come there but they would not break into the storage granaries; they would not take food from the sacred cows that they saw eating in the streets. They sat there just dying. Yet, my friends, three months later, I was picking them up as if they were leaves fallen from a tree. This feeling: we have had it with this or that cause and thus we go on our jitterbug: then it's ecology, it's war, it's hunger, it's women's rights, it's gay liberation, it's oil. And the fact of poverty remains there and we push it under the rug.

But there are infinitely more factors. For most of you, when your white ancestors came here, they did not need education and they did not need training. Nobody talked about giving the Italians and the Greeks and the Jews and others who came, training. Thank God they were imaginative people and after they got work, then education was their first desire. But they could sell their muscle power; the economic situation permitted it. Now we have 60 percent black unemployed in our ghettos and nobody wants to buy their muscle power. We are producing goods and distributing goods very differently than we did in the early twentieth century. Only a few weeks ago, 12,000 longshoremen were fired; not because they were black, but because we use containers now and we don't need longshoremen. It was not because people were black or because of black people that the needle trades have left New York, leaving the blacks (not only in the needle trades but in every other labor-intensive industry) to starve, while you and I are buying one out of every fourth garment that we wear from Taiwan or Singapore or Poland or Japan. Those industries didn't say, "We're moving because we don't like black people;" they said, "We're moving because we can get cheap labor, we can get tax deductions, we can get much easier water power for less money."

The fact is that although segregation and discrimination are still with us, if we continue to ride that horse to death we'll obscure the more fundamental problems that are keeping us down. I do not believe for a minute that any international corporation sat in New York and said, "Well, in order to brutalize the blacks let's move overseas." Not at all. Automation and cybernation have taken jobs; for every black who can not get a job in this society because he is black there are five who cannot find work because of technological developments. And therefore for blacks to sit around constantly talking about discrimination is to obscure their examining deeper problems.

There is a problem of the middle class moving to the suburbs and the businesses following them. And for anyone who wants to talk about the white flight from the cities and how that is brutalizing blacks, I will point out to you in New York, Chicago, and St. Louis, the percentage of blacks who have left is proportionately 1 percent higher than whites. Surely nobody is sitting in a corner saying, we're going to run out of the cities just to spite black people. There are many many factors that must be understood. Consider for example, the electronics industry. Right after World War II, blacks just fled into the electronics industry. Now about 60 percent of all the electronics things that you and I use are made in Japan. This example points out the conditions within which blacks are expected to utilize whatever power they have. Economic changes continue to outspeed the rate of education and training. The result is double disastrous; if you leave people long enough with no work, something very terrible begins to happen to their character, they do not respect themselves or the society that produces their despair. I receive two million dollars a year from trade unions, foundations, and others to get blacks to the polls. And as the black situation in the ghettos deepens, and there is more and more despair, the number of people who will go to the polls is greatly reduced; from 45 percent a few years ago to 33 percent now. What am I to say to a woman on a Harlem street who says, "Mr. Rustin, I appreciate your telling me to vote and I always thought it was important. But I voted for the last four presidents and each time I voted, my economic situation has got worse."

That is the kind of political apathy and individual despair that is rampant in our society. We are also up against something very sublte—the white prejudice of the confused and sometimes sickening lower working class. Bestial behavior is bestial, if a black does it or if a white does it. But I am anxious that we understand the nature underlying some of the problems that we think are merely bestial. Let's look at South Boston—white, Catholic, Irish, Italian—but let's not just leave it there. Let's see who these people are. They are the people, proportionately higher taxed than college professors, proportionately, the aristrocrasy and the poor who get something from the government. They are the people who have an extra car in order that the wife can work to try to bring in more money, but neither car is paid for. They have a refrigerator that isn't paid for, they're trying to grab money to get their kids to go to college with $5,000 and $6,000 tuition, where the very poor can get scholarships and help, but they make just enough not be able to get it. They are distraught, they are angry, and they turn their frustrations on whatever they find to turn it on. In other words, if we are interested in making this a better place, we cannot do it on the backs of the lower working classes and expect them to keep still. They will sow social dissention. It is a very curious thing that people will put up with hardship, but they do not want to put up with hardship plus injustice. And now the city of Boston comes along and says we will take the two poor parts of the city and integrate them, leaving the center city where the well-off and the outer ranges of the city where the rich live with no responsibility for integrating the city, and they blew up.

Unless there is a fantastic adjustment in the tax structure of this country, there is no way in which blacks will have the ability to appeal to the best in white people. Furthermore, there is another factor: Educators know better than I that over 3,000 school districts in our country either stopped school early or opened up late, dismissed gym teachers, music teachers, psychiatrists, and the like because these parents were not willing to have a bond issue passed that increased their taxes. What makes anybody sane think that these people who will not educate their own children will vote for money in the billions to uplift the poor of this country? There is a fantastic educational job to be done; the power for blacks begins with blacks, but its true relationship is what it can do to get the majority, now, to face the class problem of poverty and its implications in our nation.

Let no educationists sit in their ivory towers talking about training that great mass of untouchables or educating them to be able to work again. I am talking about the people whose mothers were on welfare, they are on welfare, their children are now on welfare, and their children's children will be on welfare as economic untouchables. Unless we are prepared to do a dramatic thing.

In World War II there was a commitment to win that war from Hitler, thus there was a political commitment to put people to work and we scrounged all over to find people who were ignorant, like women who couldn't work in factories, blacks who were lazy, Puerto Ricans who were dumb, we just looked all over for these sick people. Then, we built some factories. We said to them, that's a hammer, that's a chisel, that's a saw, etc. And we took John Dewey one better. Learning while doing while being well paid. No talk about training, no talk about their ills. And in three months, they were making planes that actually flew. Unless we are prepared to do a dramatic thing.

Now you might say, "Mr. Rustin, that's great, those are some great ideas, but will they work politically." Well why do I have to give great ideas that are going to work politically? The fact of the matter is, there is nothing I'm going to propose that is politically possible. But that's where you come in. Because if you don't grab a hold of it now and propagandize for it, it will never be politically possible. I remember almost fifty years ago when I started to work with Norman Thomas and A. Philip

Randolph and others on minimum wage. And thank God we got started fifty years ago. Because if we hadn't, instead of getting it in '34, it might have been '38 before we got it. There's a big job to be done; we have to be prepared to do a dramatic thing.

I want to go back for one moment to the statement I made in which I said I believe that for a democracy to function it must have respect for all groups and no group pushing another in or out. The only place that any minority group is going to get its rights is where there is democracy. I worked in four African revolutions for democracy and not a single one of the countries in which I worked in Africa ended up with democracy. The treatment of minor tribes in Africa today is not because the people there are black any more than the treatment in Northern Ireland of one against another is because they are white. The only hope for solving the problems between various groups is to the degree that we exercise democracy. And I will not stand idly by while young blacks and some liberal whites are attempting to confuse issues on the basis of special privilege for blacks now because we have been mistreated.

I want you to listen very carefully to me and I'm sure I may be run out by some of the students before I have finished. I am for affirmative action, yes. I am unalterably opposed to quotas. First, I'm opposed to quotas for moral reasons. Since I do not want to be a number, I cannot concieve of any other human being wanting to be a number. Or being included not for what I am, but for what somebody may or may not have done to my grandfather. I want to feel that wherever I stand I stand on my two feet. For political reasons, all right, if blacks set a precedent that 12 percent of those entering anything must be black, how long will it be before the Mexican-Americans insist on their precentage? Or women, who are quite numerous, demand their 52 percent, or the Italians their percentage. That is not the way we can build a democracy. Also consider the question of breaking down seniority lines to let blacks in the trade unions. I was speaking to a group of black men one night and I said, "Would you admit that black women are more mistreated than black men in our society?" "Oh yes Mr. Rustin." Well any black man in here who has ten years seniority and who is willing to give it to a black woman who has eight, raise your hand. No hands went up and I thereby proved to them it was not a racial question. It was a question of the maintenance of democracy. At the point there is any violation of the principles of democracy, any minority group is hurt. And to put yourself in the position where you're saying to other people who are equally prepared, "Because of what happened to me you must roll over and get out of the way so that I can go up" simply will not work. It simply cannot work.

Now what is the Supreme Court doing in the Bakke case? If it does what it usually does, it finds the comma around which it can make a decision. But sooner or later the maintenance of quotas will be finished. Now, I say I am for goals and timetables. I am for the goal that this university should have more blacks, Puerto Ricans, Mexican-Americans, and other poor. My goal is that they come in, but they don't hop over anybody. The university finds the money, goes out and looks for potential youngsters,—not among those from Boston, or Philadelphia who are going to go to medical school anyhow, by hook or crook, but some of these lumpen kids who have ability—brings them on campus for a year and a half. Give them all kinds of remedial training, but when the day for examination comes of going into the university, you have reached your goals and they come in on a par with everybody else and they take it or leave it with everybody else. Otherwise you are doing them a profound injustice. These kids have been brutalized over and over. And to be brought into a program where they are probably going to fail because of some jumbling of numbers does not help them.

Furthermore, I am of the opinion that the giving of special aid can destroy the fabric of this society if it is given along racial and religious lines. It must be given along class lines—to those students in America who are anxious to be in college and have some potential, whose parents make less than . . . (and you select an intelligent figure). For them there will be goals and in that group there will be some Irish, some Italians, some blacks, some Puerto Ricans. Because we must, above all, maintain democratic processes. Democracy is not a place down the road that you go to. Democracy is the road itself that you travel. There is no way of giving special privileges to some at the expense of others on arguments that to the great majority are specious. Furthermore, if there is anybody who once owned slaves, will he please raise his hand. You cannot pass on to other generations anything other than the responsibility for their own generation and they'll do jolly well to do anything about that.

In conclusion, my friends: after over fifty years in this movement, what have I learned that is the most important thing I can leave with you? I've learned that if you are black and being mistreated, you may think that is the real problem. But it is not. Otherwise in Africa, many of the African leaders with whom I fought side by side would not be mistreating their own black people who are different tribes or religion than themselves. If you're Jewish, you may think that the way Christians have brutalized Jews over the centuries and the Romans and the Assyrians and everybody else, that the problem really is between you and them. That is not the real problem. The simple problem is that men and women and children are capable of selfish and sometimes not so understood reasons of brutalizing each other. Once the problem is put in that prospective, then one can know that he is subject to this human malady. And like Isiah, and Jeremiah and Amos, we will call for being against all injustice and especially that in oneself. Jeremiah pointed out to the Jews—you think you're a Jew because you do not mix milk and meat in the same pot, or because you have been circumcised, or because you keep the Sabbath and go to the Temple. That is not what makes you a Jew. What makes you a Jew is that you are dedicated to eliminate the suffering of whomever, wherever, and to look at yourself.

Many people criticize me for setting up the Black Americans Support Israel Committee. I did not do it because the Jews gave Martin Luther King half the money he had to work with, though that would have been a good reason. I did not do it because my own people learned from the Jewish experience, although that might have been a good reason. I did it because Israel is the only democratic state in the Middle East and because I know that the economic upward mobility of the Arabs is as much in the hands of Israel, who is prepared to give them the technological assistance they need. Ultimately, if Israel is destroyed in the Middle East, and democracy is destroyed there, what have I to look forward to in this world? "Nobody in his late sixties is going to come through with the answers." In a sense, we struggle with the last generation. It's going to come from somebody who is going to be a Eugene Davis or a Norman Thomas or a Martin Luther King and provide new insights as to how we can deal with the problem of man's inhumanity to man.

Copyright © 1979 by Bayard Rustin.

Caroline Bird

Women, Power, and Powerlessness

A native of New York City, Caroline Bird studied at Vassar College, has a B.A. in American history from the University of Toledo, and a M.A. in comparative literature from the University of Wisconsin.

Bird has been a member of the editorial staffs of Fortune, Newsweek, *and the* New York Journal of Commerce. *She has written more than 200 magazine articles on economic and sociological subjects. Her books include* The Case Against College, The Invisible Scar: The Great Depression and What It Did to American Life From Then to Now, Born Female: The High Cost of Keeping Women Down, Everything a Woman Needs to Know to Get Paid What She's Worth, *and* Enterprising Women.

A provacative writer and lecturer, Bird is not afraid to challenge some of society's most firmly held beliefs. In The Case Against College, *she argues that college is not for everyone and that many of the benefits of college are a myth.*

In Born Female, *Bird puts forth the position that the economic dependence of women is the source of all their other problems. "Money is a civilized invention," she says, "the root of all freedom. What we need is more women taking advantage of equal opportunity to aspire to the top."*

She is a member of the Society of Magazine Writers, the Women's Equity Action League, the American Sociological Association, and the National Organization for Women. She testified before the Bayh Committee on the Equal Rights Amendment. In 1972-73, she was Froman Distinguished Professor at Russell Sage College in Troy, New York.

When invited to join the series of lecturers on the subject of power, it was explained that it was important to include somebody who was powerless.

It was a wise decision. As a matter of fact, powerless people are the only ones who know anything about it. The very idea of power comes from the experience of those on the receiving end of it.

People who talk about power don't have power. People who talk about health don't have health. People who talk about "exclusive neighborhoods" don't live in exclusive neighborhoods.

Power is always something that somebody else exercises over you, never something you exercise over other people.

Take, for instance, university professors. They exercise absolute power over your future. College faculties decide who shall get the degree that employers demand for the powerful jobs. They could make you all take Greek in order to graduate and you'd all take Greek. Never mind that few jobs depend on knowing Greek.

Professors hold the keys to the kingdom of good jobs on this earth and they exercise that power as arbitrarily as the medieval Popes doled out the keys to the gate of heaven.

Now the interesting thing about the power of what I have called the professoriate is that the students know they have this power, but *they* (the faculty) don't know it. They really don't. They say such things as, "Sure employers go by the degree, but we can't help it if they do. We aren't trying to tell them who to hire. We couldn't care less."

As a matter of fact, the power of the professoriate is the most dangerous kind of all: it is unaccountable as well as unconscious. Professors don't have to account to employers for the decisions they make about who shall get the sheepskin. As a matter of fact, the very idea that anyone else should have anything to say about these rules strikes them as immoral "interference." *Only members of the Guild know the truth.*

Same with doctors. If they are to be accountable for the power they exercise over your body, they want to be accountable not to you, but to other doctors.

Well, I don't think the doctors are going to get away with it. Congressmen are not getting away with the special privileges they have always had. And since the world is really falling apart—according to the power wielders—maybe even the professoriate will have to demystify its decisions.

My credentials for dealing with the topic of power are, then, gilt-edged.

I do not have a Ph.D. I am not a professor of anything. I am not a government official. I am not a director of a large-scale enterprise. But more important than any of these qualifications, I can talk with authority about power *because I am a woman.*

What, oh Lord, do women want?

The question stumped Sigmund Freud, the psychiatrist who knew what you wanted when you didn't know what you wanted yourself. Simpler men have never been puzzled. They *know* what women want without ever asking them.

I've been coping with this certainty for a long time now.

Twenty years ago, when I worked for a public relations firm, I asked why our automobile clients couldn't make car doors so that little kids couldn't open them from the inside. If you want to sell women, I said, you have to sell safety.

The men on the account smiled indulgently. The only thing women care about in cars, one of them told me, is the color and whether the upholstery goes with their clothes.

I said *I* wasn't all that interested in colors.

"Which just goes to show," the man said, "that you don't know what women want."

That was before Ralph Nader. Now everybody cares about safety.

Ten years later, it happened again. The male editors of the *Saturday Evening Post,* then a flourishing magazine, asked me to find out whether there was any truth to the rumor that women were being kept down in business. I hadn't given the proposition much thought, but I dutifully found out, and when I found out I was furious. Well, the *Post* wouldn't buy my article because they said I didn't understand that women *really* wanted home and family.

Born Female, the book I wrote, about what I found, appeared in 1968. Since then, there's been a massive, national consciousness raising. In 1977, *Born Female* is a middle-of-the-road statement of the female condition in America. But it grieves me to report that it still seems to be needed.

Men still think they can speak for women. This spring, for instance, I was explaining the ERA to a history class in a Lutheran college in Minnesota. I told them it followed inevitably from the logic of a constitution founded to preserve *individual* rights. Men in the class agreed with this philosophy—as an abstract issue.

"But the trouble with ERA," one of them observed, "is that the women don't want it. They want homes and families."

It was then that I realized that not one of the women in the class had spoken a word.

"How about that?" I asked them. And one by one, they told that young man that they expected to have home and family plus a career, and that they expected equal rights.

They were saying what a majority of college age women now say. That's a switch—less than ten years ago even young college women wanted to be homemakers—but headline writers turn it around to say that if you count all women, the old ones too, most women want homes and families same as they always did. Headline writers, mostly male, know what women *really* want.

This year, something new has been added. Congress has formally asked women what they want.

Now there is nothing new about federally funded conferences for the specially situated. We've had them for old people. We've had them for young people. We've had them for the handicapped, but never before in the whole history of our country has Congress funded a delegated, national conference on the status of women. They've appropriated a whole big dime for each and every women in the country for it. Some think that's too much.

And that's not all. When you hear this, you'll know that the act was written by congress*women*. According to the law, *the president has to answer.* One hundred twenty days after he gets our final report, President Carter is going to have to submit to the Congress recommendations with respect to matters considered in it. We don't know whether he'll give us what we will ask for, but we have been talking to stone walls at our own expense for so long that it's great to have a law that makes the head man say *something* more than "Yes, ma'am."

What, oh Lord, do women want?

We want, we keep saying, to be people. That doesn't mean that we envy the male plumbing fixture that meant so much to the good doctor Freud. What we really envy are the choices society offers those who happen to be born with it.

The one thing all women want is the same freedom men enjoy to choose their goals and the rights men enjoy under the law, in politics, on the job, in religious institutions, unions, the media, and even the family.

Don't we have it? Millions of Americans think we are equal now. And it's true that we have made some progress. The Alaska pipeline has had women working in capacities that require hard hats. There's a woman rabbi and even a black woman Episcopal priest. President Carter has appointed two women to the cabinet. But the enthusiasm with which the media photograph those women telegraphs the message. In spite of the progress women are making, they remain rarities in the seats of real power. There is no women presently elected to the United States Senate, and while there have been blacks on the Supreme Court and the Federal Reserve Board, neither of these citadels of clout have ever had a women.

Does it make a difference what sex these people are? You bet it does! Take the Supreme court. Can you imagine any women disallowing sick pay for disabilities arising out of pregnancy on the ground that pregnancy is a *voluntary* act? Listen to what Congresswoman Pat Schroeder of Colorado says about the Gilbert decision:

> If you go skiiing and get hurt, you're covered.
> If you race cars on weekends and get hurt, you're covered.
> If you jump horses and get hurt, you're covered.
> Even if you've had it and attempt suicide—you're covered.
> Now all these things are entered into voluntarily. But the courts say pregnancy is the one voluntary act for which you must pay 100%.

Pregnancy will become voluntary only when marital rape is established as a crime—and we won't get away with *that* until all nine of the Supreme court justices are women!

No, women don't get the equal protection of the laws. Most women don't brood about the ways in which our culture cuts us down. We're told we can earn money and we can. The laws of the land try to insure that if we are good enough we can get ahead. That's progress and I'm not belittling it. But as Bella Abzug, presiding officer of the IWY Commission, once put it, what that really means is that a female Einstein can get to be an assistant professor in a really good mathematics department. Anyone who has worked in a large organization can think of some man who has risen to the level of his incompetence because some woman secretary, deputy, assistant, or aide has not been allowed to rise to the level of *hers.*.

There are a few more women in policy-making jobs, but only because there are more of these jobs as the population increases. That means a few more faces for the newpapers to blow up big, to prove that you have come a long way *Baby*—and they had better smile when they print that word. The fact is that women have hardly dented the top of the earnings pyramid.

The big change at the top of the career ladders in this country has been not the sex of the people at the top, but the dollars it takes to get there. In 1966, you were among the top 5 percent of earners if you were paid $12,372 or more. Six years later in 1974, it took $20,316 to get into the top 5 percent. And were more of these top earners women? Well, yes. *Three-tenths of one percent more in 1966,* just 2.5 percent of the top 5 percent earners were women. In 1974, 2.8 percent. Who knows, maybe when the data for 1977 are collected we will have cracked the 3 percent level.

The number on the bottom of the pyramid affects many more women. In 1975, the Bureau of Labor Statistics found you need $10,000 to support an urban family of four in what they call "a low standard of living." In that year, *only 11 percent of employed women* earned that much.

Women are a bonanza for employers, Most wives now have to earn, but the gap between men and women is widening as they crowd into the "pink collar ghetto" of office clerks, store clerks, bookkeepers, cashiers, hairdressers, waitresses, domestics, elementary school teachers. These underpaid pink collar workers can honestly stay that they are not paid less than men because most of them have never heard of a man doing their work. According to Paul Samuelson, the author of the textbook from which most of us learned our economics, employers profit by this segregation of women in so-called "women's jobs."

Working women are a *bonanza to taxpayers.* If they are married, they pay taxes at the rate that begins where the bracket of their husbands leaves off. Every deduction on that paycheck is bigger or worth less in benefits than the deduction on the same amount paid to a male head of household. Because they are paid less, and quit work before they qualify, women are less apt to collect the pensions to which they are forced to contribute. And if they are married, the nick social security takes from their check may not buy them much more in benefits than they would get as homemaking wives.

Unemployment insurance taxes pay regardless of gender, but a women can't collect if she is moved out of town by a husband or forced to quit because of pregnancy or sexual harrassment on the job.

As for health insurance deductions—well, that Gilbert decision of the Supreme Court is a judicial disgrace. An employee can collect for a hair transplant or a vasectormy but not for a disability related to pregnancy.

Finally, working *women are a bonanza for the economy* and those who invest in it. One of the reasons unemployment hasn't hurt as much as it did during the depression of the thirties is that almost half of all unemployed husbands are married to wives who have jobs.

If all wives stayed at home baking cookies, few familes could afford to have homes of their own. The average single family house now costs so much to build that the average American family can't afford to buy one, yet housing starts rose last year. How come? Well, last year mortgage lenders began to obey the new laws requiring them to consider the income of a wife in deciding how big a mortgage a family could carry. Previously, banks discounted a wife's earnings on the ground that she might get pregnant or quit.

But what about the other half—the wives who don't earn? Aren't homemakers the women there laws and customs are intended to protect?

Few of them realize that the unpaid work they do in their homes doesn't count in the eyes of the law. In the 1970s homemaking has become a risky occupation with no unemployment insurance.

Consensus projections say that one of every three women under thirty will experience a divorce or separation. The experience will plunge them into unexpected poverty. According to Isabel Sawhill of the Urban Institute, only 3 percent of families headed by females received enough in child support or alimony to keep them above the official level of poverty. The divorced or separated wife has to earn money, but if she has been out of the job market keeping house she is forced into the "pink collar" ghetto of "pin money" pay.

The law doesn't go out of its way to victimize women for being unattached. It just looks right through them as if they didn't exist.

Most wives don't learn until they become widows that their husband's pension died with him unless he elected to take lower benefits on retirement for his own lifetime.

Most wives don't know that divorce ends their claim to a husband's social security unless the marriage lasts twenty years.

Only when a homemaker is divorced does she discover that she has no credit of her own, or that she may not lay claim to her own cooking pots unless she moved to establish those rights before the divorce. In most of our states the presumption is that her husband bought everything so it all belongs to him unless she can prove otherwise.

Barriers to women don't sound like barriers. They are often intended as "protections." For years we have been "protected" out of well paying jobs and the practice dies hard. The latest is an attempt to bar women from working where lead and vinyl chloride fumes might affect an unborn child. These fumes could affect sperm cells, too. We expect a man to make his own decision about risking his fertility, but every woman must be "protected" for the sake of the future of the race whether she is willing or even able to bear a child.

The laws "protect" women against theoretical hazards that lead to well-paying jobs, but crimes against the person of women are laughed out of court or blamed on the victim. Rape is the ultimate crime against women, but a judge in Madison, Wisconsin, says that a boy who raped a girl in the stairwell of their high school was reacting "normally" to sexual permissiveness and women's provacative clothing. Well this was too much. The citizens of Dane County recalled that judge and replaced him with a woman.

The old common law said that a man could beat his wife with a stick no bigger than his thumb, and to this day police officers let husbands do it. Not poor, deranged men alone, either; well-educated, high income men do it—and they're more apt to get away with it, too.

If prostitution is a crime, it must be a crime against women, but the women is charged, not the man. It's an odd sort of crime that makes the victim the criminal too.

Finally, women criminals, once convicted, are punished more severely than men guilty of the same offense. Nothing much happens to a teenage boy who runs away from home, but an underage girl is clapped into jail—you guessed it, *for her own protection.*

Rich or poor, black or white, schooled or unschooled, young or old, married or single, *all* American women live under laws and customs made by and for men—laws and customs that define them in terms of their relationship or lack of relationship to a man.

Rich is better than poor, but any rich wife who thinks she is sitting pretty and doesn't need the Equal Rights Amendment should try going to a lawyer to make a will. Many a wife who relied on the farm for security has had to sell it to pay inheritance taxes when her husband died. The law doesn't count the work she put into it. It's all his to *give* to her as a legacy unless she can prove she put money into it.

Schooled is better than unschooled, but when jobs are scarce, women Ph.D.'s find themselves "overqualified" for the only jobs available *for women.*

White is, alas, still more privileged than black, but white wives have less to say in thier own homes than black wives, the sociologists tell us, because the pay gap between white men and women is so much wider than the pay gap between black men and women. But after you say this you must add very quickly that black women are on the very bottom of the income totem pole.

The gaps on that totem pole are worth reciting because they govern the relationships of millions of human beings to each other:

At the top, *white men* average	$12,000
Next come, not white women, but *black men*	9,000
Behind them, at a respectable remove, *white women*	7,000
And at the very bottom, *black women*	6,000

What these numbers mean, of course, is that if you are a woman and you want a mink coat, the best way to get one is to attach yourself to some man. But they also mean that everything that ails you is going to be worse than it would be for a man.

If you're *black* and a woman, it's a double whammy.

If you're *poor* and a woman, it's a double whammy. Discrimination in employment puts you down and the notion that you're naturally without ambition keeps you down. If our women's movement sometimes seems middle class, it's only because there are fewer self-made women in this country than there are self-made men. Nobody lends you a helping hand up if you're female.

If you are *unschooled* and a woman, it's a double whammy.

Lack of job training causes rich women to retreat into the suburbs and poor women to retreat into childbearing.

It's a double whammy if you're single and woman. Single women are brighter, healthier, and better educated than bachelors. But they get lower salaries and fewer invitations to dinner.

If you're *divorced* and a woman, it's a double whammy.

Few divorced men support their children, and fewer still their former wives. Discrimination in employment means that she is *poorer* after the split while he is *richer*—and it's a rare loving husband who has never even for a moment thought of this incentive to split.

It's a double whammy if you're *old* and a woman—and since women are outliving men by a wider margin, it lasts longer, too. Gray hairs do not command respect or pay in pink collar jobs and older women are especially unlikely to have any other skills.

Finally, it's a double whammy if you're unemployed and a woman. Like blacks, the old, the young, the undereducated, and the handicapped, women are the last hired and the first fired. As newcomers to the labor force, women are suffering more than men from the recession right now.

Restriction to the pink collar ghetto limits their chances for work just when high prices drive housewives into competition with each other for those pink collar jobs that Louise Howe so movingly describes in her book of that title.

Many of us would like the National Women's Conference in Houston to attack all the ills that worry women—unemployment, poverty, nuclear arms, pollution, health care; but Congress hasn't asked us for a laundry list of what's wrong with the country—or even the things that hurt more women than men, like unemployment and poverty. They've asked us to identify what puts us down as women. And that sticks in our craws. Part of our trouble *as women* is that we've been conditioned not to ask for anything for ourselves.

It is easier for women to demand full employment for everyone than to demand enforcement of the laws that guarantee equal access to all jobs for ourselves.

It is easier for us to demand a minimum income for all persons than to demand equal opportunity for women to rise out of poverty.

It is easier for many of us to urge comprehensive health insurance for everyone, particularly the poor, than it is to demand that health insurance policies treat the disabilities of women on an equal basis with the disabilities of men.

It is easier for us to demand public service employment and unemployment insurance systems that benefit everyone who is unemployed than to complain when these programs give unemployed husbands more protection than unemployed wives.

It is easier to demand more aid for poor children in developing nations than more women in the posts that determine this aid. That sounds too much like asking for something "just for ourselves."

Now women don't all agree on these issues. Why should we? Men don't agree on all issues, either. But there is one thing that all women do want.

We all want access to the forums where these issues are decided.

We all want at least as much power over the decisions affecting our lives as men have over the decisions affecting their lives.

The real differences among us are on how to get this power. Some of us fall for the cruel American myth that says individuals can work their way out of oppression by individual effort. If you're poor, it's your own fault. If you don't get ahead, try harder.

As recently as 1972, 80 percent of a sample of Americans said that the best way to handle the problems of discrimination is for each woman to make sure she gets the best possible training for what she wants to do.

Again and again, women say that they are for the *goals* of the Women's Liberation Movement. It's just their *tactics* that they don't like.

Other women—and happily their numbers are growing—realize that it is not individual men or women who put us down, but laws and customs that treat us as women instead of as persons. No one of us, however clever or diligent, can change those laws and customs by individual effort. We have to get together and demand change. By definition that's not ladylike.

Yes, there are specific changes that almost all women want.

We want enforcement of equal employment opportunity laws that give women a real choice of occupations—including occupation housewife if they want it.

We want laws that recognize the contribution homemakers make to a marriage.

We want special programs to help women who have missed opportunities because of past discrimination and family responsibility—women who are casualties of our changing sex roles.

We want real reproductive freedom to control our own bodies.

We want the equal protection of the laws, including family law and government programs and practices.

We want an end to discrimination in education and training, health care, housing, credit, and insurance.

We want accurate and serious portrayal of women in the media.

We want more women in policy-making posts.

We want good child care on the basis of ability to pay.

We want what the Equal Rights Amendment will do for us. And don't let anyone tell you that women don't want the amendment! The latest Harris Poll of April this year shows 54 percent of women favor the ERA and even more men.

We got the vote before a majority of women wanted it. We got integrated schools for blacks before a majority wanted it. A majority of women want the ERA, but a majority aren't willing to fight for it. Sounds too much like asking something just for ourselves.

We got the vote. We got some protection of civil rights for blacks. Surely we can use our majority to get the Equal Rights Amendment all women need.

Copyright © 1979 by Caroline Bird.

Rollo May

Psychoanalysis and Power

Dr. Rollo May was born in Ohio in 1909. He received a bachelor's degree from Oberlin College in 1930, a Master of Divinity degree from Union Theological Seminary in 1930, and a doctorate from Columbia University in 1949.

He has taught at several universities including Harvard, Yale, Princeton, and the New School for Social Research. He currently works as a psychoanalyst in New York.

His writings and interests are interdisciplinary, dealing with psychology, psychotherapy, philosoophy, literature, the classics, and religion. Dr. May's writings include: Power and Innocence *(1972),* Love and Will *(1969),* Psychology and the Human Dilemma *(1966), and* Man's Search for Himself *(1953).*

> *. . . . I have described the human dilemma as the capacity of man to view himself as object and as subject. My point is that both are necessary—necessary for psychological science, for effective therapy, and for meaningful living. I am also proposing that in the dialectical process between these two poles lies the development, and the deepening and widening, of human consciousness. The error on both sides—for which I have used Skinner and the preparadox Rogers as examples—is the assumption that one can avoid the dilemma by taking one of its poles. It is not simply that man must learn to live with the paradox—the human being has always lived in this paradox or dilemma, from the time that he first became aware of the fact that he was the one who would die and coined a word for his own death. . . . Between the two horns of this dilemma, man has developed symbols, art, language, and the kind of science which is always expanding in its own*

> *presuppositions. The courageous living within this dilemma, I believe, is the source of human creativity.*
>
> *(From "What is the Human Dilemma?" in* Psychology and the Human Dilemma.*)*

When I wrote *Power and Innocence* about four or five years ago, I found that power is a subject we American don't like to discuss. We sweep it under the carpet, hide and repress it as we used to repress the discussion of death. Nevertheless, it is very important. There are many different kinds of power, but none is more important to us than human power. Not human force that is called influence or coercion, but more important than that, the power we generate in our own psychological development.

The original meaning of the word "power" (its original stem in Latin) is "posse" which means "I can, and I will." This is significant because as we will see from citing cases in psychoanalysis, the acquisition of power, the power within one's self and the awareness that one can influence other people, is absolutely essential to the confidence and mental health of a person.

I want to begin by pointing out that the things about power that most effect us psychologically come from technology. Technology today directs our lives. We go to the moon, not because there is any tremendous scientific purpose in getting to the moon, but because we have the technology to take us there. We are tied to technology as we are tied to a tiger's tail, and we cannot let go. What this does to most of us is to give us the feeling that our lives are lived by our techniques. What we do, we temporarily think we do on our own, but there is always somebody to explain to us that we do this because of the external forces upon us. We are mesmerized by the power and the hypnotism of our technology and this seems to take away human will, human freedom, and human responsibility.

This progression has been rationalized by many authors in the past ten or twenty years, and particularly by such books as Skinner's *Beyond Fredom and Dignity*. We are told that our freedom is an illusion, and our will is nonexistent. We do things because there have been other conditions that have forced us to; that has made us into the kinds of persons who would do those particlar things. We are only a complex mass of conditioning. But the strange thing is that people cannot live on that philosophy, so they grasp for something that will tell them that they also have some sense of ower, some semblance of power, some capacity to will and some responsibility.

Along comes Warner Erhardt with his organization to tell us that everything that happens, happens because we chose it. This message is eagerly lapped up by hundreds of thousands of well-heeled middle class people. It is lapped up as an assurance that it counters the idea that we are a mass of conditioning. But one of those extremes is just as false as the other. As long as there is a Skinner, there will be an Erhardt, and as long as there is an Erhardt, there will be a Skinner, and both sides leave us cold.

We know that everything that happens does not happen because of our own choices. We also know at the same time that our own choices and our own responsibility must have some function and some meaning. If we are going to understand this issue, we have to start back with the question how do people learn? There are two ways of learning that I want to emphasize. The first one I call by the very original title "Learning I." This kind of learning is the aquiring of new facts, new data, and new behavior patterns. The law of learning that you learned in psychology (at least the laws or learning that I learned in psychology) all have to do with the kinds of facts where you simply pick up the new facts, the new data, and new habits. Now we are partially aware of the values that are behind this kind of learning. For example, a soldier is aware of the value of patriotism as he learns the manual of arms, but there is no change of values. The awareness of all these values is all that we can expect. All we do is acquire the new data, new facts, and new behavior patterns that go with that kind of learning. Error is very simple at this point; it's simply a distortion of the facts. Rote learning fits this category, but we shouldn't think rote learning is to be discredited. For example, most of us learn mathematics and how to spell by rote learning. If we had to wait until we understood the theory and philosophy of mathematics, it would be unfortunate for most of us indeed. "Learning I" is what stabilizes the culture. We learn what our parents learned and a little bit more; but it's the same type and kind of data and patterns that existed for them. "Learning I" is learning what is not related to human responsibility and will. This is what occurs for example in behavior therapy. The therapist helps the client to adjust to his teacher and his subject matter. He also helps him to make a realistic assessment of his capacities. As we say in psychoanalysis, it helps his ego adjust to the world more realistically. Apparently, he then can go out into the world and do what he should. But the real problem is what should he do? And that's where the catch occurs. We live in a culture in which you cannot pass the old values down to the younger generation—the old values change within ten years. Marriage is changing, the sexual customs are changing, technology is radically changing, our economic views are changing, our geography is changing, our relation to technology (for example to energy) is radically changing, We cannot pass the old values down, so have to ask what kind of learning is there that will help us to find the new values, the new criteria, the new context with which we can learn. And so I some to "Learning II."

"Learning II" is where we learn to learn. "Learning II" is the shifting of the context in which the learning of facts occurs. It is what we in psychoanalysis call the transference reaction. Somebody can come in to see me every day for two or three months and then suddenly comes in one day, and says "Heavens, I thought your hair was red." Now my hair could be many different colors, but one of them would not have been red. This person is continuously projecting on me the image that he or she has of male authority figures, and when this changes (and this sounds rather absurd, but it certainly is not absurd when you see it happening) all the facts that he or she picked up also change and the facts have an entirely different meaning.

As as example of this, Helen (a false name) is presently a patient of mine. She is twenty-eight years old, has been married and divorced twice. Her problem was that she could never be spontaneous. Obviously she never could genuinely fall in love with a man. Always when she sat down in the chair opposite me, I could tell that she was trying to dope out the strategy with which she would react to me. Now it turned out in the first couple of sessions that her father had beaten her cruelly when she was a child; but that wasn't the cause of her neurosis. A person can take a whole lot of beating and not get neurotic about it; but what he cannot take is the beating to occur when he doesn't know that it's coming. What was the basis of her neurosis? She couldn't dope her father out, she couldn't figure out what infringement was going to cause a beating, and what infringement would not. She developed this attitude toward the whole world, including me and the man she married. Obviously there could be no genuine or lasting trust or love.

Now I could have helped that woman learn more facts. I could have told her about how she reacts to me, what's wrong about it, what's right about it, and so on and so forth. This would have been "Learning I." But that would not have helped her a bit. It would have helped her only to do more of what she'd been doing. What was necessary and what we are working into is a change in her whole way of looking at the world. Some people are cruel, other people are not cruel, other people are consistent, and so there must be a "Learning II" that occurs— a shifting of the context, a shifting of the whole attitude toward life. Now this is human will and it is a central part of psychoanalysis. When people come to me for therapy its terribly important that I always emphasize the fact that they have some will that's involved, that stands against the power—let us say the power of technology—the power of external forces affecting them. Now we begin on a very elementary level. What is important to see is that I don't think any therapy can get any place without the consideration of human will being brought into the picture. What's important to the therapist is that no matter how small the will of the other person is, whether it involves only putting one foot in front of the other, coming in and sitting down in a chair; what is important is that it be worked upon, that it be the basis for an ultimate shift of context and an ultimate sense of responsibility.

Now I said that we called the kind of error related to "Learning I" simply distortion of the facts. Error certainly exists in "Learning II," but there we call it something quite different. We call it dogmatism. We call it rigidity. We call it cowardice.

People can avoid "Learning I" simply by laziness, but they cannot avoid "Learning II" that way. The only ways of avoiding "Learning II" are by hallucination and by repression. Now in case you believe that hallucination exists only among mental patients, let me tell you that hallucination occurs among all of us, and that it occurs dozens of times a day. We see things differently from what they are, because we have a need to see them in certain ways. Remember in the presidential election of 1972, Nixon was reelected with a large plurality. Now not many people liked Nixon in California. They had posters with a picture of Nixon's face and the question underneath, "Would you buy a second-hand car from this man?" Most people would *not*, they would look at his face and would be saying to themselves, "He's not trustworthy," "This man is in some way or another, a crook." Yet we elected him president. We elected him president because throughout the whole country at that time there was, and there still is, a kind of panic that was based upon our great anxiety about overpollution, the atom bomb, unemployment, and about almost every other phase of life. What this anxiety leads to is the panic that makes the hallucination that we use to distort the fact and the context in which things occur in the world around us.

If you want an example closer to home because you didn't have to vote for Nixon, let me give you an example of falling in love. Falling in love is partially hallucination. It's a kind of curtain. A transparent curtain, drops over our beloved and we see there not only what is there (which we partly see) but also what we want to see. We also see there projections of our own needs and aspects of the world that we want to learn something about. Altogether these make a kind of film that projects an infinite number of people into marriages of finite compatibility. Incidentally, that projection is a very valuable fact because what you do is project on your loved one's aspects of the world that you want to live and know something about. This helps you to develop them into yourself. This is the psychological basis of the idea that brings out qualities in us that we didn't know we had. It really does, and many love affairs can demonstrate that very clearly. But there is also the hallucination, and hallucination is a normal function, just as repression is a normal function. In the Vietnam war we had to repress our awareness of what was going on in the bombing of those villages in Vietnam—especially what was happening to the children in these villages. We had to repress this in order to exist day after day. There are certain times in the life of a society when the anxiety and panic becomes greater than at other times. It is at these times that people become unable to control hallucinations and their repression; we live in such an age.

I believe we are living at the end of the period that began with the Renaissance and worked very well for about four centuries. This twentieth century—which began as a century of peace, a century of the League of Nations, a century in which there would be no more wars—this twentieth century has had more wars in the last seventy years than in the 700 years previously in European history. Rome and Greece in the Middle Ages also went through their ages of transition. Back in the classical period in ancient Greece, the philosophers talked about truth, beauty, and goodness. You will find this in the writings of Plato, Socrates, Aristotle, and other early philosophers. But, at the end of the Greek period in the first century A.D. or B.C., they no longer talked about truth and beauty. What they did talk about was "How do we find security?" that was a period of disintegration. At the end of the Middle Ages there also came the century where everyone was concerned with the occult, superstition, penance, and other various kinds of mystical experiences. All of these things, which can be duplicated today, are springing up all about us. At the end of the Middle Ages there were all sorts of new religions. Our's is the day of Sun and Moon. It is the day of Transcendental Meditation, the day of 101 different religions. All of these are symptoms of an age that has lost the stable values that began at the Renaissance. The values of rationalism, which were destroyed by Freud, are not available. We know that what we think rationally is also related to the vast unconscious that is just under the surface. Gone is the value of individualism, which came at the Renaissance but now has to be very much changed and overhauled. It's at this time that psychology becomes tremendously important.

We didn't have very much psychology back in 1910 or 1900, but nowadays it's one of the most important subjects in graduate schools. We learn counseling, psychoanalysis, and psychotherapy. There's a different psychotherapy for practically every ailment. All of this is a symptom, or symptoms, of the fact that we live in an age of radical transition. This is precisely the time when anxiety and panic become stronger and it is harder for us to engage in "Learning II." It is easier for us to hang on to technology and hedonistic values that promise some kind of comfort and to the values that we already have known.

With this kind of appeal I want to get back to human beings. I want to define human will and human freedom. I don't know how well you like definitions, but being a professor part time, I am addicted to them, so I shall perpetrate this one on you. I define "will" and "freedom" as the capacity to pause in the face of various stimuli that are coming toward us and then to throw one's weight toward this stimuli, toward this response rather than that response. Every question we ask is an exercise of human freedom and human will because it means that the person who asks it believes there is more than one answer to the question and if there is more than one answer, there must be some choice among these different answers. This moment when the stimuli comes upon us, as it does at every moment, is the moment also when we form symbols because the intensity of the experience cannot be solved simply. Even the rational thoughts come at us as a group of stimuli. The intensity of the experience can be handled only by working these together in the form of a symbol. The symbol brings together the different possibilities and then indicates or pushes us toward some particular solution.

Now you may think this a rather complex way of defining will and freedom. It seems to me actually when you stop to think about it a relatively simple definition. The testimony of one of the prisoners in San Quentin, who was interviewed by Phil Zinbardo, a colleague of mine in psychology at Stanford, tells us about this kind of will. This prisoner was apparently in San Quentin because of some political infringement. He was housed for five years in solitary confinement—this was when Zinbardo interviewed him. (They call their solitary confinement by the ironic title "Maximum Adjustment Center.") He seems to also have been a Chicano and a poet. What he said to Zinbardo was as follows: "They have separated me from my family, they have deprived me of touching my young boy, they have exchanged their concrete and steel for earth and flowers and everything warm and soft. They have left me with nothing except an inner core, a secret private place which they have not yet found out how to get to. This private place is where I think of who I am, where I try to understand the what and the why of my enemies and where I keep alive my will to live." Now you notice what he said so far is, there is a core within me, a secret private core, and this is where I keep alive my will to live. This is where I understand who I am in this will to live. "I live in a hill where I am made to feel like nothing, at best an animal, a wild animal in captivity." He then goes on, "Although I sometimes get depressed and feel like giving up, the discovery of myself and my thoughts gives me joy, for until they find a way to take my thoughts away, I am free. A man can live without liberty, but not without freedom." These are tremendously powerful sentences. I think that most of what he says about himself is what I was saying about psychotherapy. There is an inner core; and what I have to do as a therapist and an analyst, is to build on the core of this person that led him to take the steps into my office and sit down in the chair. Now in this core there is the will to live and in this will to live he is free. Man can live without liberty, as he was living without liberty. If we have to live under a fascist government we can, but we cannot live without freedom. This is part of what I try to call "Learning II." What the prisoner was saying was, I have to get in touch with the central core (which is his word) "this is what they have not found out how to get to. This is where my inner thoughts are and this is where I am free, even though I may not have liberty."

You may also think that this kind of will and freedom requires too much courage. Most people can't do that, you might be thinking, they can't confront the issues directly. If you think that, then you are thinking exactly what Dostoevsky wrote in his *Brothers Karamozov* in the parable of the Grand Inquisitor. If you have read that book then you remember that the short story within the large novel is the story of Jesus coming back to earth preaching that the truth shall make you free. At night the Grand Inquisitor, who is apprently a Cardinal of the Church, has him brought into the cathedral. The Cardinal speaks to him as follows: "Go back to Heaven, people don't want you on earth. They don't want the burden of freedom and their own will. what they want rather is to be fed, to be taken care of, to be made comfortable. We in the Church know how to do this. We know how to use mystery and miracles. Let us take care of them. Go back to Heaven and leave us alone." Now this is a tremendously interesting thing. It does represent how very many people feel and how many of us feel part of the time.

This is a sellout. It's a copout. It's giving up one's hopes temporarily at the core of one's self, a core that is necessary if we are to be free and if we are to have any kind of willpower to set against the great forces that come upon us from the outside.

There was another person who talked about the same thing in a different language about fifty years before Dostoevsky. This was Søren Kierkegaard. His whole writings could be summed up in the problem of the will. "A man's true vocation is the will to be himself or one's true vocation is the will to be one's self." To Kierkegaard freedom is possibility. We could say at the same time, will is possibility. "Possibility" comes from the same stem as "power"; "possibility" come from "posse" "I can," freedom is I can and I will and this comes to the crucial point—freedom inevitably brings anxiety because people get scared.

Anxiety is inescapable awareness that there's more than one choice. There are many different responses that we can make to the experience of stimuli coming in, and where there is more than one response possible, there is anxiety. Anxiety is the dizziness of freedom, Kierkegaard also said. My patients in psychotherapy sometimes say to me—but they have a wry smile when they say it—"I liked it better when I had my old neurosis because there there was only one thing to do and now all these different possibilities confuse me." The wry smile really means that they don't mean it, if they did mean it, they wouldn't be in psychotherapy. But it is true that freedom and will bring anxiety and in the act of bringing anxiety they also make us authentically human. Spinoza said, back in the seventeenth century, "freedom is the awareness of determinism and the anxiety comes from the fact that the choices that we make will run up against deterministic factors."

When I was thinking about what's the relationship between this freedom and will on one side and determinism on the other, I went back to the ancient Greeks (I know that civilization very well having lived in Greece for three years and also having studied it a great deal) and asked myself how did the ancient Greeks settle this problem of freedom and will on one side and determinism on the other.

One incident among many is a story that is in Homer. It is an account of how the Greeks were encamped around Troy during the Trojan war. They had been there for several years and could not yet scale the Walls of Troy. The men were getting restless. In this period, Agamemnon, who was the commander in chief of the Greek army, stole the mistress of Achilles out of Achilles' tent. Achilles happened to be the best fighter in the Greek army. When Achilles came back to his tent and found out what had happened, he was terribly enraged, and these two men stood confronting each other. The thoughts in the heads of all of these Greek soldiers standing there outside of Troy were, "Will the whole expedition from Greece to Troy be ruined by the fight between these two men?" Then Agamemnon says something. What he says to Achilles is not "I was the cause of this act," but "Zeus and the furies who walk in the darkness caused it. It was they who put wild *atae* (meaning frenzy or madness) in my understanding on that day I took Achilles' prize from him. So what could do? Diety will always have its way." Now he is saying my conditioning did it. My unconscious did it. Well you may think he is saying that, but actually he is not. He's setting the stage so that he can take the responsibility. Agamemnon goes on to say, since I was blinded by *atae* and Zeus took away my understanding, I am willing to make my peace and give abundant compensation. Achilles answers, "Let the son of Atrusius (Agamemnon) go his way for Zeus the counselor took away his understanding."

For Homer and the ancient Greeks, when something happens to you from your unconscious, it happens to you from the gods. The gods spoke in those days in the unconscious. It happens to you by *aeta,* which is the mad frenzy that takes you over. But even though this is the cause of it, it is not a reason why you do not have responsibility. Responsibility is the beginning of the human will that limits the power of Zeus. That's a very interesting thing. Agamemnon declares himself a free man: As we recall from Sartre's drama, *The Flies,* Aristries stands against Zeus and when Zeus says, "I made you, I'm the one that has all the power," Aristries says, "Yes, but you made one mistake, you made me free and now that I am free, I can act."

What's the relationship between human freedom and the will on one side and between determinism, fate, Zeus, if I were an ancient Greek, *atae* if we use the ancient Greek language on the other side. I think that the answer to all of these questions is human freedom; will with freedom. Human freedom and determinism give birth to each other. Take, for example, when Freud began to write about the unconscious and how our irrational urges determine our values, everybody said you are making monkeys out of us. It's a complete determinism. We don't like it. But after we got over being angry at Freud, we discovered what he really was saying was that the human mind is much broader than anybody yet had thought. There is not only the consciousness; there is preconsciousness; there is the collective unconscious; there are a whole lot of layers that make up our mind and that relate us to every other person who ever lived. Jung put this in terms that each of us stands at the peak of a mountaintop of consciousness and this consciousness is related to all other human beings who lived before us.

Freedom comes in new ideas, and it comes with anxiety. The anxiety comes at the exercise of will, which is essential in getting of new ideas. An example of the anxiety came to me in verse as I tried to think through the relations of freedom and will: "Other friends have flown before, on the morrow he will leave me." I know that that verse was a coverup for a great deal of anxiety that accompanied these ideas, which were new to me. And that the verse was a kind of humorous way of trying to seduce me into forgetting the whole thing. At the time I wrote down my ideas, I kept thinking about that poem, the couplet from the poem. Many of you are already aware of where it comes from, but I thought a moment and then I got down some books of poetry and I found that it comes from Edgar Allen Poe's poem, "The Raven." Remember that Edgar Allen Poe is sitting in a room late at night, 2 or 3 o'clock in the morning probably. He is alienated, he is lonely, he is anxious, he possibly is under the influence of some drugs, when a raven comes to the window and sits on the windowsill. He talks to the raven and at one point Poe is lonely and he says, "on the morrow the Raven also will leave me. Other friends have flow before, on the morrow he will leave me." Now what does the Raven say? The Raven says, "Never more." Now I think this is the way of saying, in a symbolic form—and I being a psychoanalyst can never let these symbols go without hanging on to them until they tell me their names. I think it's a symbol for the fact that all of us human beings are caught forever in the human dilemma, which is that there will be power on one side, the power with the determinism and the power with the fate, the power with Zeus and on the other side there will be human freedom, there will be human will and that we will never escape that dilemma. When Poe says, "on the morrow he will leave me," the Raven says "no, never more."

Now you and I as long as we live and as long as we continue to think, continue to be conscious, we will be, whether we are completely aware of it or not like that prisoner in San Quentin, we will be finding that core of ourselves. Whatever we can call free still comes from the center of ourselves where it is also the source of our will. Do you remember William James, who was our greatest philosopher and psychologist in America, who lived back in the beginning of the twentieth century? When William James was studying in Europe between the ages of twenty-seven and thirty-three, he was under continuous depression and in this depression he kept writing back to his friends in America, "Please send me a proof for free will." The depression came from the fact that he could not believe that his actions meant anything. This is, incidently, the chief reason we get depressed. People now in psychotherapy and psychoanalysis cannot believe that their actions will have any effect or their putting one foot in front of the other will take them anyplace. Nobody could send James a proof because freedom and human will is something you cannot prove. One has to believe in it before it exists. It's like love. Nobody can prove love, one has to believe in it before it can exist. Freedom, like beauty, like love, and like goodness, belongs in a category of realities that require belief in order to have their own validity. Nobody could write James any proof, but finally he hit upon an answer and this answer was what he called "taking the option." The option was that he would believe the morning of each day. He would believe for one day at a time that there was a freedom and there was human will that made a difference and he would see how that worked. He tried that and he found that that was the beginning of his controlling and transcending his depression. It didn't do away with his depression. He came back to this country and became a professor of psychology and philosophy. The very fighting of his depression with whatever will and freedom he could draft for himself was in itself a cause, a source of his creativity. You find that if you can struggle with the problem there comes out not only a solution to the problem but also some development of creativity in yourself, and this has a great deal to do with the fact that William James because our greatest psychologist and our greatest philospher.

Human will also is a kind of power. It's a way of saying I can and I will, and it occurs against determinism even though at the same time you take determinism into your awareness and your reality. It's a way of making your choices in a way that you can then take some responsibility for them. I have indicated that our society greatly needs this kind of freedom. The belief of this freedom by persons and this kind of will against the powers that come from technology and all of the other forms of power around us overwhelm us at times, as James's depression threatened to overwhelm him. If freedom means anything at all, it means taking courage; this also takes some will, to confront one's anxiety, and then one can live out one's potentialities. One can move ahead actualizing his potentialities in spite of the risks.

Copyright © 1979 by Rollo May.

Thomas S. Szasz
Power and Psychiatry

Thomas Szasz was born in Budapest, Hungary, in 1920. The Szasz family moved to the United States soon after the Nazi invasion of Austria. In 1939, Szasz enrolled at the University of Cincinnati, earning a B.A. with honors two years later. He received his M.D. degree in 1944 at the College of Medicine of the University of Cincinnati. He was trained in pscychiatry at the University of Chicago Clinics and in psychoanalysis at the Chicago Insitute for Psychoanalysis.

Dr. Szasz has taught at the Upstate Medical Center at the State University of New York, the University of Wisconsin, and Marquette University.

In The Myth of Mental Illness: Foundations of a Theory of Personal Conduct *(1961), Szasz challenged the use of the term "mental illness," arguing that illnesses are disturbances or malfunctions of the body. Since the "mind is not part of the body, the concept of mental illness is faulty. The term "mental illness" is, in reality, applied to "problems of living" concerning moral and social conflicts. "I hold," he wrote, "that the concepts [of mental health and mental illness], used strategically to advance some social interests and to retard others, are used much as national and religious myths had been used in the past." (Interview in the* New Physician, *June 1969.)*

Szasz is also the author of Law, Liberty and Psychiatry; The Ethics of Psychoanalysis; The Manufacture of Madness; The Myth of Psychotherapy; *and of other books and numerous articles in professional journals and popular magazines.*

I want to speak to you about psychiatry and power. When I have done so in the past, people have sometimes asked me, "But what does psychiatry have to do with power? Doesn't it have to do with illnesses and treatments." It might seem so. But it isn't so.

What is power? Speaking informally, one could say that power is the ability of a person or a group or an institution to make someone do something he doesn't want to do. The formal, political, definition or power is, however, more important for our present purposes. Formally, power is the ability to invoke the force of the state to make someone do something to to make him stop doing something. The best example of that sort of power is the criminal law.

Actually, there are two basic ways in which a person can be deprived of liberty in the United States. One is by breaking the criminal law; if you do that, you may get locked up in prison. The other is by breaking the mental hygiene law; if you do that, you may get locked up in a mental hospital. Wait. Don't say that's not so, that people get locked up in mental hospitals because they are sick and need treatment. Words are important in this business, and it's important that you not prejudge the matter. Obviously, most words prejudge the subject to which they are applied. If *you* call psychiatric confinement "hospitalization," that implies it's good; if *I* call it "imprisonment," it implies that it's bad. I recognize that. So let's call it "loss of liberty." If you are committed to a mental hospital, you can't leave the building. In the United States today more people are locked up in mental hospitals than in prisons, despite the fact that the number of mental hospital inmates has decreased dramatically during the past decade or two.

Why is that? What are the justifications, in a free society such as ours, for depriving people of liberty who have not broken the law? To be sure, some people who end up in mental hospitals have broken the law; instead of charging them with a crime, the authorities commit them as crazy. I won't be talking about them, at least not for a while.

Typically, the person who gets committed to a mental hospital has not broken law. He get locked up because he has what is called a "major mental illness"—such as depression or schizophrenia—and because he is said to be "dangerous to himself or others." As you may know, I happen to believe that there is no such thing as a mental illness. Mental illness is just a convenient name to pin on someone, especially if you want to get him put away in the madhouse. Take depression. Whatever depression is, it is obvious that it is not illegal and that it is not an illness. I am not saying that it is pleasant or good to be depressed. What I am saying is that although feeling sad or that life is futile is unpleasant, that does not make having such feelings an illness or a crime. Not everything that's painful or unpleasant in life is an illness or a crime. It is precisely because of that simple fact that words like "depression" and "schizophrenia" are so important: they give unsuspecting people the impression, which is totally false, that certain persons exhibiting certain unpleasant behaviors are sick; and that makes it seem legitimate to incarcerate such persons, because their sickness is really craziness and they don't know what is in their own best interests. That's a socially useful arrangement: it allows some people to dispose of some other people who annoy or upset them.

Obviously, any such arrangement would, in its actual implementation, affect some individuals or groups more than others. Who are the people most affected? The powerless. That is why poor people, uneducated people, people who don't speak the language well, children, and the very old—these are the people who are most likely to get committed. This was always the case, and it still is. The poor, the old, and the young get committed to mental hospitals. Because they have more schizophrenia and depression than others? Because they are more dangerous than others? Of course not. It's because they have less power than others. How often do psychiatrists or lawyers get committed? I suppose it happens, but I have never heard of such a case.

But let me stop criticizing commitment, and let us look at it more closely. After all, commitment is a form of social control. And social controls are, in principle, not necessarily bad. In fact, there can be no society without social controls. Whether a particular form of social control is good or bad depends on what sort of society we want or like. It's meaningless to assert that a particular kind of social control is bad unless we have a clear idea about what sort of moral and political order, of rights and duties, we consider to be good. Let me explain why I think that psychiatric social controls—epitomized by commitment—are bad.

One of the fundamental moral choices people must make is between freedom and order, between individual liberty and social tranquility. As a rule we cannot have social arrangements that maximize both. If we have more of one, we may have to be satisfied with less of the other. Modern Western democracies, especially England and the United States—that is, the so-called free societies—are characterized by having legal and political arrangements that tend to place a very high value on individual liberty. That is exemplified by the Anglo-American criminal law. It is a system that affords many protections to persons accused of lawbreaking. And, of course, it affords complete protection to people who are not accused of crime against being imprisoned in jails or similar institutions. Precisely because that system of social controls is so fine, so protective of individual rights, it leaves a wide range of behaviors that are socially disturbing outside the scope of criminal law. Thus, in Anglo-American law, people have a right to be depressed or to talk crazy. At the same time, however, the so-called normal people in society don't want to put up with such behavior. Since they can't control it one way, they'll try to control it another way. That is how psychiatric sanctions have come into being and that is why they have become so popular: they satisfy a popular need for controlling certain behaviors that are not illegal but which "normal" people want controlled.

A brief review of the history of psychiatry may be in order here. The idea of regulating social behavior by psychiatry is only about 300 years old. The first madhouses (mental hospitals or insane asylums) were built in France and Germany and then England around 1650. The people confined in these institutions were the homeless, orphans, poor people with infectious diseases, prostitutes, vagrants, and other such "misérables," as Victor Hugo would have put it. If we examine the development of these institutions, we see that the history of psychiatry is the opposite of the history of medicine. In medicine it was always obvious that there existed diseases that made people sick and killed them. Doctors, medicine, and hospitals came later. In psychiatry it was the other way around. First came the mental hospitals, then the mental diseases. In an important sense, mental diseases are social artifacts.

The first step in the history of psychiatry was the building of madhouses. That development created two populations, the keepers and the kept. There you have the role of power in psychiatry writ large. Who has the keys? Prostesting the use of mental hospitilization in Russia, Solzhenitsyn declared, "The incarceration of free-thinking, healthy, people in mad-houses is spiritual murder, a variant of the gas chamber, and even more cruel." It seems to me that there is something terribly wrong with that statement. If incarcerating sane dissidents is worse than putting them in a gas chamber, how can it be good for mental patients? Shouldn't one be even nicer to sick people than to healthy ones?

I think Solzhenitsyn is wrong, logically as well as morally. Nevertheless, his views reflect "enlightened" public opinion-namely, that it is okay to lock up crazy people in insane asylums, but it is not okay to lock up sane people in them. That is why it is now so popular a pastime in the West to protest the mental hospitalization of Soviet dissidents. Of course, the Russians say that they don't lock up "dissidents," they lock up "mental patients." In my opinion, the Russians are wrong, and the critics of Russian psychiatry are also wrong. The Russians are wrong because they have a poloitical system that's evil from the ground up. Locking up dissidents in madhouses is just a part of it. The Western critics of Soviet psychiatry are wrong because they flatter themselves with selective indignation. They object to involuntary psychiatry in Russia, but not in the West. They object to incarcerating dissidents in mental hospitals, but do not object to incarcerating everyone behind the "iron curtains" of their own national borders.

Let me cite a recent case of commitment in the United States reported in the press to illustrate what is wrong with Solzhenitsyn's critique, and with the Western liberal critique in general, of Soviet psychiatry. Some months ago the Chicago police arrested a man named Robert Freedman for begging for dimes in front of a downtown bus station. He said, "Don't take me in, I am not drunk, I didn't know this [that is, begging] was a crime." When he opened the briefcase he carried with him, police found $24,098 in small bills. A few days later in court, a judge, who said he was protecting Freedman from possible bodily harm by thugs who might be after the cash he carried, committed Freedman to a mental hospital. But Freedman did not suffer from a disease. Nevertheless, according to the papers, he "has seen half his life savings eaten away by hospital fees and doctors for treatment ordered by the court to keep him at a mental facility he fought to stay out of. The courts even ordered him to pay the fees for the lawyer who argued for his commitment." Three months after he was committed, Freedman was dead. Why did the judge commit him? Because, as he said after the commitment hearing, "I wonder what my decision would have been if he wasn't carrying $24,000 around. From the evidence, I decided that the man lacked good judgment. If he didn't have the $24,000 my interpretation of his judgment would have been different." That is what commitment is all about: deviant behavior and powerlessness on the one side—meddling, paternalism, and power on the other side. In the past, paternalism justifed slavery, colonialism, male chauvinism. Now it justifies coercive psychiatry—and threatens to justify an increasing number of coercive medical interventions as as well.

I have, of course, presented only one side of the story—the argument against psychiatric power. However, as John Stuart Mill so wisely observed, no one really understands a conflict unless he understands both sides of it. This warning is especially relevant to the controversy about involuntary psychiatry—because the people who protest against the "abuses" of coercive psychiatry are often the ones most eager to preserve its "proper uses." That, I think, is something that cannot be done, and here is why.

As I mentioned at the beginning, coercive psychiatric interventions are actually extralegal methods of social control. Their purpose, in short, is to take up the slack left by a criminal law "too protective" of individual liberty. But such a system of criminal law is emblematic of a people's devotion to the rule of law and the value of personal freedom. If and when a people decide to place a lower value on individual liberty, they usually revise their criminal statues to reflect such a sentiment—for example, as the Russians do in making emigration a criminal offense, and as we do by making the use of certain drugs a criminal offense.

The very essence of the mental hygiene laws is thus to serve a purpose quite different from, indeed diametrically opposed to, the preservation of individual liberty. What is that purpose? It is to preserve and promote a common ideology or world view—that is, a shared sense of what is "normal"; it is also to preserve and protect the family from its excessively disruptive members—that is, from parents, children, or aged relatives who interfere with the well-being of the dominant members; and finally, it is to do so under medical and therapeutic, rather than penological or punitive, auspices—thus overtly muting rather than polarlizing conflicts in the family, on the job, in society as a whole. In short, just as individuals need "tranquilizers," so society, too, needs to have its conflicts defused and pacified. In past ages, the organized religions fulfilled that task. Now psychiatry does. What we need to remember is that that task usually conflicts with the protection of individual dignity and liberty. Hence, it seems likely—indeed, I think is certain—that not until we renounce or abolish involuntary psychiatric interventions will we develop mechanisms for defusing human conflicts that are less injurious to our most treasured traditional values than are the present methods of insitutional psychiatry.

If we are honest with ourselves, we must recognize that neither the modern Communist state nor the modern non-Communist state likes people who challenge its core values or whose behavior disrupts the traffic of everyday life. Faced with a choice between tolerating such behavior by looking the other way (or by some noncoercive method), and repressing it by means of psychiatric "treatment," every modern society opts for psychiatric sanctions. It is, let me repeat, the very existence and attractiveness of psychiatric methods of social control that fuels the engine of coercive psychiatry—its vocabularly, its imagery, and its specific techniques. Although there is no mental illness, modern society, to paraphrase Voltaire, finds it necessary to invent it. There is now no need for involuntary psychiatric interventions, but neither was there a need in the past for religious intolerance and persecution. Still, no one ever got a medal for being compassionate or tolerant—but many have received medals, and more, for persecuting people for their own good. The doctor who developed lobotomy—since prohibited both by the Soviets and the Vatican—received the Nobel Prize in medicine for it, the only such prize every given for a so-called psychiatric discovery. Therein lies a lesson about the relations between psychiatry and power that people ignore at their own peril.

Copyright © 1979 by Thomas S. Szasz.

Theme 5
The Limits of Power

Charles Reich

Power and the Law

Charles Alan Reich was born in New York City on May 20, 1928. He received a B.A. degree in history from Oberlin College in 1949 and an LL.B degree from Yale Law School in 1952. While at Yale, he achieved one of the highest averages in the school's history. He also edited the Yale Law Journal.

Reich was law clerk to the late Supreme Court Justice Hugo L. Black from 1953 to 1954. He practiced corporate law for a number of years with a Washington firm. In 1960 Reich joined the Yale Law School as an associate professor teaching property and constitutional law. In 1964 he was promoted to the rank of professor. He taught there until 1974.

While at Yale, Reich received permission to teach a special undergraduate course entitled "The Individual in America." With an enrollment of as many as 600 students, the course was rivaled in popularity only by Erich Segal's "Classical Civilization."

In 1970 Reich published The Greening of America, *which outlined the problems of contemporary society and the corporate state while suggesting an alternative life-style. The book was an instant success and quickly climbed to the top of the bestseller lists.*

Reich has also published in numerous law journals as well as the Nation, *the* Yale Review, *and* National Parks and Conservation.

> *There is a revolution coming. It will not be like revolutions of the past. It will originate with the individual and with culture, and it will change the political structure only as its final act. It will not require violence. It is now spreading with amazing rapidity, and already our laws, institutions and social structure are changing in consequence. It promises a higher reason, a more human community, and new liberated individual. Its ultimate creation will bring a new enduring wholesomeness and beauty—a renewed*

relationship of man to himself, to other men, to society, to nature, and to the land.

(From The Greening of America.*)*

I have been assigned a topic, "Power and the Law," and I have been preceded here by a number of other speakers who may or may not have used the word "power" in the same sense that I will use it. So I think in an excess of caution I should try to say the way I'm going to use the word, and it means to me pretty much the same thing as freedom. Power is a thing that everybody wants the most that they can possibly have of. That is, skiing is power, sex appeal is power, the ability to make yourself heard by your congressman is power, anything that comes out of you and goes out into the world is power and in addition to that, the ability to be open, to apprecieate, to receive love, to respond to others, to listen to music, to understand literature, all of that is power. By "power" I mean human faculties exercised to the largest possible degree. So in a way, in a large sense, by power I mean individual intelligence. Now when you reach out to another person through the energy or creativity that is in you and that other person responds, you are exercising power. When you make somebody else do something against their will, to me that is not power at all, that is force, and force to me is the negation of power. So all those people who are called in our society power brokers, the people who exercise force, seem to me to be essentially powerless within the way that I define the term, because, you know, they can't make anybody respond simply beause of the energy within them. They've got to come with a club or with a threat or with the ability to punish you in some way in order to get you to attend to them. That is clearly the negation of power as I use that term.

Now power is something that you must develop, and the way in which it is developed is a process that I call nurture. Nurture is anything, whether it's education, whether it's love, whether it's law that gives you certain kinds of freedom, whether it's the privilege of attending a university—nurture is anything that enhances you as an individual and gives you this added strength, this added ability to project yourself in other directions or the ability to open up and listen to others. Now law and power may be related in many different kinds of ways. For instance, law might be a very severe restriction upon power, but the way I want to talk about law is in an affirmative sense—a law that enhances power, that gives you more freedom—and therefore, the general aim of my remarks is in the direction of human rights. In the direction of what law can do for people to make them more free and more powerful.

Now perhaps an illustration will be more graphic than these abstractions. Suppose that you are traveling abroad and you're by yourself and you find yourself in a country that will be nameless because it could be so many countries today, and suppose all of a sudden, without warning, you are arrested by secret agents and thrown into a prison. And in that prison there was nobody to tell you why you were there, nobody to tell you when you could get out if ever, nobody to talk to, nobody to love, nobody to respond in any sense, and the days went by and the months went by an no one knew where you were. The United States, perhaps, had no diplomatic relations with this country. The country had no laws, nothing but a dictator or tyrant and you couldn't even find out the charges against you. So as you rot there without a book to read, without a thing to do as the days go by and the months go by, you will experience powerlessness in the sense in which I'm using the terms "power" and "powerlessness." Now that's a situation where you could be immensely helped by law. Because if you happen to live in a country where there was such a thing as a writ of habeas corpus, and that simply means a writing from a court saying to the people who are holding you in prison "Explain why this person is there and free this person if this imprisonment is not justified," if you lived in a coutnry with a writ of habeas corpus you would have a chance to have a lawyer and you would have a very good chance of receiving a fair hearing.

A right is just a power. It's power that's written into law and it really shouldn't be called anything different than an instrument that gives you power. A writ of habeas corpus is no different from a pair of skis in the sense that it's something that gives you more freedom. Something that allows you to do something that otherwise you would be powerless to do. And so all kinds of instruments—whether they are legal or whether they are made out of wood or plastic or something else—that confer freedom and power can be classified together in this way. The prison image is not so foreign to our experience for we have all read about Steve Biko and South Africa and I think my description of imprisonment was scarcely an exaggeration of what happened to him. It is also true that there are a great many people who feel somewhat the same way, have the same sense of powerlessness right here in the United States of America, even though here we have plenty of laws and a Constitution. I'd like to read a letter sent to the San Francisco Chronical, dated November 15,

> Dear Editor, I have been reduced to a state of quivering terror and will be under the bed. I am afraid that the dams will break, the rain will not come, of communism, of fascism, capitalism. Of sugar in my cereal, cancer caused by Zylitol,

bacon fat, water, saccharin, microwaves and thousands of other hitherto innocent substances. I am petrified that I will be mugged, that I will offend a minority, that my social secutiry is worthless, that I will get fat, have a heart attack, become less than number 1, fail to be aggressive, be overlooked by EST, never be graphed, miss a performance of Turendo, be poisoned by nuclear waste, my car will run out of gas, the money will inflate, the economy will deflate, the stock market will collapse, I will be spied on by the CIA, FBI, IRS, and I will get VD. And there's one last word, HELP.

There are many people who feel that way in the United States today. But if we look around us and see some of the things that are wrong with this country, we will see that in almost every instance they may be attributed to one or another form of powerlessness. If you think about addiction, if you think about crazy violence, if you think about boredom, despair, depression, the people who hate their work, the people who are insensitive to others, the people who feel so terribly alone and lacking in the community, just to give you a few, a catalogue that could be carried on and on and on, you'll see that this is a country that has a great many symptoms of powerlessness. And of course, since we are the best and the richest, we are number one in the world, we have to ask ourselves, why is this so? Why have we so many powerless feeling people in a country that is so well-to-do and so happy as the standards of the world go? Well I should like to suggest that we have a case of starvation that has not yet been adequately diagnosed. And I propose simply to name it but not to argue it very hard because I think it's just something for you to think about and see whether you think I'm right or not.

There are two basic kinds of nurture that every human being needs, and if any of you found yourselves on a desert island or if you found yourselves on a brand new planet with none of our civilization, you would soon be aware of this division of nurture. There is material nurture; you need shelter, you need something to eat, you need clothes. And then there is nonmaterial nurture. You need somebody to hold you, you need somebody to hold your hand. And those two kinds of nurture are equally important, as you would find in the desert island or the new planet. You would find, for example, that if you were without the second kind you would be in very bad shape indeed. Perhaps you would disintegrate mentally and emotionally before long even though you had shelter and enough to eat and everything else. Because nonmaterial nuture is as essential to life as food. And it's just that in our society, we don't think very clearly about nonmaterial nurture. We either take it for granted or we assume that everybody will find it on his own or we think it's not as important as the material kind. And indeed we spend so much of our time gathering up the material kind that the pursuit of material nurture becomes the undoing and the destruction of nonmaterial nurture. Just as if somebody works all day making money, they're not going to have any time to give love and they won't have any time to receive love. So that if these two kinds of nurture get out of balance trouble is sure to come. And I think the undiagnosed ailment in America is nothing more complicated than a material glut accompanied by a nonmaterial starvation. And we even have individuals who exemplify this: Howard Hughes, Elvis Presley, and Montgomery Clift, if you've read their biographies. Over and over again we see people who had everything in the world, materially, and yet in some way were being driven crazy by what could only be described as nonmaterial starvation. How can this be? How can we be so ignorant, so stupid, so lacking in intelligence that we starve ourselves in this one way while we glut ourselves in the other.

Well the answer is that we repress the need for and understanding of and the knowledge of nonmaterial nurture. We simply keep insisting that it's not very important. We run it down. Nothing could illustrate this better than what has been demonstrated by the women's movement in this country. Because women have pointed out successfully, at least as far as I'm concerned, that what they do—the nurturing of children, the maintenance of a home, the nurturing of men—that is work and it ought to be treated as essential work, as important work, as valuable work, just as any other work might be considered. And the fact that it is devalued, that it is not honored, that it is not paid for, that you don't get to be chairmen of the board by bringing up a child, that illustrates a form of repression in which we don't forbid that kind of nurture but we just put it so far down and give you so little credit for doing it and leave you so little time for doing it that it is continually in short supply. And so I think that the balance that nature would ordain between these two kinds of nurture has been undone in this society and it's not very easy to overcome that condition. All you have to do is be a person who's aware of women's feelings or a woman who's aware of her own feelings and look at TV. You will want to smash the set, because over and over again the woman's role is devalued, put down, made trivial, made silly, made empty, made unimportant, while the man's role is built up into something immensely important. And so we are the victims in a sense of our own propaganda, the victims of our own conditioning, and our starvation has become a self-perpetuating and self-induced process. So that we can't correct it because on every side the lie is blared out that you don't need this and you need more of this.

Look at the so-called energy crisis as a perfect example of this. What's the real energy crisis in this country? It's the crisis of human energy; the fact that so many people are not motivated, so many people don't care, so many people hate their work, so many people don't want to help their neighbor. That's the important energy crisis, and if that were focused on and dealt with and we occupied ourselves with that, we would just use less of the other kind of energy because we wouldn't have time to bother. And we'd begin to restore a balance. But every time that we talk about this kind of knowledge, this kind of knowledge that involves the nonmaterial needs of human beings, we are told we are being self-indulgent, that we are wasting the time that should be spent in doing important things, and this statement is simply a total reversal of the truth as far as I'm concerned.

Some of you may know E.F. Shoemacher's book *Small is Beautiful*, but you may not know another book by him called *A Guide for the Perplexed*. In the second book he refers to the putting down of nonmaterial nurture, the putting down of self-knowledge, and then he comments as follows:

> Meanwhile world crises multiply and everybody deplores the shortages or even total lack of wise men or women. Unselfish leaders, trustworthy counselors, etc., it is hardly rational to expect such high qualities from people who have never done any inner work and would not even understand what was meant by the words. They may consider themselves decent, law-abiding people and good citizens. It makes very little difference how they dream about themselves. Like a computer, they carry out prearranged programs. The Programmer is asleep.

And so what we see is a society where one kind of intelligence is exalted and another kind of unintelligence is exalted. Another kind of stupidity is created and it's willfully created stupidity in the sense that we are not that stupid. We know better, we know more about ourselves than we are allowed to think or say. This puts us in a position today where there's a huge but sort of secret conflict going on in this country. A conflict between those who say that the answer to our problems is more and yet more material production and those who whisper because they hardly dare say it out loud that we don't need anything more material, we need less material things. What we need is far more nonmaterial nurture. That conflict has been growing for years, and it's reached a point of great intensity today, even though it is not really acknowledged as such.

The conflict puts the individual in a truly difficult spot because we are compelled both to make our living and survive in the material world, that is the world of here and now, and at the same time if we are at all wise, we should be learning as much as we can and doing as much as we can in the nonmaterial area as well because the material world simply cannot make up for the nonmaterial world. And so we are in the difficult position, each of us, of straddling two conflicting worlds, trying to make the best of one and trying to educate ourselves in the other. The unfortunate things about this second education is that it is a curriculum that is not taught anywhere that I know of. Only, perhaps in the tiniest bits and pieces can one come across it. But there are really no formal institutions that teach you self-knowledge, that teach you nonmaterial nurture. So while we struggle to learn the one curriculum that everybody is told is the only important thing to learn, on our own we must learn the other, unless we are prepared to be caught short at some point in middle age being materially successful or perhaps unsuccessful, but, by then starving nonmaterially, as these other examples illustrate. And then, if our marriage breaks up, if our children are discontented, if our lives are depressed and miserable, we have no way out. We are trapped because this other education is totally lacking. And our job then is to develop an intelligence beyond that which most of us now have, an intelligence that is able to know what is good for us and what is bad for us in a new area.

The best example I can give you of this kind of leap of intelligence is simply the example of old-fashioned fly paper, which some of you may be too modern to know about. But anyway, if you've ever seen it, fly paper is just a roll of gooey paper that you hang in a room that's full of pesty flies. One by one they land on the paper under the illusion that it's something delicious and they get trapped in it and they die a most unpleasant death as they get more and more mired in this rubbery goo. Their problem is that they don't know the difference between what is good for them and what is bad for them. It's just that simple. And that is our problem as well. We, too, are flies who flock to what is dangerous and bad and detrimental to us and are unable to distinguish what we really need, and we, too, are likely to end up being strangled in our own mistakes in this same horrible way.

A good illustration of this is the innocent young woman or man who goes to law school as I did without any conception of the terrific emotional drain that law school involves. And therefore, without any idea of what provisions one ought to make to survive law school. It's a very good experience for your mind. It's very good training for lots of different occupations and it does definitely sharpen the wits. But! It is an incredible emotional drain. And I would say that you should have about six lovers at a minimum before you would even think of attempting to go to law school. You should also have people to be parent surrogates, people to go and cry on their shoulders, people to keep you afloat if you plan to go and get battered by such as the likes of me in law school. Because law school consists of three years of being put down and being put down by experts, and who's going to help you to get back up again? Every day you leave the class reeling, your ego has been destroyed. Who's going to tell you what a great person you are?

What I'm suggesting is that it's the job of everyone to perceive these dangers in life and to undertake what they must with adequate provision for their own safety and well-being. It is equally indispensible, it seems to me, to know what is good and what is bad for others. Because those who are superintelligent in their careers, in business, in law, or whatever, but are ignorant of their effect upon other people, are headed for disaster in their personal lives and often in their professional lives. And so just as you must know yourself, so you must know what's happening to other people, if you want to be intelligent in this way.

Now the trouble is you can't believe what anybody tells you. Because in the field of nonmaterial knowledge, everybody is a liar. Everybody conceals what he really knows and what he really feels. And I'm not trying to make anybody feel the worse for this, it's just a fact. Nobody tells the truth in this area. Especially, we don't get the truth from the media, from advertising, from television and even more we don't get the truth from our leaders. Do we have leaders who scream, "Help, Help, I don't know what's going on" as they must surely feel everyday? No! They lie! There isn't anybody in Washington, D.C., that knows what's going on, or more than just a little bit of the time. If they would admit that, we'd all be better off. We'd be able to understand ourselves and them and the country in a good way. So I'm just saying that the problem of the self-educated person in this field is to believe nobody. Not even yourself.

What you have to do is become an experiment, you have to try new things. You have to do bizarre things. You have to alter reality in every possible way and then you have to see what happens. Check out the results. See how you feel. Does it make you feel better, does it make you feel worse? This will make you into a scientist of your own self and by that process gradually you will accumulate a store of truth. And then you have to have the guts and the courage to believe yourself and disbelieve the whole rest of the world. And that, of course, is quite a struggle, but the winning of that struggle is the becoming of an autonomous person. That is, you become a person who listens to himself as authority before he listens to anyone else or everyone else. And that, of course, is a great achievement in freedom. And so it is a desirable thing even though it is desperately hard.

Now, this process of learning and education is not going to do very much to help the world because, if there's any idea that I think we can see illustrated everywhere today, it's that knowledge and insight alone don't change anything. We all know better, but everything stays the same. Everybody in the country knows better than the way the country is now, but nothing happens. Anyone of us is wiser than our government and yet nothing happens. Why is that? Because action is the only thing that changes anything. In your own life, in anybody else's life, or the life of society, only action creates change. And so, if we are suffering, as I believe that we are, from a terrible shortage, a starvation in the area of nonmaterial nurture, we are going to have to start acting to manufacture it. And manufacture is the word I use because, just as you manufacture the material—you apply science, you produce machines—you make up nonmaterial nurture in any way that you can. And you learn how to produce it for others and there is no limit to how much you can learn. Just as we learned that there was no limit to the amount of material that we can produce.

So, for example, even if you are not attempting anything so arduous as law school, it wouldn't hurt every person to manufacture his own survival kit. And a survival kit is nothing but your own little bag of portable nurture. For some people it's a hot bath. For some people, it's peeling vegetables, you know, for some people it's watching the sun set, for others the sun rise. Usually it's a whole collection of things. But the important thing is to have it and understand it and understand yourself well enough to that you don't become a public charge. So you are not a walking disaster area. So that your friends don't flee when they see you coming, because they see a huge bundle of needs and they think you are not able to take care of yourself.

Even in this most elementary sense, one can manufacture nurture. It's much better of course to get your friends to manufacture nurture for you and with you than it is to do it all alone. And I think that that will usually prove to be a somewhat better process. But you need to make agreements of mutual nurture with other people because one of the greatest evils in this society, besides the starvation that I have already mentioned, is exploitation or lack of mutuality between people, typified by the man who takes emotionally and doesn't give and the women who gives emotionally and doesn't take. The stereotype of course is, we hope, slowly being changed. Nevertheless, it is very easy to find takers who have no intention of giving you much back. If you want a relationship on those terms, it is easy. You can find loads of people who will freeload off you emotionally. But if you want a mutual relationship with anybody, I recommend a simple device, and this is for a relationship whether it is a beginning relationship, the first date you ever have or whether it is a marriage, I recommend a kitchen timer. You set it for thirty minutes of nurture from one person and then "bing" and then thirty minutes from the other, and you'll learn something that way. You'll learn who's giving and who isn't giving. And one of the best ways to kind of characterize the giving and the nongiving situation is to talk in terms of big and small, just because it kind of gives a picture of it. Standing up here talking to all you people, I am being big. Later, alone, hiding under a blanket, I will be small. These two must balance. Because it is another rule of nature, you know, that everybody has to balance and the bigger you are the smaller you have to be. And so between two people, the same rule takes place. And so men as a group need to learn to be small and need to really show that side of themselves more. They need to learn to cry. They need to learn to show their feelings, they need to demonstrate that whole dimension they have repressed and, of course, women have to study biggness and learn that side of themselves. And it is really enormously important to see this as a thing that you can keep switching back and forth. You be big, I'll be big, You be small, I'll be small. It works in any situation because it is a way of identifying the essential need for mutuality in all transactions.

In the same vein, you can say to yourself that everything that is a chore must also be seen as its own reward and so every time that you do anything that is hard for you or draining for you, you must go after the reward that is in it or else reward yourself in some other way. If you want to learn how to motivate yourself, do it by rewarding yourself in a very clear and explicit way. Some people like to be bribed ahead of time and some people like to be bribed afterwards. So assuming that the reward for the moment is an ice cream cone, although there are other noncaloric rewards that will work just as well, you may say to yourself, "You may have this ice cream cone if you will do a half hours work." Or you may say, "I'll do a half hours work and then I'll have an ice cream cone." Don't underestimate how childish you are. Because you'll lose out on the amazing effectiveness of the manufacture of nurture. It really works and it works at the absolute highest level, that is, no matter how high the intellectual endeavor that person might attempt, for instance, trying to write a Ph.D. dissertation. Still, you will succeed better if you bribe yourself with a series of rewards, and they can be pretty low-level childish things and they will still work. So this concept is simply a way of identifying the truth about human beings and, of course, the way every person works is a little bit different, so you need to know each one individually.

I came here to talk not about developing nurture but about law. And what law is in my terms is nothing but the manufacture of nurture on a larger and more general scale. That is to say it is taking people's needs and generalizing them, giving them priority for a whole group in society. And a really clear-cut example of this would be, let's say, the demand of the handicapped people, which we have just begun to hear about in the last few years. Let's say the demand for the building of ramps so that a person in a wheelchair can get into all kind of places that they would be excluded from going. Now that is asking for a law to provide you with freedom because a ramp is freedom, a ramp is the same as a ski or a ski slope. A ramp is the same as a writ of habeas corpus for a person with a wheelchair. So asking to have a law passed that restaurants and other public places have to have ramps is asking that human needs be given priority at a level of generality where an entire society gets back of that need and says all of us have a stake in human dignity. All of us may some day be handicaped people. All of us, therefore, insist upon valuing freedom in this particular way. Well, ramps cost money, and so what a right is, besides being a generality, a right is a statement that something is more important than material nurture. It is a statement that the nonmaterial nurture is more important than the material. And so, law is used over and over again to establish the balance that is needed between the material and the nonmaterial that has become upset over the course of time. For example, suppose there is inhumane treatment of people in mental asylums, inhumane treatment of people in institutions for delinquents, inhumane treatment of people in prisons, what are you going to hear over and over again? No money! And that is true, there is no money. The way that that situation can be remedied is that you enact a right that says that people must be treated up to a certain standard, cost what it may. And then, it's going to cost. It's going to come out of the material side of life; just as if we ever get to work seriously on improving our cities, it's going to come out of some other aspect of our material well being. *But every single one of the whole catalog of human rights that is now being demanded is in essence an effort to revalue human beings above material needs in a particular way.*

I just have a laundry list here of some of the rights that occurred to me. The rights of the handicapped, the rights of women, the rights of the aged, the rights of the poor, minorities, people who are bored with their work—incidentally work can be made more interesting if you want to pay the cost—the rights of children, the rights of gay people, the rights against political persecution, the rights of war protestors. Environmental rights are a really good one to stop on for just a second because there you can see it really clearly, there you can see that the preservation of nature is in square conflict with material production and that you need to make a choice. And evey time there is a battle over human rights, it is an effort to get up to make a new choice, to insist upon a different choice. Now when our political leaders tell us that we can have it both ways, they are not doing anybody any good. They are not doing themselves any good because they can't deliver, and they're not doing anyone else any good because they're not confronting us with the choices that we must make. If we want to preserve our natural environment, if we want to give more dignity to human beings, it is going to come out of the material things that we have now. And there is no other way. There is nowhere else for it to come. Because human energy produces both kinds of nurture and the energy that goes for one does not go for the other. If you want to give the special care and love and concern, let's say that the retarded deserve in a society that cares about human dignity, then it is going to cost money and you are going to have less of something else. So every one of these involves a choice and the human rights movement as a whole is a search for revaluing in this area.

Rights also are an effort to make people think about unclaimed rights. For example, there is a great and painful battle to day on the subject of abortion that is deeply devisive and deeply hurtful to the society as a whole. But one thing that needs to be said much more than it is being said is the right that children have to be wanted if they are born, if they are alive, if they are going to grow up to be normal human beings. That is not the only right involved, there are a number of rights involved, but you don't hear very much about the right of every child to be wanted and that is an example again of failing to see the whole picture because we tend over and over again to push human rights down out of sight because they cost money. It is just that simple. Because they are inconvenient, because they represent an investment that is going to have to come from somewhere. Caring for a child is one of the most enormous investments that any person could possibly make and it is really something to think about before one brings any child into the world and most especially, an unwanted child.

Now something else should be said about rights that isn't said often enough. And that is that rights don't exist because nature gives them to you. Rights only exist because you claim them. Because you say that is what human beings deserve and every right must be claimed. There is no such thing as a right that simply floats around in the world or is given to you. So, therefore, you must see rights as being in their ultimate essence arbitrary claims. Think about a couple who go out and they hve a quarrel and one person says, "I'm not going to be treated that way." Well, somebody else would accept that kind of treatment. The claim that the first person will not be treated that way is essentailly arbitrary; it is a statement that says something like this, "I value myself so highly that I will not be treated this way." The other person says, "Either I don't value myself so highly so you may continue to abuse me," or else he says, "I'm waiting for that great parent in the sky to do something for me which I refuse to do for myself." Neither of those latter two will get you any rights. So rights essentially come from no one but ourselves. We manufacture them in the same way that I suggested that we manufacture nonmaterial nurture.

I can't resist the temptation to talk about one example of revaluing that is an option that we might consider for just a moment. Under the Constitution, the Supreme Court of the United States may consist of *any* number of Justices, any number of any sex of any age, having any education or no education, no Justice needs any other kind of qualification. So, the Supreme Court is really a rather wide open body. It doesn't need to be nine men, it doesn't need to be twenty-nine men. The Supreme Court functions as the ultimate determinant in our society of formal human rights. It doesn't just decide legal questions such as whether you are taxable under a certain section of the Internal Revenue code. It decides the fundamental priorities of our society. And so, when you think about that as an example of an institution in this society, you might say to yourself, does it really represent the people of this country?

As far as I know, there has never been a woman on the court in the two hundred year history of the court. There has only been one minority person in the two hundred year history of the court. There are no young people, there are no poor people, there are no people who are not lawyers and maybe this is the way you want it. O.K., that is fine, but my point is, you don't have to have it that way. Not at all. We could do something like this. We could pass a simple act of Congress and we could raise the number of justices to say thirty-three, we could insist under the Bakke case that half of those people be women. We could insist that some reasonable proportion represent the rest of society and we could do this legally, constitutionally, through proper procedures. In fact, President Franklin D. Roosevelt tried to do something very much like this a number of years back and he proposed adding to the number of Justices at a time when they were, as it seems to me they are now, utterly out of tune with the needs of most of the people of the country, and he said this. "We must find a way to take an appeal from the Supreme Court to the Constitution itself. We cannot yield our constitutional destiny to the personal judgment of a few men who, being fearful of the future, would deny us the necessary means of dealing with the present." Well, the Supreme Court heard that radio speech too. And they switched their votes so the court number was never increased beyond the nine simply because they began to get with it. But, I am calling your attention to this sort of thing because we have so many more options under our Constitution than we think about. My purpose is to suggest to you the choices. We do have the choice of having a representative Supreme Court and that to me would be a step in the direction of human rights. In the direction of having a tribunal that understood the needs of people today and did something about it. I merely point that out in Delaware, because this is one of these states where they say the Constitution originated, because it is a good place for new thinking about the Constitution to originate. New thinking about what kind of a country this is. Suppose that in 1789, they had decided to be satisfied with what was then in existence; there would have been no Constitution, there would have been no Bill of Rights. Why should we be any less shy in our day and our time to deal with our own needs in the same bold and brave way that they dealt with theirs.

Now, just to show you that there are those who don't wait around for the constitutional scholars. I would like to give you an example of the manufacture of freedom that is in another realm. Out in San Francisco, we have a lot of lovely hills and they are all paved over with concrete, and only in the most recent times have little kids started to asert their own freedom over those concrete hills by skateboarding down them, by dancing down them, by doing ballets down them, by zooming and whirling and having incredible fun and declaring an amazing amount of autonomy and invention and freedom and creativity in the use of all this old concrete. So there you have what I suppose was a creation of rights, a creation of a new space that was almost instinctual, because I don't think you could possibly interview very many of these kids and find out that they were creating constitutional rights or that they were nonmaterial nurture or anything of that sort. They would, I am sure, reply that they were having fun. But there are some interviews, and I read the skateboarding magazines carefully, and the kids say a little bit more. The kids say that the purpose of what they are doing is to be radical, to show off, to feel how free you can be, to explore the ultimate limits of yourself. And so, in some very deeply nonverbal way, skateboarding is a form of self-knowledge, skateboarding is a form of intelligence, skateboarding is a form of exploring your limits. And, what I am suggesting is that that spirit is exactly the same as every human rights proposal; it is exactly the same as changing the Supreme Court. All of these things involve saying that we people have needs that are more important than the needs of the inanimate things that we see all around us. Consider this letter to the editor of *Skateboarding World* magazine:

Dear Editor, I have always viewed skateboarding as a sort of harmless rebellion against the concrete covered wasteland I live in (he lives in California). Ever since I've been old enough to think, I've always felt cheated that progress has called for the slow destruction of all natural beauty in southern California. So being able to get off on all that stupid cement that's laying all over the land is a way of having a last laugh. Sometimes I take my board out really late at night and explore the industrial park not far from my home. It is really neat because the whole area is lit up but nobody is around but me and my board. It is like being the only person alive.

Well, everybody seems to be dreaming today about new space. We have all gone to see *Star Wars,* we have seen *Close Encounters,* we are reading science fiction, we are reading fantasy books, we are letting our imagination tell us that we want more space; we want to be more free; we want to start dreaming. And that should tell us something more than simply the idea that we want to create a different future from the present that now exists and it should tell us that all of us are dreaming about creating a different future and that such a future is possible. Suppose that we were here at the close of the Middle Ages before the machine age had begun, before the age of science had begun. And suppose we had some crazy person up here talking about going to the moon or something like that. It would have sounded as improbable as the dreaming of a new social system. The dreaming of people who are more intelligent, more caring, more compassionate, the dreaming of a people who know how to create a community, who know how to make a world in which everybody will feel better about himself and better about those that he loves, but those are things that we can create just as well as we can create the material wonders of today.

At the beginning of the modern age, which I would say was in the 1930s, an economist named Stuart Chase said that we had created a billion horsepower but that we hadn't yet created the minds to use it right, to do something with it, to make something beautiful of it. And he, at least, saw the terrible danger that was coming. He said, "From our brains have sprung a billion horses, now running wild and almost certain sooner or later to run amuck. Where are the riders with their whirling ropes; where are the light-hearted youths to mount, be thrown, and rise to mount again?" (*Men and Machines* [1929], p. 348.)

Well, we haven't yet answered that call, we haven't yet answered that vision, but I am not telling anybody that they *have* to do anything. That they don't have to do anything whatever about their lives except just let it all happen to them. My message is that you can do something, and you can whether society changes or not. That even if no one else in the world changes, you can create more space for yourself. And my point is that it is something that you should know. You should know that it is your birthright. You should know that it is your inheritance. You should know that anybody can revalue themselves. Everyone has that freedom. You should know that any two people in the world can form an alliance for mutual support and that by making an alliance like that they can make periodic visits to another world together. You should know that while it is possible to hang ten on a skateboard and it's possible to hang ten on a surfboard it is also possible to hang ten in your life and that that will last.

Copyright © 1979 by Charles Reich.

William H. Rehnquist

The Nature and Exercise of Power

William Hubbs Rehnquist was born October 1, 1924, in Milwaukee, Wisconsin, the son of William Benjamin Rehnquist and Margery Peck Rehnquist. He attended public elementary and high schools in Shorewood, Wisconsin, a suburb of Milwaukee.

He served in the United States Army Air Corps in this country and overseas from 1943 to 1946. He was discharged with the rank of sergeant.

Justice Rehnquist received both a B.A. and an M.A. degree from Stanford University in 1948, an M.A, from Harvard University in 1950, and an LL.B. from Stanford in 1952.

From February 1952 to June 1953, he was a law clerk for Justice Robert H. Jackson, Supreme Court of the United States. He engaged in private practice with an emphasis on civil litigation, in Phoenix, Arizona, from 1953 to 1969.

President Nixon appointed him assistant attorney general, Office of Legal counsel, In January 1969. He was nominated associate justice of the Supreme Court of the United States by President Nixon on October 21, 1971, and was sworn in on January 7, 1972.

Justice Rehnquist has contributed numerous articles on legal subjects to various periodicals.

The subject, "Power: Its Nature, Its Use and Its Limits" is both provocative and wide ranging. I realize that during the course of the series you have already heard from distinguished persons in a variety of fields, and will have the opportunity to hear from others in future lectures. While I feel fortunate in having carved out a much smaller topic, "The Nature and Exercise of Judicial Power," from this huge area, even my own more limited subject is one that could be explored in depth and at length in many different ways.

I shall endeavor to show in these remarks to you that there are at least two ways in which judicial power differs from other kinds of governmental power exercised in a constitutional democracy such as ours. I will then go on to indicate to you how each of these two peculiar aspects of judicial power both serve a useful purpose but at the same time are subject to abuse, a virtue and a vice that they share with virtually any governmental power. The final portion of my remarks will touch upon existing checks against the potentials for abuse of judicial power, which it seems to me during our history have prevented it from getting out of hand.

Perhaps the best way to illustrate the first of these differences between judicial power and other kinds of power is to recall for you the ofttold story about the argument between the bishop and the judge as to whom was the more powerful. The judge began the argument by saying that he was the more powerful, because he could say to a criminal defendant before him, "You be hanged." The bishop responded: "Ah, but I can say to a man, 'You be damned.' " But the judge had the last word; he pithily rejoined, "Yes, but when I say you be hanged, you *are* hanged."

Under recent decisions of the Supreme Court of the United States, the sentencing judge is no longer free as he once was to say, "You be hanged," but the story rather dramatically and appropriately illustrates the first one of two significant differences between judicial power and other forms of power. Judicial power, whether it be in the form of a sentence imposed upon a criminal defendant, a judgment for money damages in a personal injury lawsuit, or in any of the many forms it may take, acts directly on a particular individual or individuals. When the governor or the president proposes laws, or when the state legislature or the Congress enacts laws, they lay down rules that say in effect that certain consequences will be visited upon persons who do certain things. But the president, the governor, the legislators, and the members of Congress do not have before them any particular individual who has in fact done the things that the law they enact outlaws; instead, they are laying down general rules to applied in the future.

And it is this future application that is done by judges after having heard evidence or arguments on the law in particular lawsuits involving real, live litigants, Obviously, no system of government based upon an established rule of law could function without some institution to apply the law in individual cases, and it is that function that the judiciary serves in most systems of government. I think you will see, upon reflection, that generally speaking it is both a more limited power than that exercised by executives and legislative bodies, and at the same time is a more awesome and instantaneous sort of power. It is limited because the judge is bound by the rules that the legislature has laid down, unless he concludes that these rules or laws are in violation of some constitutional provision adopted by the people. If the legislature has said that a claim for damages resulting from a traffic accident must be filed in court within two years after the date of the accident, the judge is not free to change the two-year limit to a three-year limit. If the legislature has said that the maximum sentence that shall be imposed for armed robbery is twenty years, the judge is not free to impose a sentence of forty years.

But as I have indicated, even though judicial power is thus limited, it is also an awesome sort of poewr because it acts directly on a particular individual. The president and the governor, the congress and the legislature, when they are contemplating the passage of a law, do not have standing before them any particular individual whom they know will be hauled into court as a result of its enactment. They are aiming only at some generalized evil or problem, and leave it to the courts to determine on the basis of evidence presented in a lawsuit whether a particular individual may or many not have violated the law. The judge, on the other hand, deals with no such generalized abstraction; in a criminal cause he may have before him a defendant who has been found guilty by a jury, or whom he himself finds guilty in a bench trial, for whom he may entertain the greatest sympathy and compassion. Yet the law may require him to impose some form of punishment notwithstanding these feelings. Or a judge may determine that an automobile driver has negligently injured a pedestrian, and may award hundreds of thousands of dollars to the pedestrian; or the judge may decide that the pedestrian shall recover nothing because the driver was not at fault. In any of these cases, the judge's determination has an immediate and dramatic effect on the individuals before him. The criminal defendant goes to jail or goes free, depending on how the judge decides his case. The pedestrian receives several hundred thousand dollars, or receives nothing, again depending on how the judge decides his case.

I do not claim to be acquainted with the judicial systems of all the states in the Union, but I do know that in most of them, and in the federal court system as well, the trial of a lawsuit is presided over by a single judge. He or she decides the case at that level, decides whether a criminal defendant is guilty or not guilty, whether a civil defendant shall or shall not pay damages, subject only to the right of appeal to a higher court. It scarcely requires emphasis that this sort of power is capable of being abused, and most lawyers who have practiced for any length of time can tell you more than one story about a judge before whom they have practiced who has fallen victim to the ever present temptation to abuse judicial power. We tend to think of the trial courts as being the lowest rung of the ladder, because their decisions may be appealed to higher courts. But this is only partially so; in a sense the trial judge is a good deal more powerful than the appellate judge simply because the trial judge is a single individual, whereas most appeals courts consist of several judges—three, five, seven, or nine—as the case may be, and no one individual member of such a court may impose his judgment on the litigants without obtaining agreement of a majority of the other members of the court. But the trial judge acts alone; for the moment, at the time of sentencing, judgment or verdict, he is the sole arbiter of the dispute before him, and all of the parties are well aware of this fact. this can lead to arbitrariness on the part of the judge and to an excessively deferential manner on the part of the people who appear before him.

Let me turn now to the second of the two significant differences that I see between judicial and other forms of power in a country such as ours. That difference is this: Within the tripartite federal system, and to a lesser extent within the governmental structure of most of the fifty states, the judiciary is independent not merely of the executive and of the legislative branches, but in the short run it is independent of the popular will. In states where judges are elected to office, this general statement is obviously less true than it is with respect to the federal system, where judges are appointed to office by the president and have, for all practical purposes, life tenure. But while no one can be intimately acquainted with the history of judicial elections in even a majority of the states that elect their judges, and I am really acquainted with the broad outlines of that history only in one state, I think it fair to say as a matter of common knowledge that it is a rare judge who, running for office, campaigns on a platform of the same type as a candidate for governor or for the legislature would. The judicial office simply does not lend itself to this sort of a campaign, and virtually any conscientious judge would, I should think, shy away from it.

I do not think I overstate the case, then, when I say that there is a distinct antidemocratic element in the role of the judiciary, and in the exercise of the judicial power, which at first blush seems out of place in a democracy such as ours. Taking the federal system as an example, a judge who has never been elected to any sort of office by the people may, as a result of his particular case, declare unconstitutional a law that has been duly enacted by both the House of Representatives and the United States Senate, and signed by the president. It is obviously unnecessary for me to remind you that each member of the House of Representatives is elected by the qualified voters in his district at two-year intervals, each member of the United States Senate is elected by the qualified voters of his state at six-year intervals, and the president of the United States in fact if not in form is elected by the qualified voters of the United states at four-year intervals. Why should the federal judiciary, headed as it is by nine *non*elected members of the Supreme Court of the United States, be able to thwart the combined will of the popularly elected legislative and judicial branches?

There are undoubtedly antidemocratic aspects to this power of the courts to declare laws unconstitutional, a power which lawyers and students of government describe by the shorthand phrase "judicial review." But the existence of such a power is more readily understandable when we remember that ours is not merely a democracy, but a *constitutional* democracy. I cannot possibly improve upon Chief Justice John Marshall's justification for the existence of the power of judicial review, which he wrote in his famous opinion for the Supreme Court of the United States in the case of *Marbury* v. *Madison*.

The ultimate source of authority in this nation, Marshall said, is not Congress, not the states, not for that matter the Supreme Court of the United States. The people are the ultimate source of authority; they have parceled out the authority that originally resided entirely with them by adopting the original Constitution and later amending it. They have granted some authority to the federal government and have reserved authority not granted it to the states or to the people individually. As between the branches of the federal government, the people have given certain authority to the president, certain authority to Congress, and certain authority to the federal judiciary. In the Bill of Rights they have erected protections for specified individual rights against the actions of the federal government. From today's perspective we might add that they have placed restrictions on the authority of the state governments in the Thirteenth, Fourteenth, and Fifteenth Amendments.

In additon, Marshall said that if the popular branches of government—state legislatures, the Congress, and the presidency—are operating within the authority granted to them by the Constitution, their judgment and not that of the Court must obviously prevail. when these branches overstep the authority given them by the Constitution, in the case of the president and the Congress, or invade protected individual rights, and a constitutional challenge to their action is raised in a lawsuit brought in federal court, the Court must prefer the Constitution to the government acts.

John Marshall's justification for judicial review makes the provision for an independent federal judiciary not only understandable but also thoroughly desirable. Since the judges will be merely interpeting an instrument framed by the people, they should be detached and objective. A mere change in public opinion since the adoption of the Constitution, unaccompanied by a constitutional amendment, should not change the meaning of the Constitution. A merely temporary majoritarian groundswell should not abrogate some individual liberty protected by the Constitution.

Marshall was writing at a time when the governing generation remembered well not only the deliberations of the framers of the Constitution at Philadelphia in the summer of 1787, but also the debates over the ratification of the Constitution in the thirteen colonies. The often heated discussions that took place from 1787, when Delaware become the first state to ratify the Constitution, until 1790, when recalcitrant Rhode Island finally joined the Union, were themselves far more representative of the give-and-take of public decision-making by a constituent assembly than is the ordinary enactment of a law by Congress or by a state legislature. Patrick Henry had done all he could to block ratification in Virginia, and the opposition of the Clinton faction in New York and provoked Jay, Hamilton, and Madison to their brilliant effort in defense of the Constitution, the *Federalist Papers*. For Marshall, writing the *Marbury* v. *Madison* opinion in 1803, the memory of the debates in which the people of the thirteen colonies had participated only a few years before could well have fortified his conviction that the Constitution was, not merely in theory but in fact as well, a fundamental charter that had emanated from the people.

The difficulties that have arisen in connection with the antidemocratic aspects of judicial review have come after Marshall's time. Today our Union consists of fifty states, many of which by themselves have populations larger than the entire United States of America did 1789. While the franchise has been substantially broadened so that very likely a higher percentage of the adult population participates in the election of public officials, the public officials tend to have larger constituencies and to be more remote from any individual citizen. Thus not only the process by which ordinary government in accordance with the wishes of the majority is carried on, but the process by which Constitutional amendments that may subject that governmental authority to limitation, become more remote from the individual citizen. The Fourteenth Amendment, ratified as one of the three Constitutional amendments shortly after the Civil War, provides that no state shall deprive any peson of life, liberty, or property without due process of law, and prohibits any state from denying to any person the equal protection of the laws. What Justice Jackson of the Supreme Court referred to as the "majestic generalities" of this amendment have been a source of constant concern to the judiciary since its enactment. From what I understand of its legislative history, it was directed in part against the so-called black codes, which had been enacted

The Limits of Power 183

by the recently seceded southern states after the Civil War, in order to deny to the newly freed slaves many of the privileges of citizenship that whites had traditionally enjoyed. But because the language that I have just quoted from the amendment was cast in such broad terms, the question with which the courts have had to wrestle in the ensuing one hundred and ten years is just how much more did the framers of the Fourteenth Amendment mean than to prohibit the southern states from having black codes.

Human nature being what it is, every judge is subject to the temptation, in deciding what the Constitution means, to incorporate in that document his own views of what limits there ought to be on the authority of the legislative and the executive branches of government. The one hundred and ten year history of the construction of the Fourteenth Amendment to the United States Constitution by the Supreme Court of the United States is not by any means a straight line between two points, but rather is like the trail left by a snake on soft ground—a rough and imprecise sine curve. Sometimes the Court has assertively insisted on a broad construction of some of the vague language in the Fourteenth Amendment; at other times it has retreated in the face of criticism, scholarly or otherwise, to allow more latitude to the popularly elected branches.

Ignoring the more debatable and the more recent eras of so-called activism, with respect to which it is impossible to say that history has yet rendered a verdict, I would like to advert for a moment to the "freedom of contract" doctrine that the Supreme Court of the United States espoused during the first third of this century. For in this particular history of judicial construction of the Fourteenth Amendment, I think we can say that there has been a verdict of history rendered, and that it has found the Court guilty of assumption of power that it was not intended to have. The Court's entrance into this era began shortly after the turn of the century in a case *Lochner* v. *New York*.

The very last part of the nineteenth century and the beginning of this century saw a wave of reform legislation in the United States. Shortly after the Civil War, there had come the Granger movement, in which the farmers in the Midwest and West organized to make their voices heard in Washington and in the capitals of their respective states. Then came the Greenback movement, in which debtor classes generally sought relief form the burdens of their debts, and from legal systems that they felt favored the well-to-do, through reform legislation on the state and national levels. Many of the proposals of these earlier groups were absorbed in the populist movement of the 1890s, and the adherents of that movement had enough voice in the Democratic convention of 1896 to succeed in nominating William Jennings Bryan as the Democratic candidate for the presidency. Bryan was defeated by the Republican nominee, William McKinley, but the reform legislation that he championed on a national level, and that other adherents of his views urged on a state level, were enacted to a greater or lesser extent during the succeeding twenty years. Antimonopoly laws, laws regulating safety conditions and hazardous industries, laws establishing maximum hours and prohibiting child labor, laws providing workman's compensation for those injured in the course of their employment, all made their appearance on the scene.

As might be expected, business enterprises that were the targets of this legislation vigorously opposed the enactment of much of it, and when they failed, as they usually did, in Congress and the state legislatures, they turned to the courts for relief. They urged upon the courts the doctrine that the United States Constitution, and particularly the Fourteenth Amendment, forbade government from interfering with the contracts negotiated between employer and employee unless some special circumstances were present.

The business groups that carried on this assault against the reform legislation of this era could claim the support of very prominent and articulate political philosphers, particularly Herbert Spencer in England and William Graham Sumner in this country. Their philosophy was loosely characterized as "social Darwinism," and may be even more loosely summarized as being based on the principle that the long-run interests of the world and the nation are served if the government keeps it hands off the business relationships, which are entered into for the purpose of getting the world's work done. The long-run interest of society is in the survival of the fittest, and this can best be accomplished by seeing who in fact does survive in the hurly-burly of free enterprise laissez-faire competition.

The case of *Lochner* v. *New York* is a household word to those who have studied constitutional law, and it is one of the handful of cases in which a dissenting opinion has been overwhelmingly vindicated by the passage of time. In *Lochner,* a New York law that limited to ten the maximum number of hours per day that could be worked by bakery employees was assailed on the ground that it deprived the bakery employer of liberty without due process of law. A majority of the Court held the New York maximum hour law unconstitutional, saying, "Statutes of the nature of that under review, limiting the hours in which grown and intelligent men may labor to earn their living, are mere meddlesome interferences with the rights of the individual. . . ."

The Fourteenth Amendment, of course, said nothing about any freedom to make contracts upon terms that one thought best, but there was a very substantial body of opinion outside the Constitution at the time of *Lochner* that subscribed to the general philosophy of social Darwinism as embodied in the writing of Herbert Spencer in England and William Graham Sumner in this country. It may have occurred to some of the Justices who made up a majority in *Lochner,* hopefully subconsciously rather than consciously, that since the language in the due process clause was sufficiently general not to rule out its inclusion, why not strike a blow for the clause? The answer, which has been vindicated by time, came in the dissent of Mr. Justice Holmes:

> [A] constitution is not intended to embody a particular
> economic theory, whether of paternalism and the organic
> relation of the citizen to the state or of *laissez faire.* It is
> made for people of fundamentally different views, and the
> accident of our finding certain opinions natural and familiar
> or novel and even shocking ought not to conclude our
> judgement upon the question whether statutes embodying
> them conflict with the Constitution of the United States.

I hope that by now the two aspects of the existence and exercise of judicial power that distinguish it from other kinds of governmental power in this country—first, the fact that it is a power exercised directly on individuals, and, second, that it is a power that is in many respects immune from direct popular control—both render this sort of power subject to abuse. But the fact that judicial power is subject to abuse is not only no reason for its abolition, but is no real argument for significantly changing it, unless we should upon examination decide that the abuse or the potential abuses are so severe as to be beyond any practical remedy that we may devise. I do not believe this is the case.

The danger stemming from the fact that judicial power acts directly on individuals is that it will be exercised arbitrarily, by the occasional judge who is not faithful to his office and who becomes, as the saying goes, "A little tin god." Most judges who try cases, find defendents guilty or not guilty, preside over jury trials, and impose sentences, sit by themselves; that it, they are not required to persuade any other judge to agree with them in order to render a judgment. The great majority are capable, conscientious public servants; a few are not. There are, however, protections against arbitrariness that may result from judgment of these later few. A person accused of crime may demand this right to be tried by a jury of his peers, and while the judge will preside over that trial, it is not he who actually weighs the evidence in order to make the finding of guilty or not guilty. The trial judge is also subject to having his actions reviewed on appeal by a higher court, almost invariably composed of several judges, who have the authority to reverse his judgment if they find that he acted arbitrarily or incorrectly under the law.

These checks on the authority of the trial judge are not, unfortunately, an invariable guarantee of fairness or consistency. More and more attention has recently been focused on the problem of disparity in sentencing within the federal courts, at least, and much concern has been expressed about how two criminal defendants, each found guilty of the same crime by a jury, and with much the same factors in their backgrounds, will received widely differing sentences from two different judges. It is not a question of establishing that one sentence is too harsh, or that one sentence is too lenient; the common ground is that both sentences should roughly approximate one another. But by virtue of the focus of public and professional opinion on this question, by the conducting of sentencing institutes, in which trial judges exchange experiences and recommendations, and by experimentation with more formalized procedures for obtaining outside opinion as to the propriety of sentencing, there seems to me considerable hope that this cause for complaint against judicial arbitrariness may be greatly reduced in the future.

The abuse to which the exercise of judicial authority to declare laws unconstitutional is subject by reason of its antidemocratic aspect is more difficult to check, because we run the risk of throwing out the baby with the bath water. If certain rights established in a written Constitution were intended to be beyond encroachment by the Congress and by the president, unless the Constitution were amended by the prescribed extraordinary majorities, the mere fact that the majority of Congress or that the majority of the country is unhappy with the result reached by the Supreme Court in a particular constitutional decision does not mean that the decision is necessarily wrong. The Court in a very real sense exists to protect claims of constitutional rights on the part of those who are currently unpopular in the eyes of the general public. If we are to have judicial review, the only principled basis for criticism of its exercise or for showing it abused, is to show to the satisfaction of objective critics that the Court's decisions are not really antidemocratic. As I have indicated earlier, I think that the course upon which the Court embarked in the first third of the century was ultimately proved to be wrong in that sense, but it probably takes a generation after the damage is done to be certain that the charge has been proven. So while professional scholarship and criticism undoubtedly plays a part in preventing abuses of the power of judical review confided to constitutional courts, it is a rather weak reed standing by itself. There is also the right to amend the Constitution, provided for in that instrument itself; but because of the cumbersome nature of the amendment process, that right, too, is not invariably a reliable check upon what critics refer to as "judicial usurpation."

But probably the most important check on the antidemocratic aspects of judicial review—the power of judges to declare laws enacted by representatives of the majority of the people unconstitutional—is the nature of the process of judicial selection. Since this process varies among all the fifty states, I will use as my example the method of selection of the federal judiciary, which is the least subject to popular will of any that I know. And yet the federal system itself is not immune from some political or popular input into the appointment process. Most of you doubtless know the manner by which the constitution prescribes that federal judges, including Justices of the Supreme Court, shall be selected: They are nominated by the president, and confirmed by the United States Senate. Once confirmed, as I have previously indicated, federal judges have what for practical purposes amounts to life tenure; they cannot be removed from office simply because a majority of the voting public may disagree with their decisions. But judges, like other mortals, grow old and either retire or die in office. Presidents do not always believe this. [Jefferson remarked about judges—few die and none resign.] Upon the occurrence of a vacancy in the Supreme Court of the United States resulting from death or retirement, the president is empowered to nominate a successor Justice, subject to the requirement that the nominee be confirmed by the Senate. At various periods of time in the history of the Supreme Court of the United States, its decisions have created sufficient controversy that presidents during their campaign for election have been led to criticize the Court. Abraham Lincoln did so in his campaign for the presidency in 1860, shortly after the Court had handed down its decision in the *Dred Scott* case. Theodore Roosevelt in 1912 and Richard Nixon in 1968 likewise criticized then recent decisions of the Court. If a president who has criticized the Court for its doctrinal trend has an opportunity to fill a vacancy in its membership, he may nominate a person whom he believes would not be in sympathy with that doctrinal trend. That nominee, of course, is subject to confirmation by the Senate, and the Senate, too, has especially in recent years exercised its prerogative to inquire into the views of the nominee with the idea of trying to ascertain how he might perform once he were confirmed as a member of the Court.

Each of these aspects of the appointment process—the nomination by the president in the first instance, and the requirement of Senate confirmation after nomination, gives some sort of indirect popular input into the process of judicial selection. It seems to me that the Founding Fathers struck a very good balance in this regard. Once a person becomes a Justice of the Supreme Court, or a judge of one of the other federal courts, he should be immune to public pressure to decide a particular case in a particular way, and to this end he is given life tenure. But when it comes to choosing a person to occupy the judicial seat in the first instance, the initial nomination is made by a popularly elected president, and subject to confirmation by a Senate that consists of one hundred members popularly elected from the fifty states of the Union. While it is thus possible for the Court in the short run to be out of harmony with the majority view as to the meaning of the Constitution, as was undoubtedly the case when the Supreme Court decided the *Dred Scott* case in 1857, in the long run a Court persisting in what the majority of the public regards as misguided interpretations of the Constitution will become such a center of controversy that the popular feeling reflected in the election of the president and of the Senators will eventually result in Justice of a different view occupying seats on the Court that have become vacant as a result of death or retirement.

With this check on the antidemocratic aspect of the power of the courts to declare laws unconstitutional, and with the right of appeal to a higher court and the authority of the legislature to change the law standing as checks on possible arbitrariness on the part of an individual judge, I think it is safe to say that the system of checks and balances with respect to judicial power has, in general, worked. We have an independent judiciary that serves two vital purposes in any constitutional democracy; first, it prevents a particular lawsuit in which an unpopular person or group may be involved from being decided on the basis of uninformed public opinion, rather than on the basis of evidence properly presented to a court in accordance with legal rules. Second, it assures that judges independent of the power of political removal will be able to decide whether or not laws enacted by Congress measure up to the standards of the Constitution, which was itself adopted by the people. While each of these vital functions is subject to abuse, there are adequate existing safeguards in our system to prevent the danger of abuse from being more costly than would be a judicial system that was wholly subservient to the executive and legislative branches of the government. In short, the nature and exercise of judicial power in this country, while spotty at some times in our history and demonstrably abused in particular cases, is, I think, both soundly and adequately checked and balanced in our constitutional system.

Copyright © 1979 by William Rehnquist.

John R. Silber

The Conceptual Structure of Power—a Review

John R. Silber was appointed the seventh president of Boston University on December 17, 1970. Dr. Silber, born in San Antonio, Texas, in 1926, is a distinguished scholar, philosopher, and administrator. At the time of his appointment, he was University Professor of Arts and Letters, professor of Philosphy, and former dean of the College of Arts and Sciences at the University of Texas at Austin.

Dr. Silber has long concerned himself with the extension of equal opportunity through higher education, and is a leading national spokesman on the problems of financing higher education, in the state sector as well as the independent sector. He has proposed a comprehensive plan for the financing of higher education, called the Tuition Advance Fund, that would make equal educational opportunity—including both access *and* choice—*available to every qualified student. The Tuition Advance Fund concept is described in his article, "The Tuition Dilemma," in the July 1978* Atlantic. *Legislation to enact Dr. Silber's Tuition Advance Fund proposal has been introduced in Congress.*

Dr. Silber received a B.A. degree summa cum laude *from Trinity University, San Antonio, Texas, in 1947, where he majored in philosophy and fine arts. He received an M.A. degree in 1952 and a Ph.D. in 1956 from Yale University. Dr. Silber also attended Northwestern University, where he studied music; Yale Divinity School; and the Law School of the University of Texas. He holds the honorary degree, Doctor of Humane Letters, from Kalamazoo College and the University of Evansville; and the Doctor of Laws from Maryville College, College of St. Scholastica, and Colorado College.*

As a teacher, Dr. Silber has won several major awards, including the Morris Ernst Award for Excellence in Teaching and the Danforth Foundation's E. Harris Harbison Award for Distinguished Teaching. He is an internationally recognized authority on the philosophy of Immanuel Kant and the philosophy of law.

Dr. Silber held a Fulbright Research Grant to Germany in 1959-60, during which time he was a visiting professor at the University of Bonn. In 1963-64, he was the recipient of a Guggenheim Research Grant for study in England, where he was a Fellow of King's College, the University of London. He is an associate editor of Kant-Studien, *and former chairman of the Texas Society to Abolish Capital Punishment.*

Dr. Silber has lectured at colleges and universities and before civic oranizations throughout the United States and Europe. He has served as a member of the board of the National Humanities Faculty and is now a member of the executive board of the National Humanities Institute. He has served as a consultant for foundations and educational institutions, including the Danforth Foundation, the Ford Foundation, M.I.T., The National Endowment for the Arts and the Humanities, and the Office of Equal Opportunity. He is a member of the Board of Trustees of the College of St. Scholastica in Duluth, Minnesota, and a member of the Board of Visitors of Air University.

I have been asked to conclude this series on the nature, use and limits of power, and especially to discuss power in the context of higher education. As I have read some of the earlier contributions to this series, I have come to appreciate the complexity of the subject.

I have also noted with some concern the implicit subjectivity that has characterized several of the lectures. More than one speaker has chosen to discuss power not in terms of its nature and its various manifestations, but rather in terms of what the speaker individually has chosen to mean by power. Thus, Professor Reich, for example, says, "Power means to me pretty much the same as freedom." Or, "So, in a way, in a large sense, by power I mean individual intelligence." Or, "Force to me means the negation of power." One might as well say that money is the negation of wealth. This is an example of the greening logic.

This methodology suggests that power can be discussed on whatever terms one wishes to discuss it, that power is not a subject whose independent nature and structure we must respect and try to understand, observe, and delineate with great care and with maximum precision. Rather, power is seen to mean whatever the individual discussing it wants it to mean, and in discussing power we are free from all rational and empirical restraints. That is: Humpty Dumpty was right. Humpty Dumpty's position reflects the dominant relativism of our time. Hand in hand with a highly subjective individualism, it now approaches the limiting condition, namely solipsism.

In this lecture I wish to resist such tendencies. I am not here to tell you what power means to me, or how I feel about power, or merely what power means to males five feet eight in height with brown hair, blue eyes, and a crooked nose. I want to discuss not myself, but power; and with the maximum objectivity. What I say will, of course, be my own personal opinion. But if what I say about power is supported by careful argument and substantial evidence, it will be much more than that. My view will lay claim to your minds and to your rational assent. It will be an objective discussion of power that, if it is adequate, will be true, or at least as true as I can make it and true enough for the evening, unless one of you tonight can discern a flaw in my evidence or argument and thereby refute my position.

Those of you who have read Plato will recognize that the position I take is essentially a Socratic one. I do not pretend to know the truth on this subject, but I shall offer what I consider the likeliest account. We should not waste time discussing the nature of power if all we do is to exchange our prejudices on the subject. You feel that it is freedom; I feel that it is force. You believe that I have it; I think I don't. Such discourse is nothing more than sound and fury and signifies exactly what Shakespeare said it does—nothing.

Power in practice may be ephemeral, lasting one day or less, but the concept of power is not ephemeral. Power may be mysterious, but there is nothing mysterious about the concept of power. The concept of power can be understood. Etymologically it comes from the Romans, through the Latin verb *potere*, which came to England after the Norman Conquest. The central meaning of *potere* is to be able. Power is the ability to affect something or to be affected by something.

If the concept is confusing it is not because its meaning is obscure or contradictory, but because its meaning is so fundamental that it is highly abstract, and thus can take on an almost infinite range of concrete meanings. There is a healing power, the power of the crown, the power of logic, economic power, divine power, the power of the state, tyrannical power, the power of grace, the power of pleasing, the power even of beauty, legislative power, executive power, the power of law, the power of the senses, the power of language, the power of harmony, the power of positive thinking, and nuclear power.

Macaulay spoke of "that power which erring men call chance." And Wordsworth wrote of visionary power:

> . . . imagination, which, in truth,
> Is but another name for absolute power
> And clearest insight, amplitude of mind
> And reason in her most exalted mood.

The richness and scope of this concept compels us, as 2,400 years ago it compelled Plato, to conclude that power is being, and anything that *is* has power. Plato argued in the *Sophist* that: "Anything which possesses any sort of power to affect another or to be affected by another, if only for a single moment, however trifling the cause and however slight the effect, has real existence. And I hold that the definition of being is simply power."

Once one recognizes that being is power, and that power is being, he will recognize that there is no such thing as either the all powerful—unless it be God and the entire universe taken together—or the powerless, for that which is totally without power either to affect or to be affected cannot exist.

Understood in its ultimate philosophical meaning, power is being, the ability to affect or to be affected by anything. It includes any and all forms of ability, capability, and susceptibility. It includes not merely the power to kill, but the power to be killed. The power to hurt depends upon the power to be hurt, the power to inflict pain upon the power to feel pain, the power to speak upon the power to hear, the power to move by speaking on the power to be moved by speech. The tiniest amoeba has the power to ingest and divide in the course of its own individual life history, and through dysentery to end the life of Alexander the Great. The match between David and Goliath, as a matter of fact, was nothing compared to that between the amoeba and Alexander.

If we recognize this root meaning of power, and that power in this ultimate sense informs every particular use of the concept, we are far less likely to lose our footing as we examine the various applications of this concept. Power in its ontological meaning is good. That is, to the extent that power is being and being is good, there can be no power that is not in that sense good, and the more power the more being. This explains in part the attraction of power. It grows with fulfillment. Put theologically, in creation God shared His own power by extending it, or created more power by creating new being.

Why then does power have such a bad reputation? Not because power is evil in itself. The evil of power consists not in its being, but in the way that it is used. For there is nothing positive about evil, unless someone has a refutation for Augustine's proof that evil is privative. Augustine argued that evil is a falling away from something good. That is, it is a privation. Augustine asked, in the *Enchiridion*

> For what is that which we call evil but the absence of good? In the bodies of animals, disease and wounds mean nothing but the absence of health; for when a cure is effected, that does not mean that the evils which were present—namely, the

> diseases and wounds—go away from the body and dwell elsewhere: they altogether cease to exist; for the wound or disease is not a substance but a defect in the fleshly substance—the flesh itself being a substance, and therefore something good, of which those evils—that is, privations of the good which we call health—are accidents. Just in the same way, what are called vices in the soul are nothing but privations of natural good. And when they are cured, they are not transferred elsewhere: when they cease to exist in the healthy soul, they cannot exist anywhere else.

In philosophical discussion it is important not to spend too much time trying to invent the wheel. It has become so popular and so commonplace to speak of the lack of progress in the humanities that we often feel justified in ignoring the history of the humanities. But as a matter of fact, substantial progress has been made in the history of philosophy. Plato assured us that we would no more identify power with right than argue that the earth is at the center of the universe. Either view is now rightly regarded as nonsense. We are no more justified in ignoring the history of philosophy than in ignoring the history of science. Yet it is a fact that philosophers are free to ignore the history of their subject in a way that physicists are not. Nature has a way of calling the careless physicist to account, while the poor Owl of Minerva is, as Hegel remarked, a lethargic bird, blind by day and rarely noticed in its evening flights.

But in a sense all education involves the reinvention of the wheel for each student. Each student is born just as savage and just as primitive as the Cro-Magnon man, and it is civilization, not biology, that makes the difference. As Hobbes correctly observed, "Man is made fit for society not by nature but by education."

When we recognize that power is the ability to affect or to be affected we shall be able to recognize the family resemblances of power in its many forms, including the concept of force and the concept of authority.

With this general background in mind, let us move closer to the aspect of power that is our primary concern. If we bear in mind the central meaning of power as the ability to affect anything or to be affected by anything, it will be easier to examine this rich concept in more limited contexts. Power may take a purely physical form, as in the stable physical reactions of the sun or a volcanic eruption or the movement of bodies in the solar system or the driving of a steam engine or the firing of a gun. In each of these examples power is essentially physical. It is force of varying intensity. Energy—that is, being as dynamic—is focused and organized in different ways to produce different effects.

When power is simply physical we may prefer to call it force. But the English language does not in common usage restrict force to this meaning. And even if it did, we should want to differentiate between various kinds of force, for the level of organization involved in atomic reactions is quite different from what we find in living nature. And as soon as we encounter living creatures who are also sentient we find still different levels of physical organization, and we have difficulty in determining whether the functioning of such organisms is physical or mental or a mixture of the two. Indeed, we begin to wonder in the case of creatures such as man if mind-body is not the proper way of discussing the entire human organism. Monistic explanations in terms of either body or mind are for the most part inadequate in accounting for human experience. And yet there are difficulties with the dualistic accounts of mind and body, for the problem of interaction is left inadequately explained.

But just as power can express itself physically in the eruption of a volcano it can express itself in purely rational and nonphysical terms as in the power of an argument, in the power of language and poetry, in the power of music. In logic A implies B. A; and therefore we conclude B. This sequence of thought reveals a necessary movement and that necessity is a nonphysical manifestation of power. It is the power of logic or the force of argument. It depends for its power on understanding, on comprehension. If a child argues that two plus two is not four but is five, one cannot refute the child by striking him. As Johnson remarked, "the power to punish is to silence, not to confute." Between these extremes of power as a purely physical force and as a power of argument there is a continuum of varying degrees of rationality and sheer physical force.

The attractiveness of a beautiful piece of music is obviously dependent upon the consciousness of the hearer and not merely upon the phsycial vibrations that are made by a musician. A beautiful human figure exerts a power not explained merely in terms of biology. It is, rather, that the beholder on seeing the object is attracted to it or finds aesthetic enjoyment in its contemplation. The beautiful object is, though finite, an unmoved mover. Thus Dryden says, "Old as I am for ladies' love unfit,/The power of beauty I remember yet." Most students may be too young to appreciate fully the poignancy of that passage.

On this continuum between physical force and pure rational necessity we can locate all forms and instances of power. The nature, use, and limits of power will vary depending upon the kinds of objects, things, persons or institutions in which it is present and over which it has influence. Power expressed in planetary space and on planets void of life will be essentially different from power as expressed among biological orders on the planet Earth.

Physical power will vary in its quality, limits, and use depending on whether it is applied to animals or to men, and by what it is applied. An animal or a man may be frightened or even killed by a volcano. So far as the disintegration of living tissue is concerned, the direct physical power of a volcano as applied to animal or man is essentially the same. But in the apprehension of the threat of a volcano, man and animal differ enormously, and hence the effect of a volcano on human beings is substantially different from its effect on animals.

Its effect is further differentiated by the intelligence or educational level of the human individual. A scientist who is expert in volcanoes can scarcely experience the terror of the residents of ancient Pompeii. And the adults at Pompeii, terrified as they must have been when Vesuvius erupted, would not have suffered the blind terror of the young child. Physical power, then, is not simple, undifferentiated force, but is modulated by the context in which it is experienced, and by the nature of the object that is affected by it. If it is exercised over human beings its power is, in part, a function of the power of the individual who is affected by it, and hence it is partly nonphysical, or mental.

It is especially this area—the exercise of power over human beings—that is, I believe, the central focus of concern in this series of lectures. It will be to this area that I devote my remaining remarks.

Power over human beings cannot be understood in terms of the tripartite analysis offered by Bertrand Russell in his book, *Power,* which I hope many of you have read. There Bertrand Russell says that power may be classified both by the manner of influencing individuals, or by the type of organization involved.

> An individual may be influenced: A. By direct physical power over his body, e.g. when he is imprisoned or killed; B. By rewards and punishments as inducements, e.g. in giving or withholding employment; C. By influence on opinion, i.e. propaganda in its broadest sense.

> These forms of power are most nakedly and simply displayed in dealings with animals, where disguises and pretenses are not thought necessary. When a pig with a rope round its middle is hoisted squealing into a ship, it is subject to direct physical power over his body. On the other hand, when the proverbial donkey follows the proverbial carrot, we induce him to act as we wish by persuading him that it is to his interest to do so. Intermediate between these two cases is that of performing animals, in whom habits have been formed by rewards and punishments; also, in a different way, that of sheep induced

to embark on a ship, when the leader has to be dragged across the gangway by force, and the rest then follow willingly.

All these forms of power are exemplified among human beings.

The case of the pig illustrates military and police power. The donkey with the carrot typifies the power of propaganda. Performing animals show the power of education.

Let us examine this classification. None of the examples with animals will explain the nature of power in the context of human society, certainly not military and police power. Loading the pigs aboard ship, we have an example of almost pure physical force exerted against the pigs. But it is not merely physical force, for a pig is terrified as a hoisted bale of cotton is not. When a man is hoisted by a bosun's chair from a small boat to a ship in order to confine him in the brig, the power used would be either military or police power, and perhaps both, but it would not be primarily physical. The difference between the terrified pig and the man who knows what is happening to him is not to be underestimated. If a man has committed a crime for which arrest and confinement is a recognized and proper punishment, he is in a very different position from the Kafka character who is transported from one place to another without knowing the rules of the game. If the man is being hoisted not in a bosun's chair, but by the neck to the yardarm, that power employed is still not purely physical.

A variety of human responses are possible to the power over one who is to be executed. Men have gone to the gallows with stoic resignation, confident of their innocence. They have also gone to the gallows with stoic resignation, confident of their guilt. They have gone with courage, with indifference, with fear and trembling, with screaming and thrashing. The power to hang is not the power to affect a human being merely in one way. The person who is hanged justly and who recognizes the appropriateness of the penalty and is aware of the wrongdoing that has brought him to that punishment experiences the power of the law and police power in quite a different manner from one who is brutalized by state power in the manner of a Jew being routed through Auschwitz by a member of the SS.

No one who wishes to discuss power should ignore these differences. We ignore our philosophical classics to our peril. More than 300 years ago, Hobbes distinguished carefully between physical power and political power. The power of the sovereign, whether in military engagement or police activity, is not purely physical. For the power of the sovereign is always affected and compromised by the power of the subject, who has, when he faces sovereign power, a variety of options.

As Warrender, in his excellent *Commentary on the Political Philosophy of Hobbes,* points out, "The possibility of political society is dependent upon most citizens or a critical number of them being prepared to do their duty once they see it, quite apart from the sanctions which the sovereign may be able to exercise against them." No sovereign—no president, no congress, no governor and state legislature, no mayor and city council, no college president and board of trustees—could govern on the basis of mere physical force. The power of the people is beyond the direct physical control of any sovereign, whether at the national, state or local level. In a civilized community, Warrender points out,

> The power that is needed is basically political, for the essential power is to be able to command obedience; it is not to be able to dispose of physical resources. The sovereign, therefore, must acquire *an enhanced capacity* to bring the will of other men into conformity with his own, and this can only be done in a lasting and stable form, through their being put into a position where they regard themselves as having the duty to obey him. (Italics added)

The sovereign must have a kind of power that is properly called authority before he can effectively maintain order and ensure the peace and fulfillment of the subject. As Warrender says, ". . . power only becomes authority when it is authorized by the subject." The sovereign is granted authority by the subject, according to Hobbes, so that the subject may gain protection, the domestic tranquility on which his own personal fulfillment and happiness depend. And once that authority is granted, the sovereign does not lose that authority and the concomitant right to obedience from the subject unless he can no longer give protection. It is when the sovereign loses his ability to protect the subjects who have authorized his sovereignty that the subject, in obedience to natural law, is free either to disobey him or to fight against him and resist him. Once the sovereign has lost that authority he can govern only through terror, and that is never sufficient.

This, incidentally, is the key to the success of present-day terrorists. As Mr. Jenkins pointed out to you, they are essentially theatrical producers. Their production is designed to leave with the people a conviction that the sovereign can no longer protect them. If the German state can no longer protect a wealthy industrialist such as Mr. Hans-Martin Schleyer, how can it protect Wilhelm Schmidt or other ordinary burghers? Terrorists by their actions attempt to convince the public that they have undermined the sovereign authority by destroying the ability of the sovereign to protect his subjects. In fact, as Mr. Jenkins observed, they do not succeed in this, but they succeed in leaving the impression that they have done so. And that impression is so terrifying and so disruptive of civil authority that the sovereign is willing to make extraordinary concessions that could not possibly be based on any rational assessment of the physical threat posed by terrorist groups. Consider the case in which $60 million was paid in ransom for a kidnapping in Argentina. This was why Germany moved resolutely to put down a terrorist group at one airport in Somalia. This also explains why the Israeli government was fully prepared to go to the lengths of a limited war in order to carry out the Entebbe raid successfully and to demonstrate before all the world that the authority of the Israeli government was intact even outside its borders; Israel showed that it had the ability—that is, the power—to protect its citizens even when the government of that foreign country was in alliance with the terrorists.

In this extended analysis of the paradigm of the pig, by which Russell intended to illustrate military and police power, I have shown that power exercised in relation to human subjects is not simply or even primarily physical; that power or force is freighted with ideas and norms and even rules of law, and that its efficacy depends finally not on brute power but rather on authority. Authority in turn depends on the authorization of those who are subject to it, and hence is a power that is constituted and legitimized by those subject to that power. It also depends on the ability of the sovereign—that is, the person or the office exercising the authority in question—to deliver those services for which the authority is granted.

Thus, the terrorist, by putting in question the ability of the sovereign to provide protection to the individual, must be stamped out by the sovereign with either police or military power. Although it is clearly possible that either military or police power can be abused, it is equally clear that there are proper and just uses for this power. But the fact that power can be used either rightly or wrongly clearly exposes the fact that power and right are not synonymous but two equally ultimate and distinct concepts, and that the exercise of power is enhanced when it is in alliance with right.

Our contemporary fascination with terrorism and the sympathy and assistance that law-abiding citizens occasionally provide terrorists is perplexing. What is the appeal of terrorists? There is the appeal of specific causes. For example, Palestinian liberation, no less than Zionism, exercises power over the imagination of many people throughout the world. But how do we account for the support given the Baader-Meinhof gang? In our own country how do we explain the support that was once given the Weathermen and similar groups? There is something in Americans that responds positively to a bank robbery wherever it is carried out, and whether by Patty Hearst, Susan Saxe, or Bonnie and Clyde. "Getting the Establishment" is to many Americans an object worthy in itself. In fact, the power to kill is the most democratic form of power, and it has fascinated and attracted the young for thousands of years. Thus, in Plato's *Gorgias,* we find Socrates discussing the nature of rhetoric with Polus, who claims that orators, who had many of the same functions as prosecuting attorneys in our society, have the greatest power in the country—an assertion that Socrates finds preposterous. "What's this?" asks the young Polus, "Don't they act like tyrants and put to death anyone they please and confiscate property and banish any one they have a mind to?" Socrates answers that "both orators and tyrants have the least possible power in their own countries . . . For they do nothing that they wish to do," but only what they, in the midst of their ignorance, believe is best. Since Socrates holds that tyrants and orators do not know their own best interest, and hence that they cannot do what they truly wish to do, he concludes that they cannot exercise great power. Speaking with all the enthusiasm of youth, Polus says scornfully,

> As though you, Socrates, would not choose to have the power to do what you thought best rather than not have it! Just as though you wouldn't feel envy if you saw another man who had killed anyone he pleased or robbed him or put him in prison! . . . so I suppose you wouldn't like to become a tyrant, Socrates?

Polus is, of course, unimpressed and unpersuaded when Socrates replies, "Certainly not, if you mean by tyrant what I do." Polus answers, "Well, I mean by it what I said just now—the ability to do whatever a man pleases: to kill and banish and do anything according to one's own fancy."

The Socratic refutation of this viewpoint may win the argument without persuading the spirit of our times. In order to persuade Polus, Socrates himself offers a paradigm of what power is according to Polus's definition. Says Socrates,

> Imagine that I am in a crowded marketplace with a dagger concealed under my arm and I say to you, 'Polus, I have just acquired an amazing sort of tyrannic power. If I think that

anyone of these men whom you see here ought to die here this very instant, die he shall. Whomever I choose! And if I think that any of their heads should be bashed in, bashed in it shall be right on the spot! Or if a throat should be slit, slit it shall be! That is the sort of power I hold in this city!' Then, if you didn't believe me and I showed you my dagger, you might look at it and say, 'Why, Socrates, everybody can have that sort of power. In this way you might burn down any house you pleased and even the Athenian dockyards and men-of-war and all the ships, both public and private.' But surely this is not what one means by having great power: to do anything one pleases.

In this exchange with Polus, Socrates refutes once and for all the notion that there is any great power in the mere ability to do what one pleases without regard to what it is one pleases to do. That is, according to Socrates we cannot speak of personal or political power in any meaningful sense in the absence of a moral context, and the only fulfilling exercise of power must be an exercise of power that is also the exercise of justice or right. The man who takes a dagger to the marketplace can wreak havoc in the lives of a few individuals, but he does not distinguish himself from other men by the possession of greater power. He has that quality in terms of which all men are equal—the power to kill! He has the power of Charles Manson, not the power of Gandhi. He has the power of Oswald, not the charisma and charm of Kennedy. He has that power that is guaranteed by the Declaration of Independence when it proclaims that "All men are created equal."

Fourth of July orators generally overlook the one capacity in which all men are equal—their power to kill. But this point of view was not foreign to the drafters of the Declaration of Independence, for they, like all English and American political thinkers since Hobbes, have been thoroughly conversant with Hobbes's ideas. And when Hobbes spoke of the natural equality of man he said,

> For if we look on men full grown, and consider how brittle the frame of our human body is, . . . and how easy a matter it is, even for the weakest man to kill the strongest, there is no reason why any man trusting to his own strength should consider himself made by nature above others: they are equal who can do equal things one against the other; but they who can do the greatest things (namely, kill) can do equal things. All men therefore among themselves are by nature equal.

This is one of the facts that Carolyn Bird seems to have forgotten when she suggested that "powerless people are the only ones who know anything about power. The very idea of power comes from the experience of those on the receiving end of it." As she seems not to have noticed, all human beings have power by virtue of their being—hence none are utterly powerless—and all also experience powerlessness by their impotence in the face of death. All men are equal before the annihilating power of death, not merely by the equality of their neighbors in threatening their lives by their ability to destroy them, but also in virtue of their own power to destroy not merely their neighbors but themselves. As Shakespeare notes,

> But life, being weary of these worldly bars,
> Never lacks the power to dismiss itself . . .

Or, he says again:

> So every bondman in his own hand bears
> The power to cancel his captivity.

It is in this respect of having power to kill and power to be killed and power to kill oneself and others that all men are equal. This is the ability that is distributed with generous evenhandedness by Mother Nature. It is not intelligence nor physical strength, nor musical nor artistic talent, but the simple ability to destroy others or ourselves. On this equal footing we begin.

And even here the equality is only approximate. The proposition holds true for all normal persons, for the average man or woman in the street. But there are those born with birth defects who even lack the ability to destroy, as derisory as this basis for equality may be. Viewed from this standpoint, the power of the individual is seen to depend very largely on the power developed in the individual by a society that will not merely protect him from his equals who are capable of his destruction, but will also assist him positively in the fullest development of his capacities. That is, a society that recognizes the rights of man and is concerned to organize the resources of the society to achieve those rights. All other equalities of man are dependent on life in such a society. Equality before the law can be found only in a society that provides it. Equal educational opportunity, equal access to medical care, are available only to those individuals who live in societies in which these conditions are met. The equality of citizens as it extends beyond their power to kill reflects the rights of citizens as they are developed and enforced by the state.

The state enhances the power of the individual by guaranteeing his rights and by providing the institutional opportunities on which his fulfillment depends. Destroy the state by means of a green romance with anarchy by giving all power to all of the people and the power of the individual will be destroyed along with his rights and along with those institutions on which his self-fulfillment depends. It is an entropic move that leads not to power, but to dissipating that power in a homogeneity indistinguishable from chaos.

Returning to Russell's paradigms, we find that the donkey and the trained animal are no more satisfactory than the pig in explaining the nature of power.

We have already seen that military and police power are not to be understood in terms of pure physical force, but that effective and legitimate power depends upon authority, a kind of power that requires the authorization of those subject to it. That authorization, in turn, is gained not by the stick, since that would reduce authority to mere force and no sovereign is capable of providing that level of force, for the loyalty even of a Praetorian Guard must also depend on the loyalty of its members to the leadership of the commander. But it is quite clear that the authority of the sovereign is won in part by that carrot of security and domestic tranquility and in the well-ordered state the authority of the sovereign is secured also by education in the highest sense of that term. The sovereign may, of course, engage in propaganda, brass bands, and rallies in the manner of a Hitler; but on a much more rational level, the sovereign may also win the support of the governed through the rational explanation of policies and, more ultimately, through the development of a school system that teaches civics in its most philosophical meaning and does not preoccupy itself with the minutiae of governing.

A very large part of the contemporary crisis in American life derives from our having removed from the curriculum of secondary schools virtually all moral and philosophical content. The Federalist Papers, Locke's Treatises on Civil Government, the Declaration of Independence and the Constitution of the United States are conspicuous by their absence. And the dependence of all these documents on Platonic and Aristotelian thought, though profound, has not been recognized adequately in the education of young Americans. Yet steeping young Americans in the philosophical basis of our system of government would do much to expose the nonsense of the idea that anarchy is the best way to organize society.

Contemporary fascination with anarchy has not been limited to the social and political order. It has also extended to the university, where it has become popular to argue that if universities exist in democratic societies they should also be democratic, and that democracy means essentially one man, one vote. But in fact this strand of contemporary

The Limits of Power   203

thought is mistaken with regard both to democracy and to education. No organization, not even a dictatorship of the left or the right, can totally dispense with democracy. The degree of consent and the extent to which the consent is voluntarily given on the basis of the power of argument, of the power of ideas, rather than on the basis of political pressure and military and police force vary substantially. But the consent of the governed to some degree is required for effective government, whether in China, Russia, Hitler's Germany, or in England and the United States. In no country, and certainly not in the most enlightened of democracies, can the doctrine of one man, one vote be interpreted to mean that everyone becomes sovereign and runs the country as he sees fit. The doctrine of one man, one vote is only a pattern for voting. It must be translated for governance through an elective and representative process to majority rule. And majority rule must, in turn, be restrained lest it become the tyranny of the majority.

In Mr. Reich's paper we can see a denial of the principle of representation altogether. The Supreme Court was said to be deficient because it did not have representatives from certain groups in the United States. The absence of any women is of course shocking in a society in which women are in a majority. But the point cannot be generalized without error. In a society as heterogeneous as this, representation in this sense quickly becomes impossible. Would we have the Estonian chair and the Lithuanian chair and the Hungarian chair, in addition to the Jewish chair and the black chair? We quickly see the need of a Sioux Indian chair and an Apache chair and a Navajo chair. If one destroys the meaning of representation by claiming that like can only be represented by like, all government would become impossible.

The notion of representation is dependent upon the idea that one person can understand others. When we assert in solipsistic manner that no one can know anything about anyone else, we have dispensed with the notion of society, because a person who holds that point of view could not know of its existence. In enlightened democracies a constitution or a bill of rights, whether written or unwritten, restrains even the majority in the exercise of their power. The authority of the sovereign is, under ideal circumstances, exercised according to a rule of law that ensures a just use of power. This state of affairs would be impossible in a society in which there were simply majority rule. And, of course, no society could exist under a policy in which one man, one vote meant that each man should rule.

In the context of the university these principles are equally valid. It is not a community in which institutional decisions can be made on the basis of one man, one vote. Neither is it an institution in which authority can be exercised without the consent of the governed. But in the context of the university the consent of the governed is not established by numerical counting in which weight is given each individual equal to the weight given every other individual. Were that the case, students, being the most numerous, would run the university. Or if the determination of policy were limited to paid employees, then the staff would run the university. In a university consent is derived by rational persuasion, but the weight of argument and the weight of analysis must count more than the mere show of hands. And the final arbiters of sound policy within a university should not be those who inherently and inevitably have a conflict of interest, but those who stand beyond the immediate interests and are in a position impartially to judge the soundness of policy without being directly affected by it. That is, in short, the justification for a board of trustees or a board of regents—to determine and endorse basic policy directions within a university.

A policy that is sound, however, must be one that can gain if not the formal consent and the vote, at least the cooperation of most members of the academic community. That cooperation is most genuine and vigorous when the members of that community are persuaded of its soundness. There is no way this persuasion can take place without their involvement in the planning and implementation of university programs. In planning and in implementing programs, however, leadership must come from the most able and qualified to provide it.

The native ability of a university faculty is, comparatively speaking, extraordinarily high, but within any faculty there is a broad range of ability from competent to superb. And in the most effectively run university the ablest faculty should, by the power of their unusually great understanding, sensitivity, artistry, and learning, carry more weight and have more influence than those of lesser abilities and accomplishments. A policy within the university should directly depend on the ability, experience, and accomplishments of its members. But there is also an additional factor that is required in the exercise of authority if it is to be exercised fairly, judiciously, and justly. That factor is responsibility. The more imaginative a person is, the greater the possibility of his acting irresponsibly, for ideas, no matter how bizarre, can be remarkably intriguing and attractive. The projection and development of such ideas, no matter how bizarre they may be, is the proper function of university professors. But the decision with regard to which ideas should be acted upon must be restricted to those who will have to live with the consequences of such action, or at least those who have soberly weighed those consequences in both imagination and in the light of general experience and taken them sufficiently into account.

For example, the faculty member in an individual department or a department chairman may decide on a budgetary policy that could, if adopted, bankrupt the university over a period of a decade. It is the responsibility of the president to reject that policy, for he cannot fulfill his obligations to students, both present and past, and to all members of the staff as well as the faculty, if he allows the institution on which their livelihood or their educational credentials depend to become extinct. I was told once by a faculty member that I should not be so abrasive, I should allow Boston University to go into bankruptcy with dignity. I had to point out that there is no dignity in bankruptcy.

This is not to deny that there might come a time when a tragic choice has to be made, where a president or a board of trustees has to close a school because of inability to provide an academic program of integrity in the context of financial viability. But short of this extreme predicament, the president of a university, despite the votes of deans or faculty, must follow a policy that ensures the financial stability of the institution. The basis of that authority is rational; it is founded on the fact that if the institution does not exist, it cannot follow any particular academic policy, whether the one presently advocated by the faculty or any other.

But we should not limit the discussion of power or authority within the university to questions of finance. With regard to curriculum it is not within the authority—that is, the rational power—of the faculty of any single college within a large and complex university to set unilaterally the criteria under which students will be admitted to its programs or even the curriculum of its programs. If its existence and fulfillment depend upon the total context of the university, it bears obligations to the entire university that call for cooperative determination. Obviously, the deans and faculty of various colleges must be consulted; for it is they who must develop additional policy objectives and program requirements. But where there is disagreement or conflict, an academic vice president or provost or president must have the authority to resolve those differences. Otherwise, there can be no university but only an academic archipelago.

The authority of the professor in the classroom comes very close to being unqualified. This is the context within the university in which one man, one vote has its most natural and accurate expression. But even here there are limitations, for the authority of the faculty member is in part dependent on the consent of his students. He need not win a popularity contest, but he must exhibit before his students that level of competence sufficient to win their respect, and he must exhibit before his colleagues that level of competence that can win the approval of professionally trained persons. It is inaccurate to claim, as Carolyn Bird did, that professors exercise power "as arbitrarily as medieval popes." This may have some appeal as rhetoric, but it doesn't meet the test of factual examination. Professors do not have the authority to grade according to whim, and if they violate the rights of students they are held to account, or they should be held to account, by any effective university administration, preferably at the departmental level. They do not have the authority to decide individually what the context or expectations of the course shall be, but have to consult with others to determine it. And they do not have it within their sole power to decide what the facts are and what rational argument consists in, no matter what their field of inquiry.

But we should not be left with the impression that conflict is characteristic of life within the university. For the most part harmony and the power of harmony prevail, even in the midst of what appears to television cameras to be campus unrest. In the midst of a very large student uprising or decanal dispute, one will likely find that all classes are being held and all laboratories are in operation, books are being written and read and the educational process goes on. Only a handful are marching around with placards, leaving the television audience with the false impression that the university is disrupted; that is a consequence of the censorship inherent in television coverage.

In a well-ordered society, whether it be a nation, a state, a city, or a university, power is exercised in accordance with right, and it is exercised to varying degrees and in varying forms by every single member of the community. None is all powerful, and none is powerless. And the more successful the society, the greater the extent to which authority is exercised on the basis of persuasion and consent. That is, power is exercised rationally. It is not propagandistic, based on psychological manipulation of belief; it is not corruption or coercion in terms of financial rewards and punishments; it is persuasion in terms of shared goals, objectives, and ideals. The right to participate in the life of a university is a right that goes with membership in the community. But the nature of that right depends upon one's position and ability within that community. And the primary right of the student is to study and learn in a context of close association with highly qualified and serious young men and women, fellow students, and in interaction with highly qualified faculty mentors.

These mentors are there to encourage the greatest personal fulfillment, that is, the greatest opportunity to enhance one's power as an individual. The faculty and administrators are not there to encourage tyranny, or to be intimidated by threats of force or violence, but from a moral no less than an intellectual standpoint to assist students to their fulfillment. Student rights exist not because students claim them, but because they are required by the nature of a university and by their nature as developing human beings.

Copyright © 1979 by John R. Silber.